W0081837

HOW COMPASSION WORKS

A Step-by-Step Guide
to Cultivating Well-Being,
Love, *and* Wisdom

JOHN MAKRANSKY
AND PAUL CONDON

*With practices drawn from Buddhism,
attachment theory, and cognitive science*

SHAMBHALA

Shambhala Publications, Inc.
2129 13th Street
Boulder, Colorado 80302
www.shambhala.com

© 2025 by John Makransky and Paul Condon

Art on p. 18: Refuge Field of Gelug Lineage; 19th century;
Central Tibet; ground mineral pigment, fine gold line on cotton;
Rubin Museum of Art, Gift of Shelley and Donald Rubin; C2006.66.141.

Cover art: annaspoka/Adobe Stock
Cover design: Daniel Urban-Brown
Interior design: Kate Huber-Parker

All rights reserved. No part of this book may be reproduced
in any form or by any means, electronic or mechanical, including
photocopying, recording, or by any information storage and retrieval
system, without permission in writing from the publisher.

9 8 7 6 5 4 3 2 1

First Edition
Printed in the United States of America

Shambhala Publications makes every effort
to print on acid-free, recycled paper.
Shambhala Publications is distributed worldwide by
Penguin Random House, Inc., and its subsidiaries.

Library of Congress Cataloging-in-Publication Data
Names: Makransky, John J., author. | Condon, Paul, author.
Title: How compassion works: a step-by-step guide for cultivating well-being,
love, and wisdom/John Makransky and Paul Condon.
Description: First edition. | Boulder, Colorado: Shambhala, [2025] |
Includes bibliographical references and index.
Identifiers: LCCN 2024034263 | ISBN 9781645471738 (trade paperback)
Subjects: LCSH: Compassion. | Buddhism—Psychology. | Well-being. |
Self-actualization (Psychology)
Classification: LCC BJ1475 .M35 2025 | DDC 294.3/444—dc23/eng/20241025
LC record available at https://lccn.loc.gov/2024034263

The authorized representative in the EU for product safety and compliance is eucomply
OÜ, Pärnu mnt 139b-14, 11317 Tallinn, Estonia, hello@eucompliancepartner.com.

"*How Compassion Works* is a balm for these times of division and uncertainty. Makransky and Condon have achieved a masterful synthesis of modern psychology and cognitive science with traditional Buddhist wisdom, offering insights and practices that are truly life changing. Not to be missed."

—WENDY HASENKAMP, science director of the Mind & Life Institute and host of the *Mind & Life* podcast

"Universal care and loving-kindness for all beings illuminate the bodhisattva path of complete awakening. In this book, Makransky and Condon offer accessible yet profound meditations that help us discover our ultimately unconditioned capacity for love and compassionate action. Their skillful integration of contemporary psychology and cognitive science with classical Buddhist wisdom creates a bridge between current scientific understanding and timeless spiritual insights. May this work help and inspire readers to awaken the inherent wisdom that lies at the heart of all."

—CHOKYI NYIMA RINPOCHE, author of *Sadness, Love, Openness*

"While we all wish to be good people, *How Compassion Works* actually shows us how. Grounded in ancient contemplative techniques and modern psychological research, Makransky and Condon demonstrate that emotional evolution is not a matter of chance; it is a matter of training. By directing attention mindfully, and developing a regular practice, anyone can open their heart without losing their balance. *How Compassion Works* is not only a handbook for the heart: it provides tools of emotional alchemy capable of changing your life forever. Indispensable for caregivers, lovers, and the human race."

—WILLA B. BAKER, PHD, author of *The Wakeful Body*

"Befriending one's mind through formal meditation practice can be thought of as a radical act of love, sanity, wisdom, and healing. *How Compassion Works* is a high-resolution guide to both the instrumental and non-instrumental dimensions of meditation practice based predominantly on Tibetan teachings yet explicitly inviting a broader inclusivity. It is also a welcome and timely compendium of scientific evidence supporting the value of this relational approach and its liberative non-dual essence."

—JON KABAT-ZINN, founder of Mindfulness-Based Stress Reduction (MBSR) and author of *Wherever You Go, There You Are* and *Coming to Our Senses*

"*How Compassion Works* is a clear, carefully researched, accessible, and practical guide on how to develop and deepen love and compassion both within ourselves and over time as we mature, to all those we meet. We learn, step-by-step, how not only to open our hearts and wisdom mind but apply these powerful discoveries to the challenges of the world."

—TSOKNYI RINPOCHE, author of *Why We Meditate*

"*How Compassion Works* has the power to transform individual lives and the very fabric of our world. The practices in this book truly work, offering a profound exploration of compassion as both an innate tendency and a skill we can intentionally cultivate. John Makransky and Paul Condon illuminate how reconnecting with the essence of love at our core is essential for individual healing and societal change. With practices to deepen love, prevent burnout, reduce bias, and bridge divides, this book is an indispensable guide for fostering connection and meaningful transformation in these polarized times."

—KAIRA JEWEL LINGO, Buddhist teacher, author of *We Were Made for These Times* and coauthor of *Healing Our Way Home*

"*How Compassion Works* offers a truly rich resource, especially from Tibetan Buddhism, to develop and enhance the defining human quality of compassion. I particularly admire how the authors—a Buddhist scholar and a psychologist—engage Buddhist compassion practices from the perspective of 'attachment theory,' a framework that has brought important insights into human behavior and relationships. This book brings a whole new dimension to our understanding of how Buddhist meditative practices, especially loving-kindness and compassion, can bring about lasting personal transformation."

—THUPTEN JINPA, principal English translator to H.H. the Dalai Lama and author of *A Fearless Heart*

"As science begins to take seriously the possibility that the Buddhist view of consciousness as the ground of all being may actually be the true reality, this wonderfully timed book takes readers on a guided tour of two paths to compassion: one called 'relative,' which is understanding how we can orientate and train our evolved troublesome brains towards compassion, and the other called 'ultimate' is compassion that arises naturally from the non-dual ground of experience. This book from two internationally recognized scholars and practitioners is a delight of insights and wisdoms. It details the way the two paths can be engaged as complementary and mutually empowering. It points the way to the nature of benevolent love as residing in our awareness of non-separateness."

—PAUL GILBERT, founder of Compassion Focused Therapy,
author of *The Compassionate Mind* and *Mindful Compassion*

"Our greatest task as a species is to cultivate the capacity to live from a place of compassion. In this wise and evidence-based guide, we are given the tools to nurture our inner well-being while offering healing and love to the world around us. Practical, profound, and deeply timely, this book has the power to uplift and serve the hearts and spirits of countless beings."

—TARA BRACH, author of *Radical Acceptance* and *Radical Compassion*

"A compelling synthesis of traditional Buddhist wisdom and contemporary scientific research, offering both practical guidance and profound insights into compassion's vital role in our lives and its relevance to addressing the main challenges of the twenty-first century."

—MATTHIEU RICARD, author of *Altruism*

"*How Compassion Works* offers a clear and carefully laid out practice path for anyone interested in deepening their experience and expression of compassion and love. This insightful offering is yet another important answer and resource supporting our evolution into a more care-centered collective."

—LAMA ROD OWENS, author of *The New Saints*

"For anyone seeking to experience the wisdom of their own heart, Makransky and Condon offer an accessible guide to the boundless love and compassion within us all, regardless of our spiritual background or beliefs."

—SHARON SALZBERG, author of *Lovingkindness* and *Real Life*

CONTENTS

TABLE OF MEDITATIONS

PREFACE

Dear Reader,

This book presents a series of meditations on love, compassion, and wisdom that have been adapted from Tibetan Buddhist traditions (especially Dzogchen and Mahāmudrā), in dialogue with several areas of modern psychology. These practices help us realize a power of unconditional care from within that can be healing and sustaining, make us more present to ourselves and others, and help empower compassionate action that can be less subject to emotional exhaustion.

The arc of contemplative practice within this book is known as sustainable compassion training (SCT). This series of meditation practices highlights our need to experience how it feels to be held in love and compassion to extend love and compassion inclusively to others, our need to be seen in our unconditional worth in order to see the same in others, and our need to become present to all of our experience with kindness to become sustainably present to others with kindness.

For these purposes, SCT meditations cultivate three modes of practice: The receptive mode helps us find access to energies and qualities of love and compassion from the depth of our awareness. This establishes the secure base needed for the other two modes of practice. The deepening mode helps us deepen into the nonconceptual source of those qualities—the openness, clarity, and compassionate capacity available in the deep nature of mind—*our buddha nature*. The inclusive mode draws on those qualities and energies to help us extend love and compassion inclusively to others. On the basis of those three modes of practice, we engage further meditations for cultivating empathy and compassion, which are designed to generate compassionate solidarity with others in a sustainable and inclusive way that helps avoid empathic distress and compassion fatigue.

The meditations here are introduced progressively for you to explore at your own pace. We do not intend each of the chapters from 1 to 5 to be read as a whole chapter in just one sitting. Rather, we suggest you read just a few sections of each chapter at a time, often trying out one of the meditations from that part of the reading. Then take a break from reading to think over and digest what you discovered in those sections, repeat the meditation a few times, and see what all that newly shows you or raises up for you.

You may wish to read the book in a linear way all the way through. But you might also enjoy and benefit from it more if you take time to reread the particular sections and meditations that you find most meaningful, revisiting those sections and repeating those meditations, before reading further.

We also suggest that you keep a notebook or practice journal (on any device) for your notes, to respond to questions that we pose about the meditation process, and to help you remember insights that emerge from your reading and exploration of the practices.

Audio recordings with guided meditations by each author are available on: shambhala.com/howcompassionworksmeditations.

John Makransky
Paul Condon

HOW
COMPASSION
WORKS

Introduction

ACCESSING OUR INNATE
POWERS OF GOODNESS

Everything we care about—our mental and physical well-being, our relationships, our ability to benefit others and the world, the deepening of our spiritual life—all depend on the power of love and compassion operative in us. The strength of that power, in turn, depends on how well we are able to access the qualities, attitudes, and energies of love and compassion; how deeply we can be healed, replenished, and transformed by them. Then we can extend that same loving power to others more sustainably and unconditionally in our attention and action. Love and compassion take us beyond ourselves, so we are less caught up in our own worries, more fully present to others, more in touch with our better selves and our purpose for living, and therefore naturally happier.

Love and compassion also help us to get real. They show us the great dignity and potential of each person—how worthy of kindness, care, and forgiveness each is—beyond the superficial habits of limited perception and bias instilled by societies. Love and compassion empower us to be with those who are suffering without having to turn away or be overwhelmed. They give us the discernment and courage to hold the sufferings of self and others within the larger reality of compassion in which they can deeply heal and transform. By returning to replenishing sources of love and compassion available to us, we can find the energy and resilience to take caring action repeatedly—even in challenging circumstances—without being overcome by all the difficulties we face or getting burnt out.[1]

Some interpreters of the British naturalist Charles Darwin's work assumed that human nature was essentially selfish, our behavior guided mainly by competitive aggression as governed by the selection process of evolution. Now that view is challenged by a growing recognition that innate capacities for care, empathy, nurturing, and compassion are part of our human nature and have been crucial for the evolutionary survival of our species.[2]

Previously psychologists had assumed that our ability to receive and give love and care was fixed for life in early childhood, depending on whether we had experienced reliably loving figures in the early part of our lives. Now there is increasing evidence that our innate human capacities for love and compassion are not just fixed for life and can be strengthened throughout our lifetime by methods effective for cultivating them, even for those who have had adverse experiences.[3] This manual teaches such methods—meditation practices that help us access the life-giving powers of love and compassion so we can be healed, deepened, and transformed by them, and learn how to extend them more sustainably and inclusively to others.

Is it unrealistic to focus on love and compassion in a world racked by so much antagonism, aggression, and violence? Quite the opposite—we must recover our own fuller humanity if we want to help others recover theirs, and the key to that is more, not less, attention to love and compassion. Modern societies are afflicted by hostility, greed, callousness, and fear because too few of us have been encouraged and enabled to stay connected to our underlying capacities of care, compassion, and wisdom through which to find deep healing for ourselves and to respond to all others in their dignity and worth. We may often feel overwhelmed by our own painful feelings of stress, anxiety, hostility, loneliness, or self-loathing, and when working with others, we may find ourselves depleted and worn down by the difficulties and sufferings that we face.[4] That is not a reason to turn away from love and compassion but to learn how to access them more fully—to open to their healing and transformative powers; to be replenished, restored, and transformed by them; to reunify with their source in the depth of our being; and from there, to help others similarly access their best potential. That is the learning of this manual.

WHO IS THIS MANUAL FOR?

Many people in caring roles and activism would like to access a power of care and compassion that can be more sustaining, replenishing, and inclusive than what they have been experiencing in their lives and work—less subject to depletion, compassion fatigue, burnout, and bias. Many modern Buddhists share that concern and also seek through their practices to become unified with the ultimate source of those loving capacities—the unimpeded openness, inner freedom, and compassionate energy to be found in the depth of human awareness, which is the core of enlightenment—our buddha nature. And many people in other spiritual traditions wish to learn not just intellectual ideas from Buddhism but how its practices may inform and empower their spiritual lives, including their capacities for more unconditional love, compassion, and discernment. The aim of this manual is to help meet all three of those needs for all three of those intersecting groups.

For that purpose, we draw especially on Tibetan Buddhist understandings of awareness and its capacities of love, compassion, and wisdom, seeking to make them newly accessible for people of all faiths and backgrounds. We draw on Tibetan Buddhism, in part, because it is the primary tradition of our own training. We also draw on it for its precision and experiential knowledge in accessing those loving capacities, reunifying with their source in the depth of awareness (our buddha nature), and responding from that place to others in their depth and potential.

The meditation practices adapted here from Buddhism are also informed by analogous patterns of practice in other spiritual traditions, including theistic and Indigenous practice traditions, and by influential theories in psychology and neuroscience, including attachment theory, social baseline theory, theories of grounded cognition and constructed emotion, and other concepts from social, developmental, and cognitive psychology.

We see great value in scientific theories and concepts as support for contemplative practice. Previously science has often been related to Buddhism in three basic ways: (1) using aspects of Buddhist thought or practice to inform new directions in scientific research (e.g., research on neural, psychological, or behavioral effects of meditation); (2) adapting Buddhist practices to help treat physical or mental health problems (such as depression, stress, and hypertension); or (3) using science to justify Buddhist ideas or practices.[5] Science has also been used in problematic ways—for example, to minimize or even erase the role of cultural context in contemplative practice. As a secularizing force, science has often filtered out ritualistic forms of meditation that have been considered crucial in the contemplative cultures of their origin.[6] Yet from the point of view of scientific theories in social and developmental psychology, these ritual forms of practice express principles that are crucial for human transformation, as we will explore in this book. For that reason, our goal with science is different from many prior attempts to relate science and Buddhism. In this manual, we explore how areas of psychological science can help modern practitioners to more fully experience the transformational effects of practices from living contemplative traditions. Throughout the book, we will introduce meditative practices alongside scientific theories and concepts that point to nuanced features of each meditation, to help us deepen in the practice of it.

HUMAN CAPACITIES OF CARE AND COMPASSION ARE INNATE TO US FROM EVOLUTION

Although competitive aggression among animal groups has previously been emphasized in writings on evolution, increasing attention is turning to a complementary proposal by Darwin that empathy, care, and social bonding were also essential for the survival of many species, including humans.[7] As human beings, we have instinctive impulses to give and receive loving attention; to nurture, care for, bond, and empathize with others.[8] These impulses are vivid in the nurturing attitudes of human parents toward their children, who require a longer period of care than other animals. In earliest human history, child-rearing practices involved multiple caretakers in extended family groups, leading some theorists to argue that capacities for empathy, awareness of others' minds, care, and cooperation were highly selected for within the human species.[9] Evidence of many forms of interpersonal care is found earlier in the evolutionary past of humans than evidence for interpersonal violence and is more widespread.[10]

Human brains are highly attuned to others' feelings and mental states, and primed for mutual care and cooperation.[11] From the age of one, children spontaneously seek to aid others in ways that were not yet taught to them by adults.[12] In one research study, children one to three years old spontaneously offered to help an experimenter who pretended to be having difficulty.[13] Almost always, when the children noticed the man struggling, they interrupted their play immediately to help, without having been asked and without prospect of any reward. As the infant grows to become a toddler and older, they seek to help and console other persons who seem to be in distress. This research suggests that spontaneous caring and helping behaviors freely manifest in infancy, long before children have been socialized by their parents into social norms. Such behaviors arise at the same age in children across cultures, which suggests that they are an innate inclination, not products of adult intervention or culture. The discovery of similar empathic behaviors in other primates suggests that such tendencies are products of evolution that are deeply ingrained in our nature.[14]

The inclination toward generosity and care persists in adulthood. Research shows, for example, that people tend to opt for prosocial choices when forced to make quick, intuitive decisions, but they sometimes become more selfish when provided time to deliberate.[15] People who engage in acts of heroism often report that they did not think about their choice—they simply acted to help another.[16] Finally, a study spanning 355 cities in forty different countries showed a majority of people returned missing wallets when finding them on the street, suggesting a basic human tendency for honesty and care.[17] As the anthropologist Sarah Blaffer Hrdy notes, "Without the capacity to put ourselves cognitively and emotionally in someone else's shoes, to feel what they feel, to be interested in their fears and motives, longings, griefs, . . . and other details of their existence, without this mixture of curiosity about and emotional identification with others . . . *Homo sapiens* would never have evolved at all."[18] Humans are physically much weaker than other primates but nonetheless evolved to become the dominant species. Cooperative capacities are the key feature of human nature that supported this evolutionary success.

COMMON BARRIERS TO LOVE AND COMPASSION

Love is a caring concern for beings that wishes them to be deeply well and happy. Compassion is the form of love that empathizes with beings in their suffering, wishes them free of it, and wants to take action to alleviate it (further dimensions of compassion will be explored in later chapters). The human evolutionary capacities discussed above became the components of our love and compassion.

Although drawing on a different cultural background and cosmological vision, Tibetan Buddhism, too, asserts that we have great innate capacities of love and compassion that are available in our basic awareness—powers that are always available to draw upon. Indeed, we have drawn on these instinctive capacities of empathy, kindness, and compassion throughout our lives in many little moments of caring connection with others, which at the time felt quite natural to us—a moment smiling at a child or comforting them, a moment cuddling a pet, a moment when we felt happy that someone was present to us with warmth and care or when we were present to another in that way, or a moment when we felt deeply connected to the natural world.

But as we know, we typically experience significant limitations to how continuously and inclusively we are able to draw on these caring capacities or to be compassionately responsive to others. Although we come prepared from evolution with innate capabilities of care, they get much reduced by inner barriers that prevent them from manifesting in a more sustainable and expansive way.

Barriers to sustainable, inclusive care and compassion include several psychological processes to which we are all subject to greater or lesser degree: (1) the lack of a secure base in ourselves to support sustainable and inclusive loving-kindness for others; (2) the tendency to mistake our own reductive thoughts and images of others for the persons themselves, which prevents caring concern for them and supports bias; (3) the tendency to experience suffering in ourselves and others as a basis of aversion or anxiety rather than compassion; (4) the tendency to feel terribly alone in our own experiences of suffering so we feel disconnected from qualities of loving-kindness and compassion. We will discuss each of these barriers in turn.

"Lack of secure base" is a concept from attachment theory in psychology. Research indicates that responsive and supportive caregivers foster a sense of security in infants, which supports the development of their capacities to care for others. To experience responsive, consistent love and care in early childhood engenders a sense of self that feels worthy of love and empowers children to explore their world because they trust that they have a reliable caregiver as a "safe haven" to return to when they feel depleted or disturbed. As such children mature, their sense of worthiness, safety, and well-being becomes internalized as a "secure base" that supports curiosity about the world; attitudes of friendliness, welcoming, care, and empathy for others; and the ability to experience positive emotions during times of stress and adversity.[19] Such people have what attachment theorists refer to as a secure attachment style.

The opposite often occurs for people who have not experienced consistently responsive love and care in their childhood, resulting in an insecure attachment style. When we lack a secure base of inner safety, self-worth, and well-being in ourselves, it becomes difficult to be present to others in a loving way that can stay in touch with their deep worth and hold them in compassion when they are suffering. Instead, we can become overly identified with self-focused feelings of fear, neediness, self-deprecation, or avoidance that block empathy for others and impede the flow of care and compassion that would otherwise be available to us.[20]

Although people emerge from childhood with diverse attachment styles, no matter what kind of upbringing we have had, we are all subject to the four barriers to compassion noted above. Even securely attached people often lose their sense of secure base when working with others in difficult circumstances, unsupportive environments, or when repeatedly encountering suffering.[21] From this perspective, barriers to compassion become operative when feelings of insecurity arise, even for those with a generally secure orientation. The lack of a secure base in ourselves at any moment reinforces all three of the other barriers to care and compassion.

When we lack a felt sense of self-worth, inner safety, and well-being (barrier 1), our minds tend to reduce others' value to their ability to meet our own perceived needs or desires of the moment (barrier 2). Our perspective on others becomes narrowed through that lens, so we may see them mainly as means to fulfill that desire or as obstacles to it. But then we cannot be more aware of others as they are in their own dignity and worth, their own life experiences and sufferings, nor more present to their needs.[22] In this way, in moments when we lack a secure base in ourselves, our minds tend to reduce others to our own reductive impressions of them.[23] Since we often look for such self-confirmation from our in-group, overidentification with our own group for that purpose can impede empathy for, and promote bias against, out-groups with whom we do not identify.[24] The same lack of inner security can make us callous toward the natural world by viewing other creatures and things of nature just as objects of our own (human in-group) desires rather than worthy in their own right of fuller attention, appreciation, wonder, and protection.

When we don't have a secure base at any moment, we don't have access to sources of warmth, acceptance, and comfort in ourselves, so we lack the sense of safety needed when encountering suffering, which can exacerbate fear and aversion to suffering rather than compassion for those who are suffering (barrier 3). Finally, when we lack a secure base that connects us to qualities of loving-kindness, we can feel terribly alone (barrier 4), which intensifies our suffering when we are in pain or when with others who are in pain.[25]

These barriers to sustainable, inclusive compassion also contribute to common afflictions experienced by people in caring roles. When we are unable to connect well to sources of replenishment and support that would empower our flow of care and compassion to others, we can feel depleted and recurrently overwhelmed by the pain of our empathy for others who are suffering. This is called empathic distress, repeated experience of which leads to increasing stress, emotional depletion, secondary trauma, and compassion fatigue—the loss of motivation to empathize and care about others. These experiences are associated with high rates of burnout in caregivers and a tendency to devalue compassion.[26]

These difficulties are exacerbated when administrators and coworkers, who are subject to the same barriers to compassion, cocreate work environments that are uncaring, unsupportive, or overly demanding.[27] Individuals who experience uncaring work environments, in turn, are affected by them in ways that can reinforce the inner barriers mentioned above.

WE CAN CHANGE OUR MENTAL AND PHYSICAL PATTERNS THROUGH MEDITATION TRAINING

Are the internal barriers to care and compassion noted above fixed in us from early childhood for life? They do not have to be. Research indicates that there is significant neuroplasticity in the brains of human beings, which means that what we repeatedly do with our minds and bodies changes our brains by strengthening neural networks that correspond to those behaviors.[28] According to a classic study of neuroplasticity, memory-related brain structures in London cabdrivers, who maintain a complex driving route each day, had a larger volume compared with bus drivers who drive a simple route each day.[29] Repeatedly charting complex driving routes over time had changed the taxi drivers' brains.[30]

And there is growing evidence that attitudes and actions of care, empathy, and compassion can be significantly enhanced, even toward members of out-groups and under conditions of mental depletion. This was first discovered through research on attachment priming, which showed that people with a less secure attachment style could strengthen their secure base temporarily by recalling caring figures from their lives or recalling qualities of love and care, which shifted their attitudes and behaviors toward others to greater care and compassion and less prejudice and hostility.[31]

Such results from attachment priming, in light of neuroplasticity, raised the question of whether repeated experience of love, care, and compassion through meditation training could increase our ability to access those attitudes and to embody them in action. A growing number of research studies on the effects of meditation training indicate that this is indeed possible.[32] Several research groups have shown that meditation increases empathic responses to others' suffering,[33] which correlates with increased generosity.[34] Meditation training also increases actions meant to alleviate others' suffering, even when bystanders fail to act.[35] Meditation training can also reduce implicit bias[36] and increase prosocial behavior toward outgroups.[37] All of these studies have employed a variety of different meditation protocols, suggesting the results generalize beyond specific laboratory, methodological, and training contexts.

In sum, because capacities of love, care, and compassion are innate to us from evolution and, in Buddhist terms, are always available in our basic awareness, and because our brains and bodies can be changed through repeated habits of thought, feeling, and action, we can learn more regularly and more automatically to experience, draw upon, embody, and act upon these innate capacities of loving-kindness and compassion through meditation training.

But to be most effective, any meditation training in compassion would need to overcome the four barriers to compassion noted above. To cultivate a much more sustainable and inclusive power of loving-kindness and compassion than what we have been experiencing, the training would need to employ practices that explicitly target and help free us from those barriers.

HOW CONTEMPLATIVE TRADITIONS HAVE PROVIDED A RELATIONAL STARTING POINT TO OVERCOME BARRIERS TO COMPASSION

How did prior spiritual traditions of contemplative training in love and compassion overcome those barriers? All four barriers stem from the lack of a secure base in oneself from which to extend care sustainably and inclusively to others.[38] This lack of secure base is addressed by patterns of practice in contemplative and ritual traditions of various spiritual traditions. In these traditions, increasingly sustainable and inclusive love and compassion emerges from a relational field of loving support that instills an infinitely secure base for overcoming those barriers. A relational starting point for that is assumed.

The ritual and contemplative practices of these spiritual traditions begin not with oneself trying to become more loving and compassionate just on one's own but with awareness that you and your world are held in the care, compassion, and wisdom of a field of spiritual presence and power. In Buddhism, this is often envisioned as a compassionate field of enlightened ones—buddhas, bodhisattvas, and lineage teachers; in contemplative Christianity, Islam, and Hinduism, as divine presence, which is felt in ways that may also include saintly figures and spiritual teachers; in Indigenous religions, as a field of revered ancestors and spiritual beings, which may also include spiritual dimensions of the natural world.[39] To experience themselves and their world as wholly encompassed in love, compassion, and wisdom has empowered practitioners of these traditions to connect with the source of those qualities in the ground of their being and to extend the same power of love and compassion to others. Through embodied forms of meditation, prayer, and ritual, practitioners learn to become an extension of the field of love, compassion, and wisdom in which they are held, by holding others in the same inclusive and replenishing qualities of love and compassion in which they are embraced.

Through the lens of attachment theory, the *relational starting point* of these practices—the practitioners' experience of being seen in their deep dignity and held in unconditional care—establishes an infinitely secure base and flow of loving energy that empowers their flow of care to others while sensing others in their dignity and worth beyond reductive labels.[40] An infinitely secure base is one that is always available and experienced as unchanging, unconditional, completely reliable. An infinitely secure base serves two key functions relevant for compassion training: (1) it establishes the secure base needed to feel safe enough to be a welcoming presence to others and extend care to them; and (2) it provides the inner security needed to become compassionately present to all parts of oneself, all patterns of thought and feeling, so such patterns can relax, become less rigidly identified with, and heal deeply at an emotional level. This is the pattern of spiritual practice that has supported the inclusive, unfaltering, and unconditional quality of love and compassion that are attributed to figures such as Fred Rogers, Dorothy Day, Martin Luther King Jr., Archbishop Desmond Tutu, the Dalai Lama, Sojourner Truth, Thomas Merton, Thich Nhat Hanh, and bell hooks, all of whom have been formed by lives of prayer, ritual, and/or contemplative practice.

THE RELATIONAL STARTING POINT FOR TRAINING IN LOVE AND COMPASSION IN BUDDHIST TRADITIONS

Since Buddhism is the main source of the trainings in the research studies noted above and the meditations taught in this manual, we might ask how this relational pattern of practice has taken shape in Buddhism through history. A relational starting point for cultivating inclusive and sustainable love and compassion has been assumed across Buddhist cultures, traditions, and periods. In many Pali scriptures, the Buddha enjoins his followers to cultivate all-inclusive attitudes of loving care, compassion, empathetic joy, and equanimity that literally encompass all sentient beings.[41] Such discourses express a way of practice transmitted through all the generations of the Buddha's followers. For a practitioner from traditional Asian Buddhist cultures to hear such a discourse is to understand oneself as one of those encompassed in that field of all-inclusive loving care and compassion, by all who have generated those attitudes before that practitioner and all who hold that practitioner in them now. To enter into such a practice is not the action of an individualistic self, who learns on one's own to generate all-encompassing love. Rather, practitioners have understood the practice as a way for them to participate in and ultimately become an extension of the field of all-inclusive care that supports them. This has given prior generations of trainees the confidence that they, like those before them, can progress in such a practice in spite of the kinds of barriers noted earlier. The Buddhist understanding of deep relationality as a foundation of practice is formalized in the notion of refuge, in which the Buddha and accomplished members of the spiritual community (realized sangha) are experienced as embodiments of the all-encompassing qualities of love and wisdom that inspire and empower many others to cultivate the same qualities.

A related practice theme is the experience of being seen as deeply worthy of loving care and compassion, an experience evoked, in part, through practices that bring the Buddha and accomplished sangha vividly to mind (*buddha-* and *sangha-anusmṛti*). In the fifth-century scholar Buddhaghosa's description, meditators focus their attention on the Buddha's enlightened qualities, which include his all-pervasive, unconditional love, compassion, and wisdom that encompass the meditator and their whole world.[42] Such practices are further developed in Indian Mahāyāna scriptures, where fields of buddhas and bodhisattvas are envisioned directly in front, gazing into the deep dignity of the meditator's enlightened potential and the destructive patterns of thought and reaction that obscure it.[43] The experience of being deeply seen and encompassed in unconditional compassion and wisdom also informs the notion of empowerment in Vajrayāna (tantric) traditions of South Asia and Tibet. The Vajrayāna teacher's pure perception of the students' enlightened capacity (Tib. *dag snang*) communicates itself through ritual forms that resonate with that capacity in the students, empowering them to begin to transcend their reductive perceptions of themselves and others by joining in the deeper seeing by which they are seen.[44]

HOW SUCH RELATIONAL PATTERNS OF PRACTICE OVERCOME BARRIERS TO COMPASSION

How do such patterns of practice overcome the four barriers to compassion noted above? The deeply relational mode of practice just described can be understood to undercut *the first barrier* to compassion, lack of a secure base, by establishing an infinitely secure base that supports an unlimited extension of compassion to others. In the relational mode, one's identity is reconstructed as someone who is lovingly seen, upheld, protected by, and in deep unity with the unconditional love and compassion of their field of care; one's whole body, mind, and world are encompassed in the loving qualities that are evoked by that field. This empowers emotional healing and increasing trust in the source of those qualities in the depth or ground of one's being, which helps the practitioner to settle deeply into that source and its wisdom. From there, the practitioner can learn to extend the same power of care to others in a more sustaining and expansive way.

This experience of an infinitely secure base helps undercut *the second barrier* to compassion—reductive impressions of others—since the inner sense of security ameliorates any felt need to view others merely as objects of one's own need to confirm oneself. This relational mode of practice also undercuts *the third barrier* to compassion—aversion to suffering—by keeping the practitioner connected to ongoing qualities of support and replenishment, an outer and inner field of warmth and acceptance that can embrace, heal, and transform feelings of suffering. This relational mode of practice also undercuts *the fourth barrier*—feeling alone and isolated in one's suffering—by experiencing all suffering as embraced in the love and compassion made present by the relational field, which also supports one's ability to make an empathetic connection with the sufferings of others. These relational mode practices also foster a practitioner's efforts to participate in social support and community building, which provide the encouragement and assistance that individuals need in their ongoing cultivation of love and compassion for themselves and others.[45]

A relational approach contrasts with many meditation and mindfulness training programs in the modern West that implicitly assume a "self-help" framework, where the person takes up meditation nonrelationally, with the felt sense of trying to improve oneself, on one's own, by taking up a practice as a self-help technique. This assumption arises from a modernistic cultural understanding that views persons as atomistic individuals who exist prior to relationships rather than as constituted by relationships, which had been the assumption of traditional cultures.[46] In this way, modern meditation programs may implicitly reinforce the hyperindividualism that further separates us from relationships and community.[47] As the neuroscientist and philosopher Francisco Varela stated, "Practices undertaken simply as self-improvement schemes will only strengthen the very egotism they are intended to dispel."[48] In other words, a nonrelational orientation to contemplative practice may exacerbate the four barriers to compassion.

THE RELATIONAL PATTERN OF TRAINING IN BUDDHISM AND OTHER SPIRITUAL TRADITIONS MIRRORS CURRENT UNDERSTANDINGS OF SCIENCE

The relational pattern of training in Buddhism and other spiritual traditions mirrors current understandings in psychology and neuroscience of human emotional and social development. We have already traced parallels in those practice traditions with attachment theory and with the recognition that we can train our brains, bodies, and minds through repeated practice. The same relational patterns of practice also correlate with another influential theory in psychology called social baseline theory, according to which the human brain is designed by evolution to operate within a context of social relationships. The brain is energetically optimized when we experience ourselves in supportive social connection to others and becomes energetically depleted much more quickly when we feel alone or separated from others. In other words, the baseline state of the human brain is social connection; to diverge from that baseline is to add an extra bioenergetic burden to the brain. In research studies, when a person with a heavy backpack stands before a hill with a friend, the hill appears significantly less steep than when standing before the hill alone.[49] And although the brain is highly responsive to perceived threats, other studies showed that holding hands with another person decreased responses to threat.[50]

According to social baseline theory, an individual's social support system functions as an expansion of the self, so the bioenergetic and emotional needs of individuals are met not primarily by individual deployment of effort but by relying on and participating in a social fabric that helps shoulder the load of each individual.[51] In sum, the brains of individuals evolved in a social niche to draw on the collective energies, goals, and resources of social groups rather than relying mainly on autonomous efforts by an isolated sense of self that are much more depleting. This view further suggests that caring connection and compassion are closer to our basic human nature than competitive behaviors and violence.

Social baseline theory and attachment theory together converge on the fundamental need for supportive social connection to thrive as human beings. While social baseline theory asserts that humans are evolutionarily designed to function in a relational field of caring connection with others, attachment theory emphasizes that we become equipped to participate in that relational field first by receiving nurturing support from others for our own neural and emotional development, from which we in turn can support others. In light of the patterns of contemplative and ritual practice discussed above, we can see that part of the wisdom of Buddhist and other spiritual traditions is how the relational patterns of human emotional and social development now established in psychology and neuroscience have been encoded in practice patterns of those traditions over the course of centuries.

SUSTAINABLE COMPASSION TRAINING: ADAPTING THE RELATIONAL PATTERN OF PRACTICE FOR PEOPLE OF ALL BACKGROUNDS AND CULTURES

The aim of this manual is to provide meditative training in sustainable, inclusive care and compassion, together with the wisdom that supports such qualities, not only for Buddhists but also for people of other spiritual practice traditions and for people in caring roles and professions, whether or not they are part of any spiritual tradition. This raises another question. The relational pattern of practice described above, which undercuts the four barriers to compassion we have discussed, has been specific to each religious tradition and culture. Buddhists begin their practices by bringing to mind the Buddha or a field of enlightened beings; contemplative Christians, Muslims, and Hindus bring to mind God's presence in ways that may also include saintly or divine figures; people who practice in Indigenous religions often think of revered ancestors and spiritual dimensions of the natural world. How can we adapt this pattern of practice, which has traditionally taken expression in forms specific to each religious culture, in a way that can be accessible to people of different backgrounds and cultures, whether they are religious or not? This book will present a way to do that called sustainable compassion training (SCT).[52]

SUSTAINABLE COMPASSION TRAINING: THREE MODES OF MEDITATION PRACTICE

SCT adapts the shared relational pattern of spiritual traditions into three modes of contemplative practice that are accessible to people of any background or tradition. It does this by inviting the participant to fill in the content of each mode of practice with material from their own life within their own worldview, whether that worldview is predominantly spiritual-religious, scientific, or both. SCT's modes of practice are called the receptive mode, deepening mode, and inclusive mode (see figure 1). Each such mode is informed by patterns of practice from Tibetan Buddhism that correlate with similar patterns in other spiritual traditions and with relevant areas of psychological science. Based on the patterns of practice that we have noted in Buddhism and other traditions, the three modes of practice are designed to help overcome the barriers to compassion explained above.[53] Those three modes then provide the basis for further meditations on compassion that generate empathy and compassion with increasing strength, inclusiveness, and unconditionality, in ways that avoid empathic distress, compassion fatigue, and burnout.

Receptive Mode

The meditation practices of SCT help us access our innate capacities of love, care, and compassion first by recalling a time when we experienced what it is like to be held in such qualities, then by reinhabiting that time to reexperience ourselves as seen and loved within it. This is called the *receptive mode* of meditation. This can be a moment when we felt seen and held in another person's love and care; a caring moment with a pet; a moment when we were a caring figure for another person; or when we experienced a place, perhaps in nature, where we felt deeply well and at home. We call this reinhabiting our *field of care*.

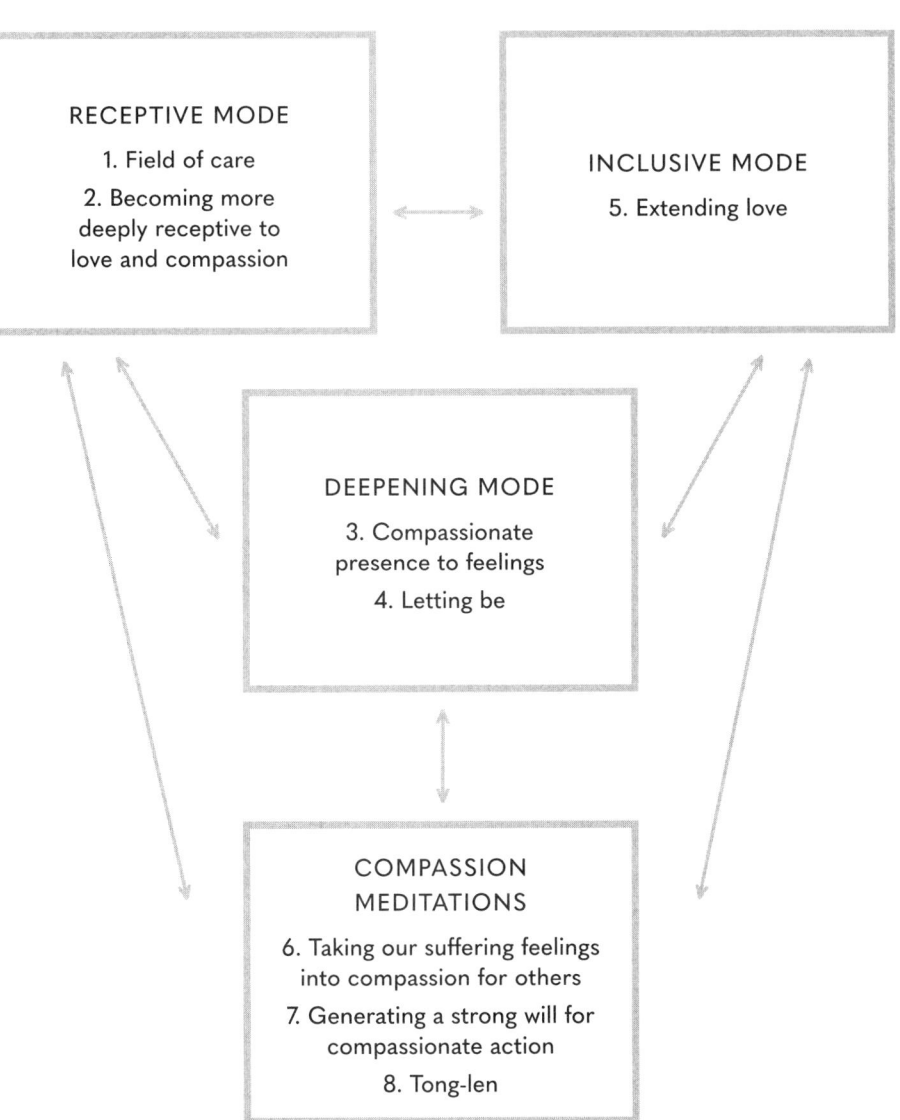

RECEPTIVE MODE

   1. Field of care

   2. Becoming more deeply receptive to love and compassion

INCLUSIVE MODE

   5. Extending love

DEEPENING MODE

   3. Compassionate presence to feelings

   4. Letting be

COMPASSION MEDITATIONS

   6. Taking our suffering feelings into compassion for others

   7. Generating a strong will for compassionate action

   8. Tong-len

FIGURE 1. SUSTAINABLE COMPASSION TRAINING MEDITATIONS[54]

By reinhabiting any such time of caring connection repeatedly and experiencing its loving energies and qualities again and again, the practitioner strengthens their secure base. This empowers the practitioner's increasing recognition of their unconditional worth and potential, which empowers them to see others more fully and inclusively in their profound worth and potential and to extend care to them. With repetition, more moments and kinds of caring connection are recalled, and a relational field of caring beings and places can emerge analogous to what has been envisioned in traditional cultures of training. With more familiarity, we learn to experience all our feelings, including suffering feelings, as encompassed in a field of love and compassion that can heal and transform them rather than as objects to push away or defend against. Another, related kind of receptive-mode practice, for those who practice within a spiritual tradition, is to bring to mind a most inspiring and empowering field of divine presence, spiritual ancestors, or saintly figures while experiencing one's whole being and world as embraced in the unconditional love, compassion, and wisdom of that spiritual field.

AN EXAMPLE OF A TIBETAN REFUGE FIELD, A SPIRITUAL FIELD OF CARE.

An important feature of receptive-mode practices is their consistency with current perspectives on grounded and situated cognition.[55] According to theories of grounded cognition, when we recall a memory from our life, it is simulated throughout multiple systems of the brain—motor, sensory, kinesthetic, affective, cognitive, and so forth. During the receptive mode of practice, practitioners envision and simulate a felt sense of security by feeling into a caring moment or spiritual field as if it is happening in the present (not as a distant memory) while noticing the felt qualities of care, love, warmth, acceptance, inner safety, peace, and so forth that come with that moment or field of connection. Such practices of envisioning and re-inhabiting fields of care, then, are not just intellectual exercises or ways of believing; they connect the practitioner with a deeply embodied experience of relationality by reenacting relevant systems and multiple modes of knowing in the brain and body.

A Tibetan Buddhist perspective on receptive-mode practice would add that others' love and compassion per se do not inject into us the feelings of warmth, acceptance, appreciation, and care that we experience when we are with them or recalling them. Those qualities are innate capacities of our underlying awareness—our buddha nature. We are not *receiving those qualities from outside of us* but rather learning *to become receptive* to them as capacities of our basic awareness. If we are receptive enough when we bring loving persons to mind, their felt presence evokes those capacities in us, to feel what love and compassion are like and to embody them for others. In this way, receptive-mode practice aligns with attachment theory—we learn to become what we are held in, to love as we are loved. And through alternative ways of entering into the receptive mode, when we are ready, we can learn how to experience the truth of that in the present, no matter what our past has been.

Deepening Mode

We learn, then, through repeated *receptive-mode* meditation with a field of care, to access loving qualities of our basic awareness with increasing facility. Building on that with a further meditation that we call Compassionate Presence to Feelings, we learn how to access those loving qualities in an even more direct manner. Through such practices, energies and feelings of warmth, acceptance, and kindness permeate our body and mind, thereby helping us to relax, heal in those qualities, and open further to them. The mind thus learns to trust the source of those loving qualities in the depth of its awareness and can feel safe enough to release its self-protective grip and begin to settle into that depth. This depth or ground of awareness is experienced as an utterly open lucidity, which is all-inclusive, undivided, and deeply peaceful, endowed with tremendous capacities of kindness, compassion, and wisdom.

This depth of our mind, often referred to in Buddhist traditions as our buddha nature, is our ultimate secure base. This process of learning to release self-grasping and settle progressively into that depth and its qualities is the *deepening mode* of meditation.[56] Subsequent meditations in deepening mode help the mind further reunify with its underlying nature of openness, inclusiveness, unity, calm, and expressive power (buddha nature) from which energies and qualities of love, compassion, and wisdom can emerge with increasing strength and freedom.

Inclusive Mode

The receptive and deepening modes of practice, in turn, empower the practitioner to enter into the *inclusive mode* of meditation and action, which involves extending love and compassion to others in more sustaining and expansive ways. This third mode of practice is *not* the activity of an isolated sense of self that is trying to become more loving on their own, which would exacerbate the barriers noted above and contribute to mental depletion and compassion fatigue. Rather, the practitioner enters into the inclusive mode of practice from the two prior modes: as someone sustained by an unconditional field of love and compassion that empowers them to access the source of those capacities and its wisdom in the depth of their mind. With that infinitely secure base and from that depth of wisdom they can learn to include others in the same loving perspective and energy in which they have been held, in increasingly sustainable and inclusive ways. This movement from receptive mode to deepening mode to inclusive mode of practice mirrors the relational training of spiritual traditions, as well as the relational pattern of attachment theory.

The three modes of meditation training described above are explained respectively in chapters 1 (receptive mode), 2 (deepening mode), and 3 (inclusive mode) of this manual. These chapters lead into chapter 4, where we learn several meditations that cultivate a sustaining, all-inclusive power of compassion and wisdom for relationship and action in ways designed to help us avoid empathic distress, mental depletion, and compassion fatigue. Chapter 5 discusses how these practices can be integrated into our daily lives to inform and empower our relationships, work, service, and activism. In each chapter, we concisely explain the elements of psychological science that inform relevant aspects of the meditation practices.

Most SCT practices are forms of meditation training. Such training involves lots of repetition over time—for example, repeatedly reinhabiting and settling into the experience of love, safety, acceptance, and comfort evoked by recalling a moment of caring connection or one's spiritual field. Over months of practice, a practitioner will have repeated this experience of secure attachment thousands of times, a process that can gradually train the brain and body for greater ease in accessing, deepening into, and extending loving qualities by continuously empowering an infinitely secure base from which to engage one's world.

THE INCLUSIVE AIM OF THIS MANUAL

A practitioner might be drawn to one of two paths in which to engage the arc of practice in this book: (1) personal healing, well-being, and growth that generally supports care and service to others, or (2) a spiritual dimension of awakening and inner freedom that draws more specifically on a nondual, unconditioned ground of awareness as the basis for deepening wisdom and compassionate responsiveness to the world. We strive to support people in both paths and encourage people to explore the practices in the manner that best fits their aspirations and needs.

As we mentioned at the start of this introduction, this manual draws especially on Tibetan Buddhist understandings of awareness and its capacities of love, compassion, and wisdom. Yet because the three-mode pattern of practice in SCT correlates with other spiritual traditions and areas of science, readers who explore its meditations will find that they can fill in the content of its modes of meditation with material from their own lives, experiences, and worldviews. Readers who practice within a spiritual community that is Buddhist, Christian, Jewish, Muslim, Hindu, Confucian, Indigenous tradition, hybrid tradition, or otherwise can easily map the three modes of practice into analogous patterns of their own tradition. Readers who primarily inhabit a scientific worldview can map the three modes of practice into that worldview, informed by areas of psychological science explained in each chapter.[57]

Our aim for this manual of practice, then, is to help support people who pursue meditation for personal well-being or spiritual deepening. For those who serve in caring roles or professions, we offer these practices to help you access a power of care and compassion that can be more sustaining, inclusive, replenishing, and less subject to mental depletion, compassion fatigue, and bias—to empower your lives and caring work with others. For people who practice in any spiritual tradition, we offer these practices with the hope they may energize and illumine aspects of your spiritual lives and service to others. For Buddhist practitioners, in addition to those benefits, we offer these practices to empower all the practices you do to become increasingly unified with the source of love, compassion, and wisdom in the depth of your being, buddha nature, from which to embody and enact those life-giving capacities for the sake of all. If that last goal also resonates with any of those in the first two groups, you are invited to explore how something similar may unfold within your own worldview, whether that is primarily spiritual-religious, scientific, or both.

CULTIVATING MEDITATIVE ATTENTION AND CALM

The Tibetan contemplative traditions that we adopted for this book are the Nyingma Dzogchen and Kagyu Mahāmudrā traditions, whose emphasis in meditation is to draw on underlying capacities for fuller attention, tranquility, love, compassion, and wisdom. These capacities are understood as powers of our buddha nature, which we can draw on to cut through self-referential habits of thought and reaction that impede those capacities.

In this section, before introducing the meditations of the following chapters, we'll share some simple meditations for cultivating fuller attention and calm through the senses—qualities of mind that help support all the other practices of this book.

Cultivating meditative attention and calm involves placing our attention on an object, such as the body, the breath, or a sound; or on an attitude like love or compassion; or on the basic openness and lucidity of our mind. Then we let that object or attitude draw our awareness into unity with it more and more. The mind strongly tends to identify with its shifting trains of thought and reaction, causing its attention to wander from the object. When you notice the mind wandering, just recall your meditation object and let it draw your awareness back to it, like a magnet. To repeatedly notice that the mind is wandering and then let the object of your attention draw you back to it is not a problem. It is the very process through which the muscle of our attention gets strengthened, by letting our innate capacity for fuller attention cut through the incessant habit of self-referential thought, calming its emotional energies.

When meditating, various isolated thoughts will probably also continue to arise in the background of your awareness, even when you are not strongly identifying with them. That is fine. Just consider whatever thoughts arise as peripheral to your attention, with the object of the meditation instruction as central.

Please explore each of the sense-based meditations that are instructed in the paragraphs that follow. After exploring each such practice, select the one most connecting for you right now and begin doing that one regularly. As you practice that over time, it can help make the other practices more accessible to you, in which case you can take up others over time.

When first starting, you can do your chosen meditation just for a short period—say, five minutes. If your mind becomes tired during that session, take a short break, then begin again freshly. As you experience benefits of such practice—such as deepening concentration, calm, meditative joy—you can let sessions naturally, gradually become longer. If you prefer to be guided by audio instruction of the meditations throughout this book, you can find audios of them at shambhala.com/howcompassion worksmeditations.

Abdominal Breathing

Sit in a relaxed, comfortable way with back straight, eyes gazing gently downward. Come down from the thinking mind into the body, relax, and settle into the grounded feeling of the body as a whole. Take a slow, deep breath, inhaling from the abdomen so it expands, then exhaling slowly and completely, letting go of all your concerns with the exhale. Relax for a moment before inhaling again. Repeat this several times.

This practice, when repeated five or more times, can be deeply grounding, helping the energies of mind and body to settle and calm. It is good preparation for any other meditation.

Settling Into Body and Breath

Begin with abdominal breathing as above, repeating it several times. Then, while still breathing from the abdomen, let the breath just settle into its own natural flow. Feel the abdomen expand and contract with each breath. Let that feeling draw you into it more and more, breath by breath. (*Pause*) When you notice the mind wandering, let the feeling of the belly moving with the breath draw you back to it, to settle into that feeling more and more fully. Let that feeling increasingly draw you into oneness with it.

Settling Into the Grounded Feeling of the Body

Begin with abdominal breathing as above, repeating it several times. Then let your attention settle into the gentle pressure of the body wherever it is most vivid, such as the pressure of your legs on the chair, your feet on the floor, or your hands on your lap. Let that gentle grounded feeling of pressure draw your awareness into it more and more. When the mind wanders, let that grounded feeling, like a magnet, draw you back to it, to settle into it more and more fully. Let that feeling increasingly draw you into oneness with it.

Settling Into Sound

While listening to any ongoing sound (such as the repeated ring of a gong or the sound of running water or the wind), let your awareness settle deeply into the sound, allowing the sound to draw you into it more and more, just hearing it as fully as possible. (*Pause*) When you notice the mind wandering, let the sound, like a magnet, draw you back to it, to settle into it more and more fully. Let the sound increasingly draw you into oneness with it.

Ongoing sounds can also be accessed online through relevant apps.

Walking Meditation

While walking at a slightly slower pace than usual, feel the sensation of walking on the feet as fully as you can, step by step. When you notice the mind wandering, let the feeling of the foot in each step draw the mind back to it, to feel it more fully. Each step is drawing you into the present moment of feeling, with increasing fullness.

Alternatively, if you wish, you may let your attention settle into the full sensory field, just seeing or hearing fully, wide open. When you notice the mind wandering, let the visual or auditory field draw the mind back to it, to sense it more and more fully, wide open.

Such meditation practices activate powers of awareness for fuller attention, calm, presence, simplicity, and oneness with what we are experiencing or doing. Those powers of mind help us to sense more of what is here now—and to start to settle into the insubstantial, lucid nature of whatever we are experiencing. They also bring fuller awareness of self and others, the natural world, our habits of reaction, what lies beyond them, and fuller presence to what we are doing ("becoming one" with our activities when walking, washing dishes, listening, etc.). These powers of attention, calm, and presence of mind support the practices of love, compassion, and wisdom that are developed throughout this book.

Key Points for Learning Meditation

The importance of motivation for success in meditation. If our motivation to do the meditations is weak, we won't have enough interest in the meditation instruction to let our attention be drawn back to it when the mind wanders. For success in meditation, therefore, prior to any practice, we need to reconnect with our motivation. One basic motivation for compassion training is to bring out an unconditional power of love and wisdom from within that is deeply healing and sustaining, beyond compassion fatigue and burnout, that can make us more fully present to ourselves and others for the sake of all.

Key principles of progress and integration: We don't need long meditation sessions if that doesn't fit into our lives. We do need a morning session as the anchor for our day. If you are new to meditation, you could start with a five-minute morning session, then let that session gradually become longer, over weeks of such morning practice, as you feel its benefits. Then touch in again on that same meditation briefly in *many* moments of your day, even for just a minute or two at a time. In the course of months of such daily practice, we will have reconnected with the practice thousands of times. It is this force of repetition that can gradually change the patterning of our bodies and minds for fuller awareness, calm, care, compassionate responsiveness, and discernment.

When first introduced to the meditations of this book, we are just beginning to imprint them on our minds, hearts, and bodies. So let's hold them lightly—there is no need to worry about getting them perfectly correct or experiencing their full effects in our first attempts. We catch on to their benefits gradually, through much repetition of the meditations, touching in on them often in our days.

Trauma-Informed Meditation Practice

Although meditation practices can, over time, give reliable access to qualities of ease, relaxation, love, and compassion, they may also trigger emotional disturbances.[58] This can happen when practitioners are introduced to new ways of being that challenge familiar frameworks of self, or when practitioners encounter difficult emotional patterns from their past or current contexts. For these reasons, we encourage practitioners to keep in mind the following principles of trauma-informed practice while exploring the practices in this book.[59]

Flexibility in choosing meditations: In this book, start with the practices that you experience as most immediately inspiring, healing, or connecting for you. Recognize that some practices will be more or less difficult. One kind of field of care practice (with caring moments or benefactors as instructed in chapter 1), for example, might be a difficult starting point for some people. Another type of field of care meditation may work better (e.g., bringing to mind a caring moment with a pet, or a different benefactor, spiritual figure, or special place in nature, etc.). For some people with past relationship trauma, starting with the Compassionate Presence to Feelings Meditation (instructed in chapter 3) may be more beneficial.

Use meditations to process difficult feelings: The Field of Care Meditation (chapter 1) and Compassionate Presence to Feelings Meditation (chapter 3) can serve as defaults for processing difficulties that arise in meditation, work, and life in healing ways. When you experience a difficult feeling during your day or within a meditation, you can default to either of those practices, whichever is most accessible, to process that feeling. Alternatively, if a meditation practice feels overwhelming, you can drop the practice and focus attention outwardly on sense experiences, taking a walk and the like.

Peer support and mutual help: Ongoing meditation practice is ideally supported by a network of practitioners that also engage in similar practices. A community of support provides a context in which practitioners can share and consult with one another as difficulties inherently arise in practice and in daily life.[60]

Meditation is not sufficient on its own: Meditation should not be considered a replacement for other forms of support that different people may need, such as supportive social relations with others in one's life, supportive structures and policies in one's work environment, mental health care, and physical care of the body. Many people have found psychotherapeutic approaches to be a helpful adjunct or preliminary to meditation practice, such as acceptance and commitment therapy, dialectical behavior therapy, emotion-focused therapy, or internal family systems therapy.[61]

1

RECEPTIVE MODE

Letting Outer Refuge Evoke Inner Refuge

WHEN JOHN WAS A graduate student in Buddhist studies, the Dalai Lama was invited to his town to offer a special Buddhist empowerment ritual over several days. John and his wife, Barbara, sought housing for many Tibetan people and respected lamas from throughout the world who came for the ceremony. John's university offered low-cost dorm space for that purpose, but spaces were limited. He and Barbara ended up having to assign Nechung Rinpoche, a renowned lama, to a dorm room that was rather dark and dingy from generations of college-student use. After the rituals were completed, Barbara and John went to see Rinpoche in his small room to say goodbye. They were horrified by the stained and scarred walls of his dorm room and apologized for the shabby accommodation, but Rinpoche just looked at them wide-eyed, as if he had no idea what they were talking about. "This place is a pure realm," he said, his face filled with joy. Barbara and John exchanged surprised looks, thinking, "He actually means it!" That dingy place was heaven to him, and the people all around were divine beings in his perception. Despite their initial bewilderment, his pure view became infectious. Suddenly Barbara and John, too, felt blessed to be there, as if it truly were a holy realm and they, with Rinpoche, were sacred beings.

In retrospect, this encounter made deep sense. Nechung Rinpoche had spent a lifetime of daily meditation practice invoking a field of spiritual ancestors and enlightened beings as a blessed environment that embraced him and his whole world in unconditional love, compassion, and wisdom. Each day in meditation, he let the power and energy of that spiritual field draw him into oneness with it in the depth of his being, to become an extension of its unconditional powers of sacred perception and love. John and Barbara had experienced the natural resonance of Rinpoche's lifetime of such practice.

INTRODUCING THE RECEPTIVE
MODE OF MEDITATION

As we saw in the introduction, the ritual and contemplative practices of Buddhism and other spiritual traditions have the power to evoke their practitioners' innate capacities of love, compassion, and wisdom. This is often done initially by bringing to mind a spiritual field of inspiration and blessing that holds participants unconditionally in those qualities—what we have called a field of care. Evolutionary theory understands those innate caring capacities to have developed in our species through natural selection.[1] Tibetan Buddhism understands them as capacities of our basic awareness, our buddha nature, which can be cultivated to increasing power and inclusivity with the right kinds of practice. The aim of this book is to make such practices newly accessible to people of any background who have the motivation to take them up.

The receptive mode of sustainable compassion training (SCT) is modeled on the field of care practice common to spiritual traditions. We bring to mind a field of care that we experience as holding us and our world in unconditional qualities of love, acceptance, compassion, and wisdom. This evokes further qualities from our underlying awareness—such as a sense of inner safety, openness, warmth, love, gratitude, and being deeply seen. In spiritual traditions of various cultures, such a field of care typically includes spiritual figures prominent in those cultures—for example, a field of spiritual ancestors, divine figures, saints, lineage teachers, bodhisattvas, and so forth. Tibetan Buddhist communities in which John and Paul practice bring to mind a collection of figures who embody the qualities of enlightenment—buddhas, bodhisattvas, lineage teachers, and other spiritual beings. Indigenous peoples of Africa, Asia, and the Americas often bring to mind their spiritual ancestors and beings from the spirit world. Contemplative Jews, Christians, and Muslims, while recalling the presence of God, may also bring to mind one or more prophets, saints, or sacred texts that embody or express the qualities of the divine. The meditations in this chapter provide ways for diverse people with a wide variety of social, cultural, religious, or scientific backgrounds to find access to the transformative power of this kind of practice, by bringing to mind a field of care in a form that works best for each individual.

Meditation practitioners in receptive mode first identify the field of care that works best for them to evoke loving qualities from their basic awareness. Once evoked, with repeated practice, those caring qualities help heal the mental and emotional barriers that had obstructed those qualities, so the qualities can emerge more fully and freely. As these loving qualities increasingly manifest in repeated meditation, they help establish the inner secure base that is needed to relax and settle into the source of those qualities in the depth of our awareness (deepening mode, chapter 2) and to hold others in those same qualities (inclusive mode, chapter 3).

To enter into the receptive mode of meditation, then, we each need to find our own most effective ways of accessing the underlying capacities of love, compassion, acceptance, warmth, and discernment that are available in the depth of our awareness, our buddha nature. In this chapter, we explore practicing with four kinds of field of care to see which ones are most effective at providing such access for each of us. Here are the four options:

1. Reinhabiting *a caring moment* from anytime in your life—a moment when somebody was lovingly present to you—seeing you in your deep worth.
2. Bringing to mind a *benefactor*, someone that you are deeply grateful has been in your life or world.
3. Bringing to mind a divine presence, spiritual ancestors from your tradition who inspire and bless you, or a part of the natural world that is sacred to you.
4. Reinhabiting a caring moment when you were a loving presence to another.

REINHABITING A CARING MOMENT AS MEDITATION

Although you may never have tried this before, it's quite possible to bring to mind a moment when you were seen and held in loving-kindness, and to reinhabit it in meditation as if it were happening now. In such a practice, we experience what it feels like to be seen in our deep worth and loved, which disrupts our tendency to mistake limiting thoughts of ourselves for ourselves. As we saw in the introduction, theories of grounded cognition suggest that to reinhabit a caring moment is not just a different way of thinking or believing but a way to actually relive the felt presence of care throughout our whole body and mind. When we imagine a caring moment from the past and reinhabit it, the imagination activates similar neural patterns now: sensory, cognitive, affective, motor, and interoceptive neural systems all come online. To reinhabit a loving moment repeatedly in meditation, then, is not just an intellectual exercise. It's a way to develop habits of mind and body that can help heal and, over time, deeply transform us.[2]

As attachment theory shows, it is incredibly powerful when others see our deep dignity, worth, and potential; take joy in the basic goodness of our being; and wish us well. They help us to recognize and accept our dignity, worth, and potential. It is from there that we too can sense the same in others. This connection between receiving and extending care, between being seen deeply and seeing others deeply, is expressed in the three-mode pattern of contemplative practice, inherited from ancient traditions, that we explore throughout this book.

Recalling a Caring Moment

To engage this meditation, you bring to mind a simple caring moment when you were with another person or being, together with the place where it happened—a moment when someone was radiating warmth and care to you, seeing you in your deep worth, listening to you, rooting for you, taking joy in you, wishing you well, or laughing with you. A moment of warm connection that makes you happy to recall or feels heartwarming. When first learning this practice, it's important to recall a simple, unproblematic moment—not a time, for instance, with someone who later cruelly disappointed you.

For example, you may recall a moment in childhood when someone was very happy to push your swing or play a game with you. John can recall his Uncle Howie laughing with him and his siblings when they were very young as they played a rousing game of Scrabble. Paul recalls peacefully playing gin rummy with his Grandma Corrine in her kitchen. Or you might think of a moment when someone was cheering for you, deeply listening when you felt troubled, or really seeing you—like when Mr. Harrison, John's high school teacher, gave John a big smile of congratulations after his theater performance. Such a moment of caring connection could be as simple as a welcoming smile or someone laughing with you—like moments in Paul's college classes when students generously laughed with him at his jokes. Such moments often also occur with strangers—like when John was temporarily using a cane after an injury and a young woman on the subway offered her seat to him with a warm, caring look. Many of us also have loving moments of connection with animals in our lives that are uplifting to recall. If we pay attention, we may notice little moments of simple caring connection virtually every day.

If the moment you have in mind makes you feel happy or uplifted to recall, you are already starting to access positive qualities of your underlying awareness (your buddha nature) through it, and it is suitable for the meditation on page 35. For some of us, it may take a little while to recall such moments, but we have all had them. Take the time you need now to remember one, together with the place or setting where it happened—how it looked, sounded, felt.

If you have difficulty accessing a caring moment in the form above, see if one of these alternatives is more accessible for you and bring it to mind together with the place where it happened: Recall a moment with another person or animal when you were a caring presence for them (which we will explore further). Or recall a moment of caring connection between others that you observed and took joy in at the time.[3] Joy in others' happiness can also occur when experiencing evocative literature, theater, or film. Or think of a moment when you were in a place that is special to you, where you felt deeply well, safe, at peace, and at home.

Identify just one caring moment, of any of the kinds described above, that when recalled puts you in touch with the heartwarming qualities that you experienced in that moment. Such qualities might include a sense of well-being, acceptance, warmth, tenderness, care, openness, inner safety, being seen or heard, gratitude, ease, simplicity, joy, or feeling at home.

Our Purpose for Reinhabiting a Caring Moment

Our purpose for reinhabiting such a moment in receptive mode meditation is to directly access loving capacities from the depth of our awareness, by interrupting what has obstructed them. These capacities are often impeded by our usual habits of thought and reaction. The loving energies and qualities we access in a caring moment can help our minds begin to heal, open, and relax into the source of those qualities in the depth of our awareness, our buddha nature. This process gradually establishes an inner secure base of love, compassion, discernment, and inner safety. This is a wonderful development in itself, and it is also needed for us to extend love and compassion more sustainably and inclusively to others.

If we are conscious that the purpose of the meditation is to provide fresh access to positive qualities from our own awareness, we can align our minds with that singular purpose rather than getting distracted from it. For example, when recalling any caring moment, we may be in the habit of ruminating about the people involved in it—evaluating whether they were always loving enough or such. But no human being can measure up to such an analysis. Or we might feel that we do not deserve to direct such attention to ourselves, and we should instead focus on generating care for others. These kinds of thoughts can shut down our engagement with meditation, but they don't have to. It is helpful to remember that we are using the caring moment only to access loving qualities from the depth of our awareness, to reexperience those qualities now, steep in them, and be drawn into them more and more. When we remember that is the sole purpose of this practice, we know to come back to that purpose whenever the mind diverts from it.

In the caring moment meditation that follows, then, after reinhabiting that moment, when you begin to experience loving qualities that come with it, shift your attention mainly to those qualities. People who have repeatedly practiced this meditation commonly report loving qualities such as warmth, acceptance, tenderness, gratitude, ease, peace, and so forth. Focus on how such qualities feel in your body, heart, and mind—not mainly on stories your mind may generate about that moment or about people involved. We access the felt sense of that moment as if it's happening now. If stories about it arise, we can let them go by letting the positive qualities that accompany the moment draw our awareness back to them, to settle into those qualities more and more.

Pause after reading each sentence of the meditation instruction to give yourself time to settle into it. If you prefer to be guided by audio instruction of the meditation below and the others in this book, you can find audio of them at this link: shambhala.com/howcompassionworksmeditations.

FIELD OF CARE MEDITATION 1: A CARING MOMENT

STEP 1. ABDOMINAL BREATHING (3 MINUTES OR SO) Sit in a relaxed, comfortable way with back straight, eyes gazing gently downward. Come down from the thinking mind into the body. Take a slow, deep breath, inhaling from the abdomen so it expands, then exhaling slowly and completely, letting go of all your concerns with the exhale. Relax for a moment before inhaling again. Repeat several times. Then, while still breathing from the abdomen, let the breath settle into its own natural flow. Feel the belly expand and contract with each breath. Let that feeling draw you into it more and more, breath by breath.

STEP 2. REINHABITING A CARING MOMENT (7 TO 10 MINUTES) Bring to mind a caring moment that makes you happy to recall. Bring this to mind not as a distant memory but as if it is happening right now, right here. You are being seen and held in deep care, compassion, acceptance, and warmth beyond judgments. (*Pause*) Relax into this experience, steeping in its loving energies, feeling its tender qualities, and letting them spaciously infuse your whole being. Accept these loving energies and qualities into your whole body and mind—into every part of your body, every layer of feeling and emotion—as if every part of you is loved in its very being. (*Pause*) Let these loving qualities unify you with them more and more. (*Pause*)

Let any thoughts or reactions that occur just be embraced in the spacious warmth and acceptance of this loving environment. Let them find their own place in their own time, by letting them all be.

If you lose the feeling of the loving qualities, freshly recall your caring moment as present here now, and let its power draw you back into the felt sense of it.

STEP 3. RELEASING (3 TO 5 MINUTES) Now let this environment of warmth and acceptance help your mind to relax deeply and release all its frameworks of meditation and concern. Let the mind settle back a bit inwardly and come to rest in the background of its awareness, which is naturally wide open and luminous, like a sunlit sky. As thoughts and feelings arise, let them just metabolize themselves and release within this sky-like openness of awareness, by letting everything be.

Processing the Meditation

Take a moment to let the feeling of this meditation continue to resonate. Let that felt sense overflow from the meditation to infuse your experience now, affecting and informing whatever you may do next.

What unfolded in the steps of this meditation? The abdominal breathing in step 1 evokes a relaxation response in the body and mind by activating our parasympathetic nervous system.[4] This helps our bodies and minds to relax, settle deeply, and become receptive to what will follow. In step 2 we settled into an embodied experience of a caring moment, steeping in the felt sense of its loving energies and qualities in body, heart, and mind. In step 3, we let go of the visualization, and let those loving qualities help the mind to trust, relax, and begin to settle into the source of the qualities—the openness, clarity, simplicity, and warmth available in the depth of our awareness, our buddha nature. Step 3 is the beginning of the deepening mode of practice, which we will explore further in chapter 2.

With these three meditation steps, we learn to become more fully and compassionately present to all parts of ourselves, including all of our physical and mental feelings, so they can begin to relax, heal, and settle, with an increasing sense of inner safety and well-being. From this secure base within, we can also be more compassionately present to others and their feelings in a more sustaining and inclusive way. That direction of practice is the inclusive mode, which we will explore in chapter 3.

Becoming Familiar with a Spectrum of Loving Capacities That Emerge from Our Awareness

Step 2 of the meditation instructed: "Relax into this experience, steeping in its loving energies, feeling its tender qualities, letting them spaciously infuse your whole being." Try now to name at least one loving quality that you felt when following this instruction. Try to name several such qualities that you experienced. Please take some time now to write them down in your practice journal before you read the next paragraph.

Here are some of the qualities that participants have commonly named after doing this caring moment meditation: "warmth," "acceptance," "tenderness," "ease," "spaciousness," "gratitude," "peace," "well-being," "joy," "felt seen," "softening," "healing," "slowing down," "simplicity," "felt at home," "felt like nothing is wrong," "felt restful," "I felt uplifted," "felt like grace," "felt like a blessing." Does this list help you notice further such qualities that you experienced during the meditation? If so, please add them to the list in your journal.

The practice of noticing and naming a whole spectrum of loving qualities helps us further engage the purpose of the receptive mode, which is to access loving capacities of our basic awareness—in Buddhist terms, our buddha nature. According to research in the science of emotion, the ability to notice, distinguish, and specifically label distinct mental states and qualities is a form of emotional intelligence.[5] Scientists call this ability "granularity." Some people have higher granularity for emotional states. They are able to use specific labels for different emotions—for example: angry, frustrated, irritated, disappointed; uplifted, cheerful, energized, joyful. Others have lower granularity, using more general, imprecise labels—for example: bad, horrible; good, wonderful. Higher granularity for emotional states has a number of benefits related to self-awareness, empathy, relationality, and resilience. It is correlated with greater emotion regulation, awareness, and emotional stability, more informed empathy for others, and more social and emotional competence with others.[6] We can develop granularity for caring experiences by attending to a variety of loving qualities that arise in meditation sessions and across a variety of caring moments. This helps us become more receptive to such qualities, which can bring out the benefits mentioned in the prior section.

Hidden Powers of Love and Compassion Are Available Here and Now

From a Tibetan Buddhist perspective, these kinds of qualities arise from the depth of our awareness, our buddha nature. The capacity to experience such loving qualities is always available here and now, but because that capacity is often held back by our ordinary habits of thought and reaction, many of us haven't known how to access it more fully. Those habits are interrupted by the caring moment meditation. *This meditation, then, shows us how immediately we can access such loving qualities from our basic awareness.* From the perspective of grounded cognition noted above, we reenact these qualities throughout our whole mind and body when we recall the caring moment in meditation.

Deepening experience of the loving qualities can be further supported by having a more granular sense of them. In order to cultivate such granularity, after each time that you do the caring moment meditation, try to identify further loving qualities that you experienced in it so they become more conscious, accessible, and familiar to you. With repetition of practice, our increasing ability to notice and feel our way into various loving qualities helps us experience them more fully.[7]

Unconditionality Is Part of the Underlying Power of Love Brought Out by This Meditation

Also notice how the meditation process purifies the qualities of love and compassion we experience, taking them into greater unconditionality. Unless we spend our days with saints, we probably start the caring moment meditation with a fairly ordinary experience of caring connection, when someone was present to us in a welcoming way, not necessarily in a totally unconditional and unrestricted way—that is, holding us in unchanging love no matter what happens and no matter what we may think, say, or do. But repeatedly engaging the instruction—"Accept these loving energies and qualities into your whole body and mind . . . as if every part of you is loved in its very being."—we experience the loving qualities as more unconditional and unrestricted. The sense of unlimited love, care, warmth, and acceptance implied in that phrasing brings out the unconditional capacity of love and compassion that had been hidden in our underlying awareness. In Tibetan Buddhist understanding, this unconditional capacity, too, is a quality of our buddha nature—an innate power within our awareness for increasingly stable, enduring, inclusive, and unqualified care, acceptance, and compassion. Repeated practice of this kind of meditation familiarizes us with the hidden power in us to experience love in an unconditional way, first with regard to all aspects of our experience—all thoughts, feelings, senses of self—and later with regard to all others.

When the mind, with repeated practice, experiences qualities of love in an increasingly unconditional way, it engenders a deep sense of inner safety and protection. Sensing this unconditional power of love as trustworthy, the mind learns to trust its source in the depth of our awareness, which is endowed with qualities of openness, clarity, profound peace, and warmth. This depth of awareness transcends the mind's habitual frameworks of thought and reaction. Repeated practice of step 3 of the meditation becomes a process of increasing relaxation, inner acceptance, and spaciousness that can be deeply healing and freeing. In this way, step 3 of the Field of Care Meditation represents the beginning of the deepening mode of meditation that we will discuss in the next chapter.

COMMON IMPEDIMENTS TO RELIVING A CARING MOMENT AS MEDITATION

Before we do the Field of Care Meditation 1: A Caring Moment meditation again, it will be helpful to note several common impediments that people encounter in this practice, so we can recognize and work with them.

Impediment 1: Our Attachment Scripts May Cause Us to Ignore, Forget, or Distrust Caring Moments

When introduced to the concept of a caring moment, some of us may think, "I haven't had any such moment," "I can't remember one," or "People don't care about me." These are common reactions, but they are not necessarily true. We have all had little moments of caring connection, but we may not have noticed them enough to recall them later. This may be because of what is called, in developmental psychology, an "attachment script" that is operative in us.[8]

As mentioned in our discussion of attachment theory in the introductory chapter, in early childhood we had various experiences with those who were supposed to care for us. Those early experiences generated sets of expectations about relationships. Such expectations become internalized as habitual ways of thinking and talking repeatedly to ourselves about our relationships, like a script. Over time, these habits of mind take the form of internal models of self and world, including our self-worth and whether the world is a trustworthy source of care. For example, we may tend to think, "No one cares about me," "People just pretend to care to get something from me," or "If they really knew me, they wouldn't love me." Because of repeated identification with these internal scripts, we take the corresponding models of ourselves and others as facts. We don't realize they are merely habits of thought—not objectively who we are.

Such internal scripts often prevent us from noticing simple moments of caring connection in our days. Then we may have difficulty recalling any such moment, even if several such moments happened earlier today! For example, someone smiled upon first seeing you, or was happy to be with you for a moment, or pleased to help you with something. (Please note that our discussion in this section refers to attachment scripts that are *out of touch with reality*. Alternatively, there may be scripts that arise that do reflect reality. For example, scripts such as "My environment is not safe" or "This relationship is not safe" might reflect truths about your current experience. We address how to work with such experiences later in this chapter.)

In addition, we might miss or neglect moments of caring connection even when they are right in front of us, due to a process researchers have called selective attention. In a famous study, people were asked to count the number of times that a basketball was passed between players on a given team. During the video, a person wearing a gorilla outfit walks through the middle of the court, waves at the screen, and leaves. In some versions of the study, up to 50 percent of people did not notice the gorilla because their attention was elsewhere, focused on the basketball.[9] Caring moments can be similarly hidden in plain sight. Because our goals often direct our attention to other things, such as competitive strivings with others, we fail to notice the energy of care that pervades our lives.

Attachment theory helps explain how caring moments, like the basketball-court gorilla, can fail to reach our awareness. The dismissal of care may be an attachment strategy that we have learned as an attempt to protect ourselves from the vulnerability inherent in opening up to care. This might take the form of thoughts that dismiss others' care, such as "They don't really care about me" or "They are just being polite" or "They are trying to get something out of me." Unfortunately these scripts can be activated in any moment of experiencing care and thus interfere with our ability to access and relax into the enlightened dimension of our nature. Avoidant strategies, such as "I don't need others; I can take care of myself" can develop if we have experienced others' care as unavailable or unreliable early in life. Then, throughout the lifespan, such reactions may lead us to dismiss or misconstrue other's genuinely caring actions, even when we are not conscious that we are doing so.[10] We may completely miss authentic moments of care. Our discomfort with vulnerability to care can lead us to filter out the caring moments that are happening all the time. Instead, we often subconsciously cling to those familiar strategies, from the sense that they offer some kind of protection and control of the external world. Throughout our lives, each of us is conditioned to develop diverse strategies and scripts that trigger various impressions of self and others that may prevent us from connecting with felt qualities of care more deeply.

To break free from bondage to attachment scripts and limited models of ourselves and others, it is helpful, then, to learn how to become more conscious of, and receptive to, moments of care. We can gain more access to our innate capacities for care and compassion by noticing the felt qualities that come with those simple moments of connection, and allowing our bodies, hearts, and minds to be infused with those qualities. In time, this can help us discover that those qualities are always available to us as capacities of our underlying awareness—part of our buddha nature. After practicing this way for several years, for instance, Paul recalled a deep caring moment of goodbye to his Japanese host family at the end of his cultural exchange program in high school. It was a joy suddenly to rediscover the power of care from that moment within his own mind in meditation.

Please take some time now to revisit the different kinds of caring moments described above, noticing this time how your internal scripts may cause you to ignore or dismiss some such moments that you have actually experienced. Because such scripts may operate below our conscious awareness, we may also become newly conscious of them when engaging in Field of Care Meditation 1. Though perhaps uncomfortable, becoming newly conscious of such scripts in a gentle, welcoming way—and exploring how the caring qualities generated in the meditation can take us beyond these habitual scripts—is an important part of making progress in these meditations.

Impediment 2: We May Not Be Reliving the Caring Moment as If It Is Happening Now

Some people can bring a moment of caring connection to mind yet not experience its loving qualities. If this is true for you, it might be because you brought it to mind only as a *memory* of the past, not with the feeling that it is happening now. Another kind of inner "script" might pop up in this context, with the thought, "Perhaps others can experience what a caring moment feels like, but I can't." This reaction might feel very real, but the attachment theory perspective suggests this is an internal script—not the final word.

The ability to experience again the felt sense of a previous experience is a skill that we all have and frequently use. As theories of grounded cognition suggest, we are constantly simulating experiences from the past throughout our body and mind. For example, we often remember moments from the past in which we felt annoyed, angry, afraid, joyful, blissful, or sad, and while recollecting such a moment, reexperience its feelings in the present to a significant degree.[11] That's why we often ruminate about things that previously happened to us: we are not just *thinking about* those moments, we are *feeling* them. For example, by simply imagining a basket of fresh strawberries or grapes, the mouth often begins to salivate. The body feels what the thought has created, as if it were real, not thought made.[12]

In this meditation, we relive a simple caring moment with the feeling of it in a similar way. Knowing that we simulate our experiences all the time, with many other kinds of moments, can help empower this possibility. If you had difficulty accessing the feeling of a caring moment the first time you tried it, when you do the meditation a second time on page 43, try more fully to relive the moment by bringing more of its aspects to mind while feeling it as though it is happening right now (how things look within that moment, or sound, or smell, or physically feel, and so on).

Informed by these points, please now select the type of caring moment from the list (pages 32–33) that you currently find most connecting, then do Field of Care Meditation 1 again. Pause after reading each sentence of the instructions to give you time to practice it. (An audio option is available at shambhala.com/howcompassionworksmeditations.)

REPEATING FIELD OF CARE MEDITATION 1:
A CARING MOMENT

STEP 1. ABDOMINAL BREATHING (3 MINUTES OR SO) Sit in a relaxed, comfortable way with back straight, eyes gazing gently downward. Come down from the thinking mind into the body. Take a slow, deep breath, inhaling from the abdomen so it expands, then exhaling slowly and completely, letting go of all your concerns with the exhale. Relax for a moment before inhaling again. Repeat several times. Then, while still breathing from the abdomen, let the breath settle into its own natural flow. Feel the belly expand and contract with each breath. Let that feeling draw you into it more and more, breath by breath.

STEP 2. REINHABITING A CARING MOMENT (7 TO 10 MINUTES) Bring to mind a caring moment that makes you happy to recall. Bring this to mind not as a distant memory but as if it is happening right now, right here. You are being seen and held in deep care, compassion, acceptance, and warmth beyond judgments. (*Pause*) Relax into this experience, steeping in its loving energies, feeling its tender qualities, and letting them spaciously infuse your whole being. Accept these loving energies and qualities into your whole body and mind—into every part of your body, into every layer of feeling and emotion. Every part of you loved in its very being. (*Pause*) Let these loving qualities unify you with them more and more. (*Pause*)

Let any thoughts or reactions that occur be embraced in the spacious warmth and acceptance of this loving environment. Let them find their own place in their own time, by letting them all be.

If you lose the feeling of the loving qualities, freshly recall your caring moment as present here now, and let its power draw you back into the felt sense of it.

STEP 3. RELEASING (3 TO 5 MINUTES) Now let this loving environment of warmth and acceptance help your mind to relax deeply and release all its frameworks of meditation and concern. Let the mind settle back a bit inwardly and come to rest in the background of its awareness, which is naturally wide open and luminous, like a sunlit sky. As thoughts and feelings arise, let them just metabolize themselves and release within this sky-like openness of awareness by letting everything be.

Processing the Meditation

After this, and after every other meditation you do, take a moment to let the feeling of the meditation continue to permeate your body and mind. Let that feeling overflow from the meditation to infuse your experience now, affecting and informing whatever you may do next.

Look back at the list of loving qualities that you named earlier. Can you name any further such qualities that you experienced this time in step 2 of the meditation?

Over the next few days, please explore Field of Care Meditation 1 with different kinds of caring moments (for example, moments of connection with different people in various situations over your life, or with a pet, or when you were taking joy in others' happiness, or when you felt at home in a place that is special to you). Just do one such kind of meditation at a time. This variety helps us find moments that provide the best initial access to loving capacities from our underlying awareness. Different kinds of caring moments may also evoke somewhat different loving qualities, which helps us access a fuller spectrum of caring capacities for inner healing, deepening, and extending to others in further practices throughout the book.

OTHER FIELD OF CARE OPTIONS
FOR RECEPTIVE-MODE PRACTICE

So far we have explored Field of Care Meditation 1, in which we relive a caring moment when we were seen and supported by another, in order to evoke loving qualities of our awareness. We will now explore three other Field of Care options for the same purpose: option 2, bringing to mind a *benefactor*, someone you are grateful has been in your life; option 3, if you practice in a religious or spiritual tradition, bringing to mind a *spiritual field*—a sacred reality or field of spiritual figure(s) felt to be unconditionally present to you and your world; and option 4, reinhabiting a caring moment when you were a loving presence for another.

Invoking a Benefactor as a Wise, Loving Presence

Think of someone you are truly grateful has been in your life or world—someone who has inspired, uplifted, or blessed you by their loving presence, wisdom, way of being, teaching, mentorship, or work in the world. This may be someone you have known personally, such as a loving relative, a caring family friend, or an inspiring teacher, pastor, counselor, therapist, or personal friend. It could also be someone—past or present—you have not met personally but who has greatly affected you through their writing, speaking, artwork, music, presence, or activity. You may have a book by such a person in your home, a recording of a talk, or a picture. To do Field of Care Meditation 2 with such a benefactor, think of that person as present here with you, supporting you with their loving, inspiring presence and wisdom.

Invoking a Spiritual Field as an Unconditional Support

Some people who practice regularly in a spiritual or religious community feel a strong connection to one or more spiritual benefactors within that tradition, as in the story of Nechung Rinpoche at the start of this chapter. Examples include a field of spiritual ancestors, lineage teachers, bodhi-sattvas, a communion of saints, or a favorite prophet or saintly figure of their spiritual community. If you have a felt sense that you and your world are held in the unwavering love, compassion, wisdom, and blessing of such beings when you bring them to mind, they will serve well as your field of care for the next meditation. In this form of meditation, imagine them to be present, encompassing you and your world in continual blessings and energies of love, compassion, and wisdom. Or, if meaningful to you, you can simply bring to mind the presence of God in that way.

Or, as in many Indigenous traditions, you could bring to mind the natural world, or some part of it, with which you feel a strong spiritual connection, such as the sky, the vast ocean, a majestic mountain, or an animal or tree that is sacred to you. Or you could bring to mind a sacred symbol, such as a light in your heart or a holy sound, or some image or icon that is rich in meaning for you. For this meditation, your image of nature or symbol needs to be experienced as present to you with qualities of unwavering love, compassion, and wisdom. You would bring such an image to mind with a sense that you are deeply known and held in those unconditional qualities.[13]

Take a few moments to consider the two options above for Field of Care Meditation 2, bringing to mind a *benefactor* or a *spiritual field*. Which of those two options is most effective right now to help you sense that you are held in a field of unconditional, uninterrupted love, compassion, and wisdom? Take that option into the next meditation. The special power of these two options is their unconditionality—we experience the figure(s) in the meditation to be holding us and our whole world in unchanging compassion and wisdom, unaffected by what anyone may think, say, or do. Pause after reading each sentence of the instruction to practice it. (An audio option is available at shambhala.com/howcompassionworksmeditations.)

FIELD OF CARE MEDITATION 2: INVOKING A BENEFACTOR OR A SPIRITUAL FIELD

STEP 1. ABDOMINAL BREATHING (3 MINUTES OR SO) Sit in a relaxed, comfortable way with back straight, eyes gazing gently downward. Come down from the thinking mind into the body. Take a slow, deep breath, inhaling from the abdomen so it expands, then exhaling slowly and completely, letting go of all your concerns with the exhale. Relax for a moment before inhaling again. Repeat several times. Then, while still breathing from the abdomen, let the breath settle into its own natural flow. Feel the belly expand and contract with each breath. Let that feeling draw you into it more and more, breath by breath.

STEP 2. FIELD OF CARE (7 TO 10 MINUTES) Now bring to mind your field of care in the form of your benefactor or spiritual field. Bring this to mind not just as a memory or an abstraction but as really present here with you now. Your benefactor or spiritual field is holding you and your whole world in unconditional warmth, acceptance, compassion, and wisdom, beyond judgments. (*Pause*) Relax into this experience, steeping in its loving energies, feeling its tender qualities, and letting them spaciously infuse your whole being. Accept these loving energies and qualities into your whole body and mind—into every part of your body, into every layer of feeling and emotion. Every part of you loved in its very being. (*Pause*) Let these loving qualities unify you with them more and more. (*Pause*)

Let any thoughts or reactions that occur be embraced in the spacious warmth and acceptance of this loving environment. Let them find their own place in their own time by letting them all be.

If you lose the feeling of the loving qualities, freshly recall your field of care as present here now, and let its power draw you back into the felt sense of it.

STEP 3. RELEASING (3 TO 5 MINUTES) Let this loving environment of warmth and acceptance help your mind to relax deeply and release all its frameworks of meditation and concern. Let the mind settle back a bit inwardly and come to rest in the background of its awareness, which is naturally wide open and luminous, like a sunlit sky. As thoughts and feelings arise, let them just metabolize themselves and release within this sky-like openness of awareness by letting everything be.

Processing the Meditation

Take a moment to let the feeling of this meditation resonate. Let that felt sense overflow from the meditation to infuse your experience now, affecting whatever you may do next.

Try now to name one or more further loving qualities that you experienced in this meditation to add to your list.

Those who feel a special connection to this form of meditation often say they feel more of the unconditional or unrestricted power of love in this meditation than in Field of Care Meditation 1: A Caring Moment. Others do not relate as well to the notion of benefactor or spiritual field and may find reliving a caring moment more accessible and connecting.

The Resonance of Love and Acceptance
Continues to Call Us Back to It

As we noted above, many people report difficulty with meditation because the mind tends to wander constantly, but this is normal and a great opportunity for deepening in practice. We may experience a benefactor or spiritual being as someone who relates to a deep dignity in us that is not changing, even when our own mind is wandering or confused, or even when an attachment script activates a sense of self that doubts or dismisses such love. Whenever we notice the mind wandering in meditation, we can allow the field of care to draw us back into its energy of deep acceptance and love. The qualities of the field of care can remain accessible in the background even when we begin to get distracted. This power of love is always calling us back to it, and we can let it draw us back. The meditation brings out this enduring power of love.

RECALLING A CARING MOMENT WHEN YOU
WERE A LOVING PRESENCE TO ANOTHER

Many people find it helpful to access their loving capacities by recalling another kind of caring moment, one in which you helped generate a field of care by being a loving presence for another being. In this meditation, you will recall a moment when you were holding another being in loving-kindness or compassion. This helps us further access, nurture, and embody capacities of warmth, acceptance, openness, care, compassion, reverence, and so forth, from our underlying awareness.

To prepare for the next meditation, please recall a moment when you were a loving presence to someone else, human or animal—a moment when you were radiating warmth and care to them—for example, when you were seeing them in their deep worth, rooting for them, taking joy in them, deeply listening, or doing something that makes them happy. Try to recall a simple moment like that from any time in your life. The focus here is not on a moment when you felt burdened by physically or emotionally caring for someone else. Instead, recall a time when you were present to another with a simple, openhearted *attitude* of loving care—for example, when you were glad to see someone, taking delight in them, speaking to their hidden strengths, encouraging them, responding sympathetically, smiling upon them, or simply wishing them well. Or it might be a loving moment with a pet, patting them just the way they like it! Pause after reading each sentence of the instruction to practice it. (An audio option is available at shambhala .com/howcompassionworksmeditations.)

FIELD OF CARE MEDITATION 3: YOURSELF AS A LOVING PRESENCE TO ANOTHER[14]

STEP 1. ABDOMINAL BREATHING (3 MINUTES OR SO) Sit in a relaxed, comfortable way with back straight, eyes gazing gently downward. Come down from the thinking mind into the body. Take a slow deep breath, inhaling from the abdomen so it expands, then exhaling slowly and completely, letting go of all your concerns with the exhale. Relax for a moment before inhaling again. Repeat several times. Then, while still breathing from the abdomen, let the breath settle into its own natural flow. Feel the belly expand and contract with each breath. Let that feeling draw you into it more and more, breath by breath.

STEP 2. REINHABITING A CARING MOMENT (7 MINUTES) Now bring to mind a moment when you were present to another person or being in a loving way, together with its place or setting. Consider that moment not as a distant memory but as happening right now—you are present in that way now with that being. Feel the loving energy and tender qualities that accompany this way of being with another. Let this loving energy flow freely. Steep in its tender qualities, letting them infuse your whole being and world.

STEP 3. NOTICING YOUR CARING QUALITIES (3 TO 5 MINUTES) Notice the loving qualities occurring in this moment, such as warmth, care, acceptance, compassion, responsiveness, peace, inner strength, discernment, courage. Let yourself fully accept, own, embody these qualities of your loving self.

Let any thoughts or reactions that arise during this meditation be gently embraced in the spacious warmth and acceptance of this loving environment.

STEP 4. RELEASING (3 TO 5 MINUTES) Now let this environment of love, warmth, and acceptance help your mind to relax deeply and release all its frameworks of meditation and concern. Let the mind settle back a bit inwardly and come to rest in the background of its awareness, which is naturally wide open and luminous, like a sunlit sky. As thoughts and feelings arise, let them just metabolize themselves and release within this sky-like openness of awareness by letting everything be.

Processing the Meditation

Let the feeling of this meditation continue to resonate. What qualities of your caring self did you notice in steps 2 and 3 of the meditation? Try to name several. As you repeat this practice over time, try to notice further such qualities. What is the practice showing you about your ability to access those qualities and to be a loving presence to others? What does the practice show you about your ability to become a loving presence to your own thoughts, feelings, and struggles?

PROGRESSING IN PRACTICE WITH ALTERNATIVE ACCESS POINTS TO OUR INNATE CAPACITIES

We have now explored a variety of options for the Field of Care Meditation that can serve as alternative points of access to loving qualities of our underlying awareness. Points of access to such qualities include: (1) recalling a simple moment of caring connection, (2) bringing to mind a benefactor to whom you feel grateful or a spiritual field that is uplifting for you, or (3) recalling a moment when you were a loving presence to another. The sign that any such option is a good access point for loving qualities is that it effectively takes you into the experience of those qualities in body and mind. Any field of care that you find effective for that needs never get old. We can repeat the same meditation again and again, experiencing it freshly every time because we are not engaging it as merely a memory or abstraction. Rather, as we repeat the meditation, we keep reentering that field of care in the present, reliving it anew, and *feeling* it more and more fully in body and mind. By practicing this way, we may even feel the power of a caring moment now more strongly than we did in our initial experience of it.

When first learning this receptive mode of meditation, it is helpful to explore several of the field of care options to identify what access points to loving qualities are most effective at present, then to familiarize yourself with those forms of meditation in repeated practice. Initially, for example, you may find a memory of one particular caring moment most effective. Over time, it will be helpful also to explore other options that may be effective—other caring moments or a benefactor, a spiritual field, or a time when you were a loving presence to another. Or a new doorway may spontaneously open. After several years of doing this practice, for example, John suddenly remembered the face of Mr. Sorley, a deeply kind camp counselor who made him feel at home at a camp he attended as a young child. John was amazed to find this long-forgotten source of warmth and belonging already present in his mind. By exploring different doors of access to loving qualities, we begin to populate our own fields of care, analogous to the fields of buddhas and bodhisattvas that Buddhists have relied on for centuries.

NOTICING DIFFICULTIES THAT ARISE
IN THE FIELD OF CARE MEDITATION

From the complementary perspectives of Buddhism and science, then, various alternatives for the field of care practice give us different points of access to underlying capacities of love, compassion, and discernment. Repeated practice gradually establishes greater ease of connection to those loving qualities and through them, to their source in the depth of our awareness from which to become present to others in more unconditional and inclusive ways.

Having now done these field of care meditations, we can draw on our own experience to revisit the kinds of impediments we discussed earlier in this chapter. Shortly after we begin experiencing loving qualities, various reactions may come up that begin to shut down our receptivity to those qualities. This usually happens while we are following step 2 of the meditation—the step where we steep in the loving qualities evoked by a field of care.

Perhaps you experienced a difficulty of some kind during that step in the meditations above—a train of thought or feeling that took your attention away from the loving qualities? If so, take a moment to recall what that felt like. If you like, you can repeat one of the meditations above now to help you recall.

What sort of difficulty arose for you? Before reading the next paragraph, try to name the most prominent difficulty you had during the meditation and describe what it was like in a sentence or two.

Here are examples of common ways of thinking that impede the meditation, reported by people in practice settings. Indeed, many of these reactions to the meditation are quite familiar to John and Paul from their own practice experience:

- "No one really cares about me."
- "If they really knew me, they wouldn't love me."
- "It doesn't feel right to focus this way on myself; I should only care for others."
- "I don't deserve love; I shouldn't be doing this practice."
- "I found myself wanting to think or fantasize about other things."
- "I spent the time analyzing what I was experiencing in the meditation rather than just experiencing it."
- "I doubted that the loving qualities I experienced could be real."
- "I doubted that any caring moment was good enough."
- "I don't fully trust anyone associated with love or care, for fear of getting hurt."
- "The person with me in the caring moment has passed away, so I stopped meditating to spend time grieving over their loss."

Is the difficulty that you named above included in that list of examples? Does that list help you remember further difficulties you may have had in the meditation? If so, please also write them down. Now recall our discussion of attachment scripts. Many of the difficult thoughts in the list above are examples of attachment scripts within which various senses of self are embedded. No matter what kind of upbringing we have had, we all harbor some inner layers of insecurity that are maintained by these scripts. But attachment theory also reminds us that these scripts express internalized concepts of ourselves that are just habitual ways of thinking about ourselves, not objective truths. As we will see, meditations of love, compassion, and wisdom can show us how to become a loving environment of warmth and acceptance in which all such senses of self can deeply relax, settle, and heal.

Why Difficulties Arise in the Field of Care Meditation

Why do such difficulties come up in this receptive mode of meditation? After all, in it we are learning to become receptive to loving energies and qualities. Why would our minds have trouble with such a good thing?

One reason has to do with receptivity itself. Another word for *receptivity*, in this context, is *vulnerability*. This practice cultivates vulnerability to loving qualities. But various parts of the mind, senses of self that our minds began identifying with in childhood, are very cautious about that kind of vulnerability. These parts of the mind associate the loving qualities we have experienced throughout our lives—feelings of warmth, acceptance, tenderness, and so forth—with people or circumstances outside of us. From childhood to now, these senses of self have been trying to help us find reliable ways of getting these loving qualities by managing our relations to the external world, often supported by attachment strategies that guide our expectations about others. These protective parts of us think we will get hurt if those caring qualities are not received from the external world in a safe enough way, which often means a way that they are in charge of.

For this reason, often the Field of Care Meditation is not just a free and easy experience. It may initiate attachment scripts that resist the practice by clinging to familiar senses of self that prevent vulnerability to loving qualities and their presumed external sources. Noticing and naming senses of self that seek to control external sources of care can further inform our meditation practice. For example, a "manager part" of my mind may arise—a sense of self that takes control of the meditation by thinking of other things. A "doubting part" may arise—a sense of self that thinks up reasons not to trust any caring moment, benefactor, or spiritual field. A "caretaker part" may arise in which I think it is wrong to focus on myself at all because I should always only be taking care of others. A "protector part" may arise that shuts down any loving experience to avoid feelings of hurt associated with unreliable figures of my past. A "self-critical part" may arise that thinks I do not deserve to experience love. An "intellectualizing part" may arise that takes me out of the meditation experience by continually analyzing it at a distance, endlessly seeking to understand the meditation at a rational, cognitive level rather than relaxing more fully into the felt sense of it. If I am a helping professional, a part of my mind may spend most of the meditation period thinking about how I will teach the meditation to others, preventing me from actually experiencing the loving qualities myself. Or a "striving part" may arise in which I am seeking to quickly fulfill some ideal of meditative attainment rather than following the meditation instruction simply to let the experience unfold in its own way. Noticing and naming such parts of the mind increases granularity for different senses of self through which we become more conscious of the patterns of thought and feeling that impede the loving qualities. We can then let those parts of us experience the qualities rather than obstruct them.

When the mind identifies with any such part of your mind, it feels like the loving qualities need to be controlled, managed, avoided, or prevented in order to protect yourself from vulnerability to their source, which that part identifies with external persons and situations that may not be fully trustworthy. When your mind is identified with any such part, it is unaware that the meditation is simply giving access to loving qualities from the depth of your own awareness, your own fuller being.[15]

ATTACHMENT THEORY FROM A BUDDHIST PERSPECTIVE

Tibetan Buddhism and attachment theory agree that we need caring figures in childhood to help bring out our innate, inner capacities of love and care, and throughout our lives to help us further access and develop those capacities. This is why attachment theory holds that we need caring people and caring moments in our lives for our emotional development—to evoke our capacity to experience, live into, and learn to embody loving qualities. Such experience helps us establish an inner core of self-worth, safety, well-being, and loving power—a secure base that enables us to explore the world with curiosity and to become present to others in empathetic and caring ways. This is why spiritual community is a central support of practice in all religious traditions, including Buddhism. Other persons serve as a scaffold for us, holding us in qualities of love and wisdom so we can learn similarly to hold others in such qualities. The need for connection with caring figures is also why Tibetans who take up Buddhist practices are often told vividly to recall their mothers' love (or that of another caring adult) as they experienced it in childhood. Doing so helps them access their own loving capacities as an inner secure base from which to experience gratitude and to become a loving presence to others.

John recalls how when he became upset as a small child, his mother came to comfort him and he would experience feelings of comfort and warmth. It felt as if the comfort and warmth came from her *into* him. But John's mother never injected those feelings into him. Her caring presence *evoked John's own underlying capacity* to experience those positive feelings. He was too young to notice that distinction. Buddhist thought holds that the caring figures in our lives, important as they are, have never actually *given* us the qualities of warmth, acceptance, or love that we experience when we were with them or when we recall them in meditation. Those qualities are part of our buddha nature—innate capacities of our underlying awareness. Being with caring figures or bringing them to mind evokes our underlying capacity to experience what love and compassion feel like, so we can familiarize ourselves with those qualities, heal in them, settle into their source in the depth of our awareness, and learn to embody them for others.

This means that the various parts of us and attachment strategies since childhood that still think that our experiences of warmth, acceptance, and comfort come just from external sources have always been mistaken.[16] Caring figures evoke such experiential qualities from our own underlying awareness, which is the actual source of these qualities. In this way, the field of care practice correlates with attachment theory—we learn to become what we are held in, to love as we are loved. This happens not by learning only to rely on external caring figures but by learning to rely on the loving qualities that they evoke from within us, and to rely on the source of those qualities in the depth of our own awareness.[17]

INCORPORATING PARTS OF THE MIND INTO THE MEDITATION IN A DEEPLY HEALING WAY

In sum, when the mind is identified with protective parts of itself, out of habit, it understands loving qualities to come only from external sources and is therefore cautious about becoming too vulnerable to those sources. So we need a way to do the Field of Care Meditation that shows these protective parts of the mind that the loving qualities it seeks are being accessed safely from the depth of our awareness. Then these parts of the mind can experience loving qualities without the felt need to shut down our receptivity to them from fear that we will be hurt, because the inner source of those qualities is experienced as trustworthy, unconditional, and inexhaustible.

For that, we will add a bit more instruction to the Field of Care Meditation in its next rendering. This added instruction will help us notice whatever part of us—whatever self-concept—arises when we begin to experience the loving qualities of the meditation. Upon noticing that sense of self and associated feelings, the mind can allow it to be held unconditionally in the spacious warmth, acceptance, and love evoked by the field of care. Then, in their own time, these patterns of thought and feeling can begin to unclench, relax, and settle into the openness and warmth in the depth of our awareness. From there, they can start to heal. Our senses of self and associated feelings can metabolize themselves in that way when provided the space of unconditional acceptance that they need for that to happen.[18] With repeated practice, this deeply accepting way of being with feelings and thoughts of self can let further energies and qualities of love and acceptance come forth from our underlying awareness, to further embrace and heal whatever wounded patterns of our minds may arise.

When the instruction comes in step 2 to let the loving qualities unify you with them more and more, let the qualities of warmth, acceptance, care, compassion, and so forth that are evoked by the field of care merge with you, making you into a healing environment of loving qualities that can embrace all aspects of your experience. Let all senses of self, thoughts, feelings, and reactions that arise during the meditation be embraced naturally in that spacious loving environment.

What if a sense of self arises that wants to take time to grieve the death of someone associated with a caring moment? All such feelings and parts of us are welcome to find their own way of being within the loving environment generated by the meditation. Some part of us may not feel ready yet to relax, settle, and heal because we feel a need to process grief or another emotion. In that case, the welcoming environment provided by the meditation can embrace that part of us and its emotions in powers of continual warmth and acceptance, in which it can start to relax, settle, and heal in its own time. In that way, this practice gives us a way to reinhabit loving moments with people we have lost, so we continue to feel their empowering presence in our lives now.

For the next meditation, choose the type of field of care that is currently most accessible to you and most effective for accessing loving energies and qualities. (An audio option is available at shambhala.com/howcompassion worksmeditations.)

FIELD OF CARE MEDITATION 4: DEEPENING RECEPTIVITY TO LOVE AND COMPASSION

STEP 1. ABDOMINAL BREATHING (3 MINUTES OR SO) Sit in a relaxed, comfortable way with back straight, eyes gazing gently downward. Come down from the thinking mind into the body. Take a slow, deep breath, inhaling from the abdomen so it expands, then exhaling slowly and completely, letting go of all your concerns with the exhale. Relax for a moment before inhaling again. Repeat several times. Then, while still breathing from the abdomen, let the breath settle into its own natural flow. Feel the belly expand and contract with each breath. Let that feeling draw you into it more and more, breath by breath.

STEP 2. RECONNECTING WITH LOVE AND COMPASSION (7 TO 10 MINUTES) Bring to mind your field of care—a caring moment, your benefactor, or your spiritual field—and experience it as happening or present to you right now. You are being seen and held in deep care, compassion, acceptance, and warmth beyond judgments. (*Pause*) Relax into this experience, steeping in its loving energies, feeling its tender qualities, and letting them spaciously infuse your whole being. Accept these loving energies and qualities into your whole body and mind—every part of you loved in its very being. (*Pause*) Let these loving qualities unify you with them more and more. (*Pause*)

If a part of you starts to have difficulty with this practice or to draw your attention away, notice that part of you, that sense of self and what it's feeling, in a completely accepting way, deeply allowing it to be here. Let that part of you be gently included in the warmth and acceptance of this loving environment. Let it have all the space it needs to relax, find its own place in its own time, and metabolize itself in its own way.

If your mind becomes tired, take a break, relax the mind, then freshly reconnect with your field of care and begin anew.

STEP 3. RELEASING (3 TO 5 MINUTES) Now let this loving environment of warmth and acceptance help your mind to relax deeply and release all its frameworks of meditation and concern. Let the mind settle back a bit inwardly and come to rest in the background of its awareness, which is naturally wide open and luminous, like a sunlit sky. As thoughts and feelings arise, let them just metabolize themselves and release within this sky-like openness of awareness, by letting everything be.

Processing the Meditation

When transitioning out of the formal meditation session, let the felt sense of this practice continue to resonate within your present experience and into whatever you do next.

THREE BASIC PRINCIPLES OF RECEPTIVE MODE: ACCESSING, NOTICING, AND INCLUDING

With this last meditation, we have now engaged all three essential principles of receptive-mode practice: accessing, noticing, and including.

1. *Accessing:* Accessing loving energies and qualities from the depth of your awareness through your most effective means of access—the kind of field of care that best evokes those qualities. This begins with step 2 in the meditations instructed above.
2. *Noticing:* Noticing when a part of you arises that is having difficulty with the meditation and is starting to impede your experience of the loving qualities. "Part of you" means a sense of self with its patterns of thought,

feeling, and reaction. You might also notice one or another attachment script arise with that sense of self, as in the examples given ("No one really cares about me," "I don't deserve love," "I don't trust anyone associated with love," and so on).

3. *Including:* Letting that part of you and any associated feelings be naturally included in the loving environment of spaciousness, warmth, and acceptance that is generated by this meditation.

Accessing loving qualities, *noticing* any troubled part of you that arises together with its thoughts and feelings, and *including* them in the gentle embrace of those tender qualities can be deeply healing for these parts and feelings, helping the mind to feel safe enough to trust and relax into the process of deepening receptivity to loving qualities and to their source in the mind.

Throughout our lives, our attachment strategies and senses of self have been trying to help us find loving qualities, comfort, and well-being from external sources—various people and places. They have also been trying to protect us from getting hurt when external sources are not reliable. These protective strategies are often encoded as attachment scripts or internalized senses of self—habitual inner voices that evaluate ourselves and others. From childhood up to now, these mental strategies have been working almost continually to manage all that. When we learn to pay new attention to them in the compassionate space of this meditation, we often discover that our minds are quite tired of endlessly laboring and struggling at those tasks. In this meditation, the mind—exhausted by its long identification with shifting senses of self and their reactions—can now begin to discern that help has arrived. The mind can let go of its burdensome effort to manage and control. It can relax and begin to sense that the loving qualities it has been seeking are already present, emerging right now from the depth of its own awareness.

Indeed, in light of this meditation, it can dawn on us that throughout our entire life, our mind has been seeking the qualities of our buddha nature all along—trying to obtain unconditional qualities of love, warmth, acceptance, compassion, ease of being, connection, and joy in a totally reliable and stable way. But it's been seeking them in the wrong place—in a conditioned external world that is never fully reliable or stable. What the mind has long sought—its buddha nature—is now making itself directly known within this practice.

UNBLENDING: LETTING OUR IDENTITY SHIFT FROM ONE NARROW PART OF US TO OUR FULLER AWARENESS

According to the theory of grounded cognition, a practice like this receptive-mode Field of Care Meditation, wherein we engage a memory as if it were happening now, connects us with a multisensory embodied experience by stimulating many neural systems simultaneously.[19] This meditation thus engages our entire being. From the fullness of our awareness, we access an all-encompassing experience that includes our senses, perceptions, feelings, cognitions, and energies, infused with increasingly unconditional qualities of warmth, acceptance, and care. In step 2, we also let the loving qualities that are evoked by the field of care gently merge with us, making us into a healing environment of loving qualities that embraces all aspects of our experience. In this way, the meditation shifts our sense of identity from just one part of us to the fuller awareness that holds any such part in unconditional care and compassion. That expanded awareness is our fuller identity, beyond delimitation by any single narrow sense of self or attachment strategy.

As the mind opens into that fuller awareness by means of the meditation, it is no longer completely identified with any one part, sense of self, attachment script, or feeling. This happens not by rejecting that part or feeling but by holding it in the unconditional care of our fuller awareness. Our sense of identity starts to shift from the part of the mind that is reacting to the meditation to the larger awareness that holds that part in unconditional care. In this way, we discover that we are the compassionate awareness that can embrace any part of us, not the part. We call this shift of identity from part to whole "compassionately unblending" from a part.[20] Importantly, this practice can increasingly widen into an experience of what in Tibetan Buddhist terms is considered our buddha nature, an intrinsically open and compassionate depth of awareness, which can spontaneously embrace all parts of us in spacious care.[21]

As all parts of the mind experience the safety and healing power of such unconditional acceptance and warmth from our fuller awareness, the various parts of the mind can learn to trust that awareness as the source of those unconditional qualities. As this trust deepens with repetition of practice, the mind becomes willing to release more fully at the final releasing phase of the meditation into the openness, simplicity, and warmth of that fuller awareness. This process of deepening trust and fuller release begins to draw us into the deepening mode of practice by helping us start to reunify with the fullness of our awareness (our buddha nature), from which further loving qualities can emerge.[22]

Just as our awareness can embrace all parts of us and feelings in unconditional compassion, the same awareness can hold others and their feelings in the same unconditional care, without contributing to mental depletion or compassion fatigue. The openness, clarity, and compassion of our basic awareness—our buddha nature—is gradually revealed by the receptive-mode meditation as our ultimate secure base from which we can extend love and compassion to others more sustainably and inclusively (extending love to others will be the focus of chapter 3).[23] Then we can take on whatever roles and senses of identity are needed in our relationships and work with greater fluidity, ease, and resilience, since we know we are not ultimately any of those roles. We are the basic awareness that can take expression in any role that is needed in different contexts, situations, and relationships.

REINTRODUCING FIELD OF CARE MEDITATION 4: DEEPENING RECEPTIVITY TO LOVE AND COMPASSION

In light of the points above, it will be helpful to do Field of Care Meditation 4 again, now with more understanding of its principles so you engage them more fully: *accessing* loving qualities, *noticing* any sense of self that reacts to the meditation or starts to draw you away from it, then gently *including* that part of you and its feelings in the unconditional care of the meditation. When you follow those three principles, notice how the meditation begins to shift your identity from just one reacting part of you to the larger compassionate awareness that holds that part in care. Repeated practice of the meditation creates the space of unconditional care and inner safety needed for more parts and feelings to reveal themselves and for the loving qualities of our awareness to emerge more robustly.

Please go back to page 57 or the audio recording and do this meditation again.

After that, return to the "Processing the Meditation" section just below.

Processing the Meditation

As always, please let the felt sense of this meditation continue to resonate after the meditation session into whatever you do next. In step 2 of the meditation, when you were steeping in the loving qualities, did you notice any further loving qualities? Try to name any further qualities you noticed. Please add them to your list of such qualities.

Did you also experience any difficulty with the meditation, some part of you reacting to it? If so, what part of you arose with that experience— what sense of self? What feelings came with that sense of self? Could you include that part of you and those feelings in the meditation? If so, how? Review step 2 of the meditation to inform that possibility for future meditation sessions.

WHAT TO DO WHEN THE MIND REACTS TO ONE PART FROM WITHIN ANOTHER PART

It is not uncommon to experience another level of difficulty in the meditation. Suppose, for example, when you begin to experience the loving qualities, a self-critical part of your mind arises with the thought, "You're hopeless; you will never learn how to meditate"—a disparaging inner voice of a kind that you have experienced throughout your life. Now suppose another part of your mind responds: "Oh, I am so tired of this self-criticism. I wish it would go away! I'll try to ignore it so I can meditate." These inner storylines can alternate in succession like alternating perceptions of the figure on page 63.

Some people first see a duck, whereas other people first see a rabbit.[24] The two distinct perceptions can alternate back and forth, but we only experience one at a given moment.[25] Just as the duck and rabbit can come in and out of focus quickly, so too various senses of self with different voices can come in and out of experience rapidly within a meditation.

In the example above where you noticed those competing internal storylines, you have successfully accomplished the first two principles of receptive-mode meditation. You have begun *accessing* loving qualities and you have *noticed* a part of your mind—a self-critical part ("You're hopeless; you will never learn"), which is decreasing your receptivity to those qualities. But in this example, you have not yet fully engaged the third principle, *including*, because you have not yet included that self-critical part of you and its feelings in the deeply accepting space of the meditation. Instead of letting that part be included in that way, you have a spontaneous aversive reaction to it ("I wish it would go away!"). At that moment, your mind is now identified with a *second* part of your mind that is rejecting the first, self-critical part. When you notice that, focus your caring attention now mainly on this second part of you that rejects the first part. Let this second part of you, this rejecting sense of self and its feelings, be included in the loving environment of the meditation, as instructed in step 2. When this second part of you begins to relax and settle, you can return your attention to the first self-critical part (if it continues to arise), letting it also be included in the compassionate, healing environment of the meditation.

If another part of your mind arises that is now reacting to the meditation in some other way—for example, wondering if you're doing the practice correctly—notice that sense of self and its feelings, and let that part of you similarly be included in the loving environment of step 2. If you notice various senses of self arise sequentially in meditation, it is a sign that you are becoming more fully conscious and granular with patterns of experience. Each sense of self that arises is an opportunity to deepen further in the practice by welcoming it into the loving space in which it can feel safe, relax, and begin to metabolize itself and heal.

Whatever Parts and Feelings Arise in Meditation Can Further Empower the Meditation

As we familiarize ourselves with this meditation through repetition, the mind can become more skilled at including parts and feelings as described above. Then as any protective part of the mind arises during the meditation, its very arising can further evoke the loving qualities that embrace that part. This process increases the mind's receptivity to the loving qualities, its trust in their source, and its ability to release into that source in the final step— the openness, clarity, and warmth of the mind's deep nature. In this way, the same parts and feelings that had previously shut down our receptivity now empower further receptivity by drawing the loving qualities to them as they arise. This process of deepening receptivity and release unfolds from repeated practice in its own time. Tibetan Buddhism is known for its ability to take difficult experiences and painful emotions in our lives as the very means to awaken enlightened capacities of love, compassion, and discernment.[26] That is what we are learning to do here in receptive mode—learning how to let painful feelings and parts of ourselves help us find fuller access to the positive capacities of our underlying awareness.

Receptive-mode practices can thus feel disruptive because they challenge long-held views of oneself and others within familiar attachment scripts. But these disturbances to our familiar identities and ways of being can be experienced as opportunities for progress in meditation. The ability to integrate such reactions in a healing way is best supported by an outer secure base that includes teachers and other mature practitioners of compassion and wisdom, which provides emotional and energetic support for deepening into the inner secure base of our buddha nature and its qualities. Such support will be discussed in chapter 5, on integrating practice with our lives. If it becomes too difficult to explore such reactions within meditation, that may signal a need for healing through therapy with a mental health professional, to explore traumas or attachment wounds.

ATTACHMENT WOUNDS, TRAUMA HISTORIES, AND GENTLENESS IN PRACTICE

Many of us harbor attachment wounds. This means that our minds may associate loving experience with a feeling of danger that we may get hurt, because of traumatic experiences that took place, often first during childhood. Such past experiences include times when we were depending on others to treat us with kindness and felt terribly let down or experienced emotional or physical abuse. When recalling caring moments, then, many of us experience senses of self that arise with feelings of rejection, shame, anger, or fear of abandonment.[27] Given these attachment wounds, we need to be very gentle with any parts of ourselves that are evoked by whatever field of care we recall. The instruction to "include" such parts in the meditation does not mean to force them aggressively into anything they do not want. These parts of our minds have been seeking unconditional love and have not found it reliably from external sources. It takes time, repetition of practice, and perhaps diverse caring moments and benefactors for these parts and feelings to learn—gradually, experientially, in their own time—that an unconditional quality of care is available now, right here, from the depth of our own awareness, our buddha nature.

We help these parts of the mind experience this unconditional care by letting them find their own place within the warmth, safety, and absolute acceptance of the loving environment provided by the Field of Care Meditation. As all parts of the mind experience that unconditional space, the mind gains the power to unblend from them more often, helping us increasingly rediscover that our identity is not any one narrow part of us. Rather, we are the fuller awareness that can hold any part in care. We are not the narrow sense of self that is having a fearful or aversive reaction to the meditation; we are the larger compassionate awareness that embraces it. To learn how these parts of our mind have been trying to protect and help us also makes us newly aware of how hard they have been working to keep us safe—with appreciation, care, and compassion for them. With that awareness, we can embrace them all in a healing way, both during meditation sessions and in our daily lives.

As noted earlier in this chapter, on the one hand, attachment scripts that are out of touch with reality can take us away from the experience of caring moments, leading us to distrust or dismiss those moments, or fail to notice them altogether. On the other hand, there may be attachment scripts that interfere with practice in ways that *do* reflect reality. For example, scripts such as "My physical environment is not safe" or "This relationship is not safe" might reflect truths about your current experience. If you feel this is the case, the field of care practice is not in conflict with the need to be attuned to that reality. In fact, the practice can be supportive for removing ourselves from dangerous situations in two key ways. First, the field of care practice not only gives us access to caring qualities but also helps shift our identity to see and experience ourselves as *worthy of care*. Second, these practices also help us cultivate the security to become more fully conscious of destructive habits of thought and reaction within ourselves and others, so we can see more clearly how others have the potential to be harmful. These meditations establish the holding environment within which we can become present to our experience in new ways and explore these two possibilities, and then remove ourselves from damaging relationships or situations with increasing discernment.

While keeping the possibilities just described in mind, we should also proceed gently with meditation, and keep in mind the trauma-informed approach to meditation discussed at the end of the introductory chapter. It is normal for some aspects of meditation to come more easily than others. Sometimes symptoms from prior traumas might emerge during meditation—for example, a feeling of disembodiment, troubling memories, a feeling of hyperarousal, a feeling of physical pain, and so on. If we are experiencing such symptoms or other strong states of activation, we may need time and support outside of meditation practice, including support from forms of therapy or connection with knowledgeable peers or other practitioners. If difficult symptoms arise in the middle of a meditation session, it may be necessary to stop the practice and go for a walk, enjoy the scenery, relax with some pleasant music, be with a supportive friend, or rely on other familiar strategies that you know are workable for you. With time and repeated practice, we may become comfortable and familiar enough with the meditations in this manual that we can start to use them effectively to work with such challenges directly in practice.[28]

If you wish, when ready, you can do Field of Care Meditation 4: Deepening Receptivity to Love and Compassion again and, while doing it, explore the possibilities discussed in the previous sections.

INTEGRATING RECEPTIVE-MODE
PRACTICES INTO OUR DAILY LIFE

We suggest that you do Field of Care Meditation 4: Deepening Receptivity to Love and Compassion daily in the coming weeks and months. Do this meditation first thing in the morning for at least ten or fifteen minutes—or longer if you have time. If you do the meditation each morning, you establish the basis to reconnect with it repeatedly during the rest of your day, even if just for a minute or two at a time. In this way, your day is permeated with repeated experiences of warmth, care, acceptance, inner safety, and so forth. Each time you do the meditation in the day, remind yourself that the loving qualities you experience emerge from your own underlying awareness. This makes you conscious of how immediately available these qualities are to you and signals to any part of your mind that arises in the meditation that the source of the qualities is unconditional and trustworthy. To reconnect many times a day in that way supports experiential access to loving qualities and strengthens the inner secure base of love and compassion needed to extend such qualities more sustainably to others. People who practice within a spiritual tradition often find that this sort of daily practice energizes and deepens the felt sense of their spiritual field in their practices of contemplation, prayer, ritual, service, spiritual activism, and so forth.

Outside of the meditation sessions, throughout the day, you can become compassionately conscious of whatever parts of your mind the meditations have raised up. Then let any memories of your life associated with those parts be held in the same qualities of warmth, acceptance, and compassion that you have accessed in the meditations. In this way, both within meditation sessions and in frequent moments of the day, the mind discovers that it is already held in the unconditional care that it has been seeking, can experience the healing power of that care, and can let itself settle into its fuller depth of awareness—buddha nature. That fuller awareness has the intrinsic capacity to respond to all parts of the mind, and to others, with the unconditional acceptance and care they all deeply need. From that fuller awareness we can take on whatever roles and identities are needed with greater fluidity and effectiveness.

TAPPING AN INEXHAUSTIBLE SOURCE OF LIFE-GIVING POWERS

What we are learning in this receptive mode of practice is how to tap a literally inexhaustible source of love, warmth, compassion, and discernment in the depth of our being. We are uncovering an absolutely reliable source of basic goodness within us, which we can tap into frequently to access those loving qualities. This can progressively strengthen the inner core of security from which to become more fully and compassionately present to all parts of ourselves and to others. We are accessing a flow of caring energy and qualities from within that is beyond mental depletion or compassion fatigue. This process of healing and deepening is further empowered by learning how to let the source of the loving qualities, the depth of our own awareness, draw us increasingly into unity with it. This is the "deepening mode" of practice that is the focus of our next chapter.

2

DEEPENING MODE
The Wisdom of Openness and Presence

AS WE EXPLORED IN CHAPTER 1, the Field of Care Meditation helps us begin to shift our identity from one narrow sense of self to our fuller, more inclusive basic awareness. How so? We let the qualities of warmth, acceptance, compassion, and so forth evoked by the field of care merge with us, making us into a healing, loving environment that can include all aspects of our experience. This helps the mind compassionately unblend from any narrow sense of self by shifting our identity from that narrow part of the mind to the fuller awareness that holds that part in care. Then, in the releasing phase of the meditation, the same loving qualities help the mind settle into their source in the depth of our awareness, which is experienced as an expansive unity of openness, lucidity, and warmth. As a result, patterns of thought, feeling, and reaction that have impeded love and compassion can metabolize themselves in a deeply healing way—relaxing, unwinding, releasing.

In this chapter, we will learn to settle even more fully into that underlying unity of openness and lucidity, the expansive awareness in the depth of our being that is beyond identification with any one sense of self or reaction, since it is the basis for all possible self-identities and ways of responding. We will learn more fully to access the innate qualities of that underlying awareness—qualities of openness, acceptance, clarity, simplicity, ease, healing power, peace, dignity, warmth, love, compassion, presence, equanimity, courage, and creative responsiveness. We do that by means of the deepening mode of meditation, which helps us reunify with that expansive awareness, which is also called the nature of mind or buddha nature.

Actually, this deep nature of mind is our most natural state of being, logically prior to our social and individual conditioning. It includes the backdrop of expansive, space-like awareness that is always present behind the narrow focus of our conscious attention and which pervades all aspects of our experience. Many of us have had moments of settling into this natural state—that background of pervasive awareness—to some degree. For example, you may have a memory as a child outside in nature—perhaps when you were in a vast forest, gazing at a starlit sky, viewing the limitless panorama of a sunset, or overlooking the ocean—when everything settled, time seemed to stop momentarily, and you felt the infinite immensity of the natural world in its mystery and limitlessness. Or perhaps a time when you reached the top of a mountain after a long hike—a moment when the outer expanse of nature evoked from within you an inner expanse of utter openness that had been hidden in the background of your awareness, accompanied by feelings of wonder, awe, appreciation, freshness, and joy. Those are qualities of our expansive underlying awareness, evoked in such a moment by panoramic experience of the natural world. In our receptive-mode meditations, we experienced further qualities of this underlying awareness, evoked by vivid experience of a field of care (which can also include the natural world).

A person's basic, underlying awareness is the preconceptual, nondual basis in consciousness for all of one's thoughts, sensations, feelings, emotions, intentions, attitudes, and senses of self. It is the awareness that takes expression in all those aspects of experience. A person's basic awareness thus encompasses their entire experience of mind, body, and world. As the basis of all one's experience, this awareness is in itself primordial, unconstructed, unconfined, simple, nondual, and open to an infinite horizon. It is insubstantial like space, lucid and possessed of expressive capacities and energies that take shape in all aspects of experience of self and world. Such qualities of our basic awareness, in the Tibetan Buddhist traditions that we draw from, are often crystallized in three fundamental aspects: (1) the essence of our awareness is empty, insubstantial, nondual, and all-pervasive like space; (2) the nature of our awareness is cognizant, luminous, and knowing; (3) the expressive capacity of that cognizant emptiness is unlimited, taking expression in all the ways that we experience the world and in the energies associated with all those aspects of experience.[1] Thus, the empty, cognizant nature of our awareness is unconditioned and unchanging, even as that awareness takes expression in all the conditioned, changing aspects of our experience.

One metaphor for this is the wateriness of the waves in the ocean. All the waves are shifting and changing according to varying conditions of wind, temperature, current, and so forth, but their essential nature, the wateriness per se, is unaffected by any such conditions—it is unconditioned, unchanging. Because the nature of our awareness, as a unity of space-like emptiness and cognizance, is unconditioned and all-pervasive, its innate capacities for love, compassion, and discernment are unconditional and naturally all-inclusive when not obstructed by conditioned, narrowly confined, self-clinging patterns of mind.

Even our so-called dysfunctional patterns of thought and reaction arise out of this basic nature of awareness on their way to expression of our social and individual conditioning. We alluded to this in the last chapter, noting how when we are identified with various narrow senses of self that emerged in childhood, we do not recognize that the unconditional loving qualities we seek are available in our basic awareness. When our minds are identified with these senses of self, we are prone to destructive behaviors, seeking to obtain those loving qualities in an unconditional way from an external world that is not their actual source and can never be totally unconditional. As we noted in chapter 1, through our social and individual conditioning, our minds get used to identifying more often with those limited senses of ourselves than with our fuller awareness—narrow self-identities whose conditioned reactions impede the unconditional qualities of our fuller awareness. In this way, our minds lose touch with the expansive, nondual, and unconditioned awareness that is their ground. But, as we learned in chapter 1, our basic awareness also possesses great hidden capacities of love, empathy, compassion, peace, inner freedom, discernment, dignity, energy, joy, and creative responsiveness, which can be evoked and cultivated to increasing power, all-inclusiveness, and unconditionality.[2]

In the Tibetan Buddhist traditions that we draw from, this basic nature or ground of our awareness is called by various names, including primordial awareness (Tib. *rig pa*), buddha nature (Tib. *de bzhin gshegs pa'i snying po*), the ground of experience (Tib. *gzhi*), and the deep nature of mind (Tib. *sems nyid*).[3]

In Christian theology, various interpretations of the image of God within human beings (Latin: *imago dei*) support diverse understandings of personhood, some of which can be viewed as analogous to the Buddhist perspective we draw on here. For example, the renowned twentieth-century theologian Karl Rahner asserted that there is a preconscious, nonobjectifiable level of awareness in human beings that is the primordial basis of all their conscious activities and which opens to an infinite horizon, manifest in the unlimited human urge toward greater knowledge, love, and freedom.[4] For Rahner, that unlimited urge toward greater knowing, love, and freedom is an urge to be reunited with God, the primordial ground of those qualities. As Buddhists, we understand that kind of urge as the longing to be reunited with our buddha nature—the expansive, unconditioned awareness that is the nondual ground of our being and source of the unconditional love, compassion, and wisdom that we ultimately seek. Analogous understandings can be found among other theologians and in other spiritual traditions, including parts of contemplative Islam such as Sufism, as well as contemplative lineages within Judaism, Christianity, Hinduism, and Daoism. Nondual kinds of awareness have also become a focus of attention in some areas of science.[5] We invite readers of different backgrounds, spiritualities, and worldviews to explore relating your understanding of the person to this kind of framework—that human beings harbor a depth dimension of which they have not been fully conscious, a dimension of tremendous potential, possibility, and freedom. The practices of this chapter can further inform that understanding beyond the merely theoretical by helping us find further experiential access to the deep nature of mind, the nondual ground of experience that we are discussing here.

Because our minds so habitually identify with one limited sense of self or thought pattern in any moment, we lose our fuller, more expansive power of awareness. Our minds don't typically know how to relax their narrow grip of self-clinging and settle into the depth, fullness, and all-inclusiveness of their underlying awareness where innate capacities for greater love and compassion, inner peace, wisdom, and responsiveness are available. The field of care practices have started to help us with that, but the deepening-mode practices of this chapter can take us further. With them, we learn to settle into the depth of our being and inhabit our expansive underlying awareness more fully. From that depth of being we can sense and respond to others in the depth of their being, beyond limiting perceptions and judgments that hide their fuller dignity and worth. From that place of depth, we can employ whatever sense of self-identity is appropriate to fulfill our roles with others, without losing the qualities of our basic awareness in that identity. We can learn to hold any needed identity more lightly; with greater flexibility, humor, discernment, compassion, and creative responsiveness to others. In that way, the deepening-mode practices of this chapter prepare us for the inclusive mode of the next chapter, in which we extend love and compassion to others beyond narrow, self-clinging habits of reaction or accustomed in-group boundaries.

When entering into deepening-mode meditations, it will be important to continue to do receptive-mode meditation regularly, alternating between both kinds of practice in our days. Field of Care Meditation (which is receptive mode) establishes a secure base in loving qualities of awareness so that the mind can feel safe enough to settle into the very source of those qualities in the deepening mode—the expansive, nondual depth of the mind.

Tibetan Buddhism offers various ways to settle more fully into the qualities and nature of our basic awareness. In this chapter, we will first explore the Compassionate Presence to Feelings Meditation, which can help us become newly present to our physical and emotional feelings with a healing power of care, spaciousness, and compassion. This compassionate way of being with our feelings helps further establish the foundation we need to enter into Letting Be of Body, Breath, and Mind, a meditation that will be discussed later in this chapter. The Letting Be of Body, Breath, and Mind meditation takes us into deepening levels of tranquil abiding (Skt. *śamatha*) and nondual experience, which bring out underlying capacities for fuller presence, attention, steadiness, openness, clarity, wholeness, tranquility, and ease. The Letting Be meditation allows mental patterns of thought and reaction to relax, calm, and settle out, to reveal the natural expansiveness and radiant clarity of the mind that is logically prior to all such mental activity. This direction of practice can permit the mind to reunify with its unconditioned nature, buddha nature—a nondual state of nonconceptual openness, pure awareness, and compassionate capacity. From our perspective, this deep nature of mind is the ultimate secure base in which is found the fullest replenishment and empowerment to become a more loving, compassionate, and discerning presence to others.

You are invited to take up the following deepening-mode meditations that are most connecting for you now, in accord with your goals for contemplative practice. As we noted in the introductory chapter, such goals commonly include one or more of the following: (1) to establish the inner secure base needed to process all your feelings in a healing way, from which to embody a more sustaining and inclusive power of care and compassion for self and others; (2) to experience Buddhist awakening; that is, to let your mind be reunified with its deepest nature, buddha nature—the infinite openness, lucidity, and warmth that knows and responds to the same hidden depth in all others for the benefit of all; (3) for those who practice in non-Buddhist spiritual traditions, to explore how these practices derived from Buddhism may experientially inform and empower practices you do within your own tradition.

BECOMING NEWLY PRESENT TO OUR EMOTIONS AND FEELINGS WITH COMPASSION

Our Field of Care Meditations have helped us access qualities of warmth and love while knowing that they arise from the depth of our own awareness (not from outside of us). To know that well is to know that those qualities are always available to us, since their source is in the depth of our own mind. In the Compassionate Presence to Feelings Meditation, we draw directly on qualities of warmth, acceptance, and compassion from our underlying awareness to become a healing environment for all of our feelings, without envisioning a separate field of care. This meditation helps us become a healing environment for feelings not only when in formal meditation but also within the ordinary activities of our day, in our relationships and work with others. This meditation also further empowers the Field of Care Meditation. Some practitioners find the Compassionate Presence to Feelings Meditation more immediately accessible to them than the Field of Care Meditation, while others find the reverse.

In the Compassionate Presence to Feelings Meditation we learn to welcome all our feelings into a compassionate space where they can relax, find their place, settle in their own time, and heal in their own natural way. "Feelings" here refers to the pleasant, unpleasant, and neutral feeling tones that accompany all of our physical and mental experiences, and to all the emotions with which they are associated.

In this practice, we learn how to become more at home with our emotional feelings, even difficult emotions. They then feel safer, since they are not being rejected, denied, or avoided. This transforms our way of being with others, since our ability to be present to our own feelings with openness and unconditional warmth is what enables us to be present to other people and their feelings in the same way. As Thupten Jinpa, a Tibetan Buddhist scholar and translator for the Dalai Lama, writes, "The more we learn to be with our suffering, the better we can connect with other people. When we suppress or resist our suffering, we lose the common ground that lets us connect to and care for others."[6]

This practice has four principles: (1) *Notice the predominant feeling* within whatever state of mind or body is occurring. (2) Allow the feeling to have *all the space it needs* to find its own place, in its own time. (3) *Rest with or within* the feeling. (4) Then *just let everything be*, with a sense of spaciousness.

This practice is adapted from the Handshake Meditation teaching of Tsoknyi Rinpoche.

COMPASSIONATE PRESENCE TO FEELINGS MEDITATION

PREPARING FOR THE MEDITATION In the meditation, you'll be instructed first to notice a physical sensation, then to become aware of an emotional feeling, sensing how it feels within your body and mind—not just thinking about it "in your head." If during the practice your mind becomes tired, stale, or uptight, take a break, rest the mind, relax the body, and start afresh when ready. If the meditation feels overwhelming, you can stop doing the meditation for a while and do something else, such as taking a walk, enjoying the natural world, or taking in your visual surroundings. If you encounter such difficulties within any meditations, please refer to the recommendations for trauma-informed meditation at the end of the introductory chapter.

STEP 1. BECOMING COMPASSIONATELY PRESENT TO BODILY FEELINGS Sit in a relaxed way, with back comfortably straight, eyes gazing gently downward. Come down from the thinking mind into the body, feeling the body as a whole, and letting the breath settle into its own natural flow. After a little while, notice the physical sensation in any part of your body and become aware of that feeling in a deeply allowing way, without trying to change it all. Just let it have all the space it needs to find its own way of being. If another physical sensation replaces it, become aware of that sensation in the same deeply allowing, spacious way.

STEP 2. BECOMING COMPASSIONATELY PRESENT TO EMOTIONAL FEELINGS Now sense whatever emotional feeling is present within you, from within your body—not just thinking about it but sensing how it feels from within. If you think that you are not feeling anything emotionally, you can probably become aware of a subtle emotional feeling that wasn't fully conscious to you—for example, a little anxiety or worry, liking or disliking a little how things are, a sense of trying to hold on to things, or feeling a little confused. Or you may feel a stronger emotion, like fear, frustration, annoyance, or joy. Or you may just feel numb. Those are all feelings with which you can practice. Or, if you wish, you can recall an emotional feeling that is quite familiar to you and let yourself feel it now.

Become aware of that feeling within you, with a sense of deep permission for it to be here—fully allowing it, gently welcoming it. Without being caught up in it, without rejecting it, without trying to solve or change anything in it, without ruminating about why it's here. Like a friend being compassionately present to a friend, let this feeling have all the space it needs to find its own place or settle in its own time. Rest with the feeling spaciously in that way, or rest within it, without trying to change anything, just letting everything be. One feeling may open into a further feeling and so on—just be with each feeling in the same spacious, accepting way.

If part of you is having difficulty with this practice, notice *the feeling within that reaction* and become compassionately aware of that feeling in the same way, letting it have all the space it needs to find its own place, to settle and metabolize itself in its own time.

If the mind wanders into chains of thinking, notice *the feeling associated with those thoughts* and become present to that feeling in the same spacious, allowing way.

As this practice deepens, you may find your mind resting right in the essence of a feeling, which may open into a space of deep warmth, calm, and peace from within. If that happens, just relax deeply into that experience and let everything be.

STEP 3. RELEASING After some time, just settle fully into this feeling of spacious allowing. Let this help your mind to relax deeply, settle back a bit inwardly, release all frameworks of meditation or concern, and become completely open like space, beyond reference points. As thoughts and feelings arise, let them just metabolize themselves and release within this sky-like openness of awareness by letting everything be.

Processing the Meditation

How was this meditation for you? Were you able, even a little, to begin to explore this very different way of being with feelings—gently welcoming and allowing feelings to find their own way of being or settle in their own time? Without ignoring the feeling, trying to change it, getting caught up in it, analyzing it, or trying to make it go away? This openhearted way of being with feelings can be quite challenging at first because many of us have been socialized to react to our feelings in a very different way.

Take a moment to reflect on this question: How have expectations of people in your family, schools, workplaces, and other settings affected your way of relating to your emotional feelings? If you wish to write some notes in your journal, please take a moment to jot down a few ways that you have become accustomed to react to your feelings in daily life due to your socialization in such environments.

LEARNING A THIRD WAY TO
RELATE TO OUR FEELINGS

Many of us have received messages in our families, schools, and workplaces to suppress, deny, hide, or distract ourselves from feelings. But there is a cost. Ignoring, denying, and suppressing our feelings over time can hurt our mental and physical health, harm our personal relationships, and contribute to burnout or a tendency to "self-medicate."

When we ask practitioners how they've been socialized to relate to their emotions, most say that they try to avoid painful feelings by attempting to suppress, ignore, or distract themselves from them; or they try to always tightly control their emotions. But then the emotions tend to return stronger over time,[7] causing us to tense up inside, which may manifest as physical tightness and chronic pain.[8] This inner stress and tightness make it difficult to open to the qualities cultivated in all our SCT practices—qualities of openness, kindness, compassion, inner peace, equanimity, and wisdom.[9] If, on the other hand, we just react to everything from our volatile emotions, we lose our agency to them—our freedom to discern the fuller reality of everyone around us beyond our habitual reactions and to become more fully present to them all.

Many people learn only two options for relating to emotional feelings: either to reject them or to act them out, often in habitual reactive ways that can become harmful to self or others.[10] The Compassionate Presence to Feelings Meditation offers a third way for relating to our feelings that is new to many of us—neither to suppress nor act out painful emotions but to become more fully aware of them in a kindhearted way that provides the welcoming space they need to feel safe, relax, settle, and metabolize themselves in their own way—ultimately a space of deep healing and releasing that opens our perspective on self and others. Emotional feelings will naturally do that when given the warmhearted space of acceptance and the freedom to do so.

But when we are first introduced to the Compassionate Presence to Feelings Meditation, the habitual strategies we have internalized since childhood for relating to our feelings often remain active, reinterpreting the practice in their own terms. In our first experience with the meditation, we may not actually be following the instruction to be with our feelings in such a fresh, openhearted way. For example, some of us may be motivated to accept our feelings in the meditation in order to get them to go away. Or some may try to avoid our feelings by thinking throughout the practice about how we will help others by teaching this meditation to them rather than actually following the meditation instruction ourselves. Or some may be thinking about other things throughout the meditation, ignoring the instruction to notice the feelings that accompany all such thoughts.

Let's do this meditation now a second time. Notice when any sense of self arises that wants to manage feelings, get rid of them, analyze them, ruminate about their causes, or ignore them to think of other things, in familiar ways that run counter to the meditation instruction. When that happens, *notice the feeling* that arises with that agenda and that sense of self, and take that feeling directly into the meditation by becoming aware of that feeling in the spaciously compassionate way that is instructed. Become conscious of that feeling within your mind and body in a way that fully allows it to be here, without any attempt to do anything to it or about it. The feeling, given such a space of unconditional acceptance, can find its own way of settling, relaxing, metabolizing itself, healing, and opening. It will naturally do so when we stop feeding into it, reacting to it, and instead simply let it be.

Recall the four principles of this meditation to keep in mind as we practice it: (1) Notice the predominant feeling within any state of mind or body that is occurring. (2) Allow the feeling to have all the space it needs to find its own place, in its own time. (3) Rest with, or within, the feeling. (4) And just let everything be, with a sense of spaciousness. In this way, we become unconditionally present to feelings, holding no agenda over them, which gives them the free space they need to settle deeply in their own way.

In light of the observations above, please keep these further two points in mind:

First, be careful not to harbor an implicit agenda of *trying to get rid of feelings* by embracing them in compassion. The teaching that this meditation allows painful feelings to heal themselves provides us motivation to do the meditation, which is a good thing. But if, when doing the meditation, we hold that agenda in mind—that we want the feelings to settle or heal themselves *so they will go away*, the meditation will not work. This is because we are imposing an agenda on the feelings rather than freely allowing them to find their own way of being and settling. So no matter what motivates us to do the meditation, during the time that we actually do it, just follow exactly what it instructs—become unconditionally present to the feeling at hand, spaciously allowing it to find its own way of being, without any agenda to get rid of it, figure it out, or do anything to it.

Second, we need to learn to do this meditation in a relaxed way but also with increasing precision. Reactions that arise during the meditation can either distract us from it or help us engage it more fully. If we get caught up in reactive thoughts, we lose touch with what the meditation instructs. Instead, try to notice how any reactive thoughts that arise are delivering feelings, the feelings that accompany those very thoughts. For example, a reaction may arise like, "I don't want to be with this feeling." That reaction is expressing a feeling of aversion or fear. Or, "I don't know what to do, I don't feel anything." That is expressing a feeling of confusion or frustration. Or other worrisome thoughts may arise, feeling like the instructions don't make sense. Make it a point to sense the feeling that is within any such reaction and become compassionately present to that feeling just as the meditation instructs. In that way, all of our reactions will empower the meditation by delivering feelings for us to practice with.

When ready, in light of the points just above, please do the Compassionate Presence to Feelings Meditation (page 75) again.

FURTHER PROCESSING OF COMPASSIONATE PRESENCE PRACTICE: THEORY OF CONSTRUCTED EMOTION

The Compassionate Presence to Feelings Meditation draws directly on underlying powers of acceptance, care, warmth, kindness, and compassion from our basic awareness as we adopt an unconditionally welcoming way of being present to all our feelings. As we learn better with practice how to follow the instruction to let even our most painful feelings inhabit a space of deep allowing, our feelings feel safer with us. Rather than ignoring, rejecting, or getting caught up in them, we are letting them have the space they need to naturally relax, settle, and metabolize themselves under their own power.

As we learn the practice better with repetition, the instruction at the end of step 2 becomes relevant: "As this practice deepens, you may find your mind resting right in the essence of a feeling, which may open into a space of deep warmth, calm, and peace from within. If that happens, just relax deeply into that experience and let everything be." As noted earlier in this chapter, the underlying awareness (buddha nature) that takes expression in all aspects of experience, including our feelings, has intrinsic capacities of spaciousness, clarity, warmth, peace, simplicity, inner healing, love, compassion, responsiveness, and so on. Indeed, those capacities are hidden within our feelings—they are capacities of the very awareness that takes shape in our feelings.

When we are caught up in a narrow sense of self that is rejecting our feelings or distracting us from them, the primordial qualities of openness, warmth, and peace that are hidden within our feelings remain hidden. In contrast, the unconditional acceptance of feelings cultivated in this meditation provides the space for our patterns of feeling and reaction to naturally settle and heal in their own time. One sign of this natural settling is that—at first occasionally, then more often—you find your mind resting right in the empty essence of a feeling, which is experienced as a space of warmth, peace, and simplicity from within. In that moment, the separation you had felt between yourself as observer and the feeling observed dissolves. You merge with the feeling within a space of stillness, warmth, and simplicity that feels absolutely safe. If this kind of experience happens, just let it be by relaxing right into that sense of simplicity and warmth.

This perspective from Tibetan Buddhism can be related to constructivist theories of emotion from modern psychology and neuroscience. The theory of constructed emotion points to the underlying emptiness of all emotions and associated senses of self. Emotions are constructed from multiple processes such as memory, interoception, language, and perception.[11] Although emotions have a relative, social reality, they are not biological essences; they have no substantial physical reality.[12] This theory holds that emotions are constructed by drawing on conceptual knowledge and memory to make meaning of our current physical sensations in connection with the external world. For example, a rise in heart rate and blood pressure can be interpreted as "anger" or "disgust" depending on the context and our past experiences with those physical sensations. Then when those physical sensations occur in a similar manner in the future, our mind quickly reconstructs those bodily sensations as anger. In this way, we are constantly relying on past experience to make meaning of the present.[13]

The Compassionate Presence to Feelings Meditation takes on new significance in light of this theory of constructed emotion. Each time we become compassionately present to a particular feeling or emotion, that quality of compassionate presence can become a part of that emotion. In other words, with repeated practice, the unconditional qualities of warmth, acceptance, and openness that we bring to an emotion become part of the experience of that emotion. When that emotion occurs in the future, outside of formal meditation, it can automatically point us back to the practice. Furthermore, because our emotions are constructed, as we learn to allow and accept them, we are no longer fueling them by reinforcing the construction process. Then they can metabolize themselves in a healing way that increasingly reveals their empty, constructed nature as a felt sense of openness, peace, and warmth from within the feeling.[14]

Thus, the compassionate presence practice (and also the field of care practice) adds to the theory of constructed emotion by establishing a *holding environment* in which emotions with narrow senses of self and other can naturally relax and self-release.[15] This environment provides an unconditional space in which emotions are not elaborated on, ruminated about, or reacted to, so our usual mental habit of constructing and identifying with emotions can relax and unwind, revealing the emptiness and healing power that is available right within our emotions.[16]

To become so unconditionally present to feelings in this practice, then, provides the spacious holding environment for the knots of our reactive patterns to unravel by themselves. As patterns of contraction metabolize themselves and release in that way, a sense of inner freedom and deep relief can emerge. We can begin to experience the unconditioned simplicity of being that is prior to all of our reactivity. To be present to experience in such a full, spacious, and nonreactive way, without agenda, has been called "unconditional presence."[17] This direction of practice is also enhanced by settling into the final "releasing" step of all the meditations in this book and by reconnecting regularly with the "letting be" meditation that will be instructed below.

We cannot force this deepening direction of practice. It unfolds in its own time, through repeated practice. But just to follow the meditation instruction above is already to enter into this process since the meditation familiarizes us with qualities of openness, acceptance, and warmth that gradually deepen into unconditional presence. The contemplative psychologist John Welwood describes "unconditional presence" in an illuminating way: "When we relate to our experience in a friendly, nonreactive, and allowing way, we open ourselves to the embrace of our larger, unconditioned nature. And it is here . . . that the healing of our conditioned self takes place."[18] Using fear as an example, he writes, "When we finally bring full attention to the fear, feeling and opening to it, our larger being makes contact with the fear, perhaps for the first time. As this happens, the fear starts to loosen; it cannot remain so tightly contracted in the embrace of our full caring presence. . . . The full presence of our being is healing in and of itself."[19]

COMPASSIONATE PRESENCE IS A GREAT SUPPORT FOR ALL OTHER PRACTICES AND ALL ACTIVITIES THROUGHOUT OUR DAY

Ideally, the Compassionate Presence to Feelings Meditation becomes a common practice throughout the day. We began the meditation by becoming spaciously present and compassionately aware of physical sensations, then emotional feelings. The meditation familiarizes us with this unconditional way of being with all feelings. As we learn the practice better in daily morning sessions, we can increasingly explore that way of being with the many kinds of feelings that come up throughout our days. In this way, we learn to do this practice with any feelings at any time: physical or emotional, unpleasant or pleasant, strong feelings or subtle feelings. If there is no strong feeling at the moment, you can do the practice with your felt sense of body and mind at that moment, even with a feeling of dullness or numbness.

All of our meditation practices introduce ways of being that run counter to what we have been accustomed to. We have seen that in the receptive-mode meditations—how various parts of us and emotional reactions get activated by the Field of Care Meditation in ways that can impede our receptivity to awakening qualities. It is similar with all of our other meditations—all stimulate reactions that contain feelings. This means that, when any meditation we do stimulates a reaction that makes us unable to follow its instruction, we can notice whatever feeling is accompanying that reaction and become compassionately present to that very feeling. When the feeling and reaction settle, we can return to the meditation at hand. In this way, compassionate presence to feelings becomes a crucial support for all the other meditations we explore in this book.

The same principle holds for all of our relationships and activities. All of our ways of being and working with others stimulate emotional feelings, often in reaction to others' emotions. When we become skilled at being compassionately present to our feelings, we realize that all of our activities function as a delivery system for feelings that can fuel this practice. As we gain confidence in learning how to be with our feelings in the safe way instilled by compassionate presence, we feel more at home with others because we no longer need to be afraid of the feelings in us that are triggered by them. All such feelings, even as they arise, can be given the space they need to find a deeply settled and healing way to be, which can open into a warmth at their core, which becomes a warmth toward others and their feelings. This transforms our relationships and activities with others. This possibility emerges not just by thinking or theorizing about it but by practicing compassionate presence a lot, first within meditation sessions, then increasingly when with others in our days.

Compassionate Presence Practice
for Professional Caregivers

Many caregivers are taught to distance themselves from feelings of empathy for suffering patients. In professions such as medicine, nursing, and social work, for example, training programs often instruct students to ignore or suppress feelings when interacting with patients or clients so as to be able to maintain a professional boundary or clinical distance.[20] But as we note above, such avoidance becomes a stressor that can lead to mental and physical exhaustion. In addition, painful feelings of inefficacy when attempting to help patients can elicit aversion toward the patients, which is associated with cynicism, compassion fatigue, burnout, and moral injury among health professionals.[21] The meditation here offers a new possibility: by taking all such feelings into the practice of compassionate presence, we can gradually learn that we don't have to suppress or become overwhelmed by the feelings that inevitably arise in caregiving work. All such feelings can be directed, as in the meditation instruction, into a path of healing rather than emotional depletion and burnout, by giving them all the space they need to relax, settle, metabolize themselves, and self-heal. But it does take practice to learn this.

We should also echo a cautionary note voiced by many health-care workers: emotional depletion and burnout is also a systemic issue that must be addressed at an organizational level.[22] Meditation practices should not be offered as a tactic to avoid investing in improvements in work environments, by placing all responsibility on individual health-care workers to improve their work lives just by becoming more mindful. Failure to establish compassionate, trusting relationships in workplaces and caregiving settings can be attributed, in large part, to systemic pressures and workload. Our hope is that the meditation practices offered here will not only empower people to avoid individual empathic distress and depletion but also empower them to work for systemic change where needed. If your current work environment is just too overwhelming to function well in, you may want to consider looking for a more supportive environment to begin to explore how becoming compassionately present to your feelings could empower your relationships and work with others. Then by familiarizing yourself with this meditation practice, you can gradually learn to handle more challenging environments and situations with greater ease around feelings and emotions.

In sum, all meditations, practices, and life experiences generate the material for compassionate presence to feelings. Over time, and with repeated practice, we can become increasingly confident in the capacities of this practice to provide a sense of safety to work with any feeling. Whenever you are having a difficult or painful reaction to any other meditation practice, any person, or any situation in your life, notice the feeling within that reaction and become compassionately present to that feeling for a while, so it can feel safe enough to relax, settle in its own time, and heal in its own way. Then notice how much more present that makes you to your meditation, the other person, or the task at hand.

Compassionate Presence and Reappraisal of Our World

Psychologists have shown that people can learn to interpret difficult feelings in a newly beneficial way. For example, we can learn to reappraise feelings of stress as beneficial—stress as helpful to mobilize the body's energy so we can meet demands of the current situation well.[23] This kind of strategy is referred to in psychology as *reappraisal*. This concept can be related to our compassionate presence practice. We are always experiencing some kind of feeling within our daily lives. Situations that elicit feelings of anger, anxiety, sadness, hopelessness, numbness, physical pain, frustration, giddiness, or more diffuse feelings of dis-ease or confusion provide an opportunity to deepen in practice by becoming compassionately present to those feelings. In this way, our feelings themselves become the very means to bring out our innate capacities of care, compassion, and wisdom. We can reinterpret our feelings not as difficult distractions but as the very means to awaken, a form of reappraisal. Buddhist practitioners have historically employed this kind of reappraisal by understanding the whole world as a teacher.[24] The whole world, by continually activating feelings in us, can point us back to qualities of care and compassion through repeated practice of compassionate presence in our days.

SUMMARIZING BENEFICIAL EFFECTS OF COMPASSIONATE PRESENCE TO FEELINGS

1. *A healing effect:* Compassionate presence to feelings transforms us into an unconditional holding environment for all of our physical and emotional feelings, which helps our minds and bodies to relax deeply, unclench, and begin to heal deeply from within.

2. *Opening into qualities of buddha nature right through our feelings:* Compassionate Presence to Feelings Meditation can gradually uncover the emptiness, lucidity, and warmth of our buddha nature, right from within our emotional feelings. Feelings are provided a safe space to open into underlying feelings and eventually into the very core of the feelings where, perhaps to our surprise, a sense of relief, warmth, and well-being can be experienced. This core of deep inner peace and security is found in the empty essence of the feelings. With this comes a readiness to appreciate the beauty in things, and to love and care for what is. This is what Tsoknyi Rinpoche, one of our Tibetan teachers, calls "essence love," the essence of love that has been hidden in our feelings.[25]

3. *Inner steadiness and courage:* This process of letting feelings open and heal from within brings out a power of equanimity toward our feelings and

the situations that activate them. There is a growing awareness that we do not need to be afraid of the feelings that people and circumstances trigger in us, which can give us more courage to work with them all.

4. *Compassionate presence to others:* The power to be with our feelings with such compassion and steadiness becomes a power to be with others and their feelings in the same way.

TO ACCEPT AND HOLD OUR FEELINGS IN COMPASSION CAN EMPOWER US TO CHALLENGE DYSFUNCTIONAL SOCIAL INSTITUTIONS AND SYSTEMS

Many people live or work within social structures and institutional arrangements, parts of which may need to be challenged for the good of all—for example, inequities in access to good education, housing, employment, health care, food and water; oppressive working conditions; and massive destruction of the natural world. Someone may think that if they become more accepting of their feelings and reactions, as in the Compassionate Presence to Feelings Meditation, they would be learning to accept dysfunctional social conditions that trigger the feelings rather than challenging those conditions. That is not the direction in which we take this practice. In an oppressive environment, we can get so caught up in our own painful feelings that we become paralyzed, unable to see the potential for change or confront what needs to be challenged effectively. In fact, burnout is a common response to the difficult emotions generated by social activism work.[26] To become compassionately present to our own feelings and reactions so they can settle and heal brings out powers of inner safeness, equanimity, discernment, resilience, courage, and creative responsiveness that can empower us to respond much better to the needs around us and to challenge what should be challenged, with real care and compassion for all involved.[27]

Let's return to the topic of people in helping professions, some of whom, when introduced to the Compassionate Presence to Feelings Meditation, have said, "I don't think I should do this practice! Because it runs counter to the way I am supposed to be in my workplace. I need to ignore my feelings so I can focus on the many tasks I have to do all the time." Unfortunately, to follow that precept is to internalize an oppressive aspect of the system in which we work that promotes burnout, by internalizing an oppressive way to be with our feelings. One practitioner commented on this point: "We need to tear down our own internal repressive system and rebuild it so that we can come from a place of real compassion in working with the systems outside ourselves." To become more compassionately aware of our feelings, giving them the space they need to unclench and heal, frees us from the repressive ways we may be accustomed to relate to our feelings. And this gradually shifts our way of being and working with others within our institutions by helping us become a more healing, discerning, and responsive presence to all involved.

What about anger at injustice? How would our practice of spacious acceptance of feelings affect that? When we perceive injustice, it is natural to feel anger as part of our motivation to respond. Anger, in that initial phase of response, can be valuable. It helps us generate the energy needed to change things, just as stress mobilizes bodily energy to meet demands in our environment. But once we are activated by anger, if we maintain a tight identification with our anger and get caught up in it, many problems follow. Anger tends to reduce other persons in our perception to just one negative characteristic. We then lose our sense of the fuller persons, who have not only faults but also positive capacities and possibilities that we could relate to if we noticed them. If we get incessantly caught up in our anger while trying to work for change, it not only wounds our own hearts and minds but also cultivates a habit of hostile reaction to others that can drive them away just when we need their support the most. This is because, when our anger has control over us, it tends to imitate the behavior of those at whom we are angry: aggressive, reactive, not really seeing others, not valuing them, dominating them, and so on.

Lama Rod Owens, an African American Dharma teacher and social activist, explains that if we continue to be dominated by our anger, we lose our freedom. "I've come to realize that when I don't have agency over my anger, it actually has agency over me. Or in other words, I am a slave to my anger." He continues: "[But] anger is full of wisdom; and with the appropriate practice, anger can actually transform into wisdom, and that wisdom is deeply liberating."[28] When we apply the practice of compassionate presence to our anger, it has the space it needs to release its fixations, clarify what it knows, and channel its energy into a fierce compassion that can confront what needs to be challenged in people and society, as an expression of real care for everyone involved.[29]

LETTING BE OF BODY, BREATH, AND MIND MEDITATION

The Field of Care and Compassionate Presence to Feelings meditations help us activate capacities of love, acceptance, inner safety, spaciousness, and compassion from our fundamental awareness that can embrace all our perceptions, thoughts, and feelings in a healing way. In the final *releasing phase* of each such meditation, those qualities help the mind feel safe enough to relax its grip on self-clinging reactions and relax into the *source* of those loving qualities—a pervasive openness, clarity, and warmth that is always available in the background of our awareness and transcends all narrow frameworks of mind. The next meditation—Letting Be of Body, Breath and Mind— builds on this releasing phase of all prior meditations to help us settle more fully into the expansive depth of our being, the pure cognizance and infinite spaciousness of our buddha nature, the source of all the awakening qualities that we are learning to cultivate. The term *pure cognizance* refers to the basic knowing quality that is present in all of our experiences and in the spacious backdrop of our experience.

According to the nondual perspectives of Dzogchen and Mahāmudrā in Tibetan Buddhism, there has always been a background of spaciousness and pure cognizance that pervades all of our experience, though often not conscious to us. As we noted earlier, you might remember a moment when that pervasive background of awareness dawned on you, perhaps when you were resting after a long walk, enjoying the panoramic view of a sunset, or relaxing along a shore and gazing upon the ocean and sky. Or when you were on the roof of a building overlooking a vast cityscape. Or when you were able to relax deeply after a long day of hard physical labor. In such a moment, a sense of utter openness, simplicity, peace, and clarity may dawn from within—a pervasive quality of awareness and limitless openness that is suddenly brought forward by the all-encompassing scope of your gaze.

That is a momentary glimpse of the infinite openness and clarity that was always available in the background of your awareness but was hidden by your ordinary patterns of thought and reaction.

The next meditation of "letting be" in body, breath, and mind helps us settle more fully into that tranquil background of pervasive openness, simplicity, warmth, and clarity of awareness. In this meditation, we settle naturally into the felt experience of body, breath, and mind in sequence. First, we let the felt sense of the body help the mind to settle deeply. The meditation instruction does not involve actively trying to make anything happen. Instead, it specifies a way to let the feeling of the body itself draw our awareness increasingly into unity with it, as if letting the body do the meditating, while allowing any physical tension to relax and settle in its own time. The same process is then carried out with the "letting be" of the breath. In the "letting be" of mind, we notice any grasping in the mind to whatever mental framework, sense of self, or pattern of thought is occurring and let that feeling of holding relax deep within. This gives the mind permission to relax its hold on its mental schema and open to the spaciousness available in the background of its awareness, beyond clinging to any framework of thought or reference point. We learn to let that unity of utter openness and pure cognizance increasingly draw our awareness into oneness with it. In this way, we are drawn toward a nondual experience of body, breath, and spacious awareness. This process strengthens our inner secure base of deepening tranquility, spacious well-being, inner freedom, and compassionate awareness from which to become more fully present to self and others. Ultimately it draws us into increasing unity with our buddha nature.[30]

This Letting Be of Body, Breath, and Mind Meditation is best done with your eyes open, so your attention is receptive to the expansive scope of experience that includes all the senses. With the letting be of body and breath, the eyes can be gazing gently downward, about four feet ahead. With the letting be of mind, it is best to raise the eyes to look straight ahead, with a gentle panoramic gaze that is open to the whole visual field, with all senses left naturally wide open.

(An audio option is available at shambhala.com/howcompassionworks meditations.)

LETTING BE OF BODY, BREATH, AND MIND MEDITATION

STEP 1. ABDOMINAL BREATHING (3 MINUTES) Sit in a relaxed, comfortable way with back straight, eyes gazing gently downward. Come down from the thinking mind into the body. (*Pause*) Take a slow, deep breath, inhaling from the abdomen so it expands, exhaling slowly and completely, and letting go of all your concerns with the exhale. Relax for a moment before inhaling again. Repeat several times. Then, while still breathing from the abdomen, let the breath settle into its own natural flow. Feel the belly expand and contract with each breath. Let that feeling draw you into it more and more, breath by breath. (*Pause*)

STEP 2. LETTING BE OF BODY (2 TO 3 MINUTES) Notice any feeling of tightness or holding on anywhere in the body and let that relax. Let all bodily feelings just settle in their own way, in their own time. (*Pause*) Deeply let be into the body by letting the body unify you with it more and more—as if the body is meditating you; as if the body is doing the knowing. (*Pause*)

STEP 3. LETTING BE OF BREATH (2 TO 3 MINUTES) Still breathing from the abdomen, feel the full inhale and exhale with each breath. Notice any sense of holding on to the breathing process anywhere and let that relax. (*Pause*) Deeply let be into the breath, letting the feeling of the breath in the body unify you with it more and more, breath by breath—as if the breath is meditating you; as if the breath is doing the knowing. (*Pause*)

STEP 4. LETTING BE OF MIND (5 TO 7 MINUTES) Now raise your eyes to look ahead with a gentle panoramic gaze that spaciously encompasses the whole visual field. Leave all senses wide open and just relax into that panoramic sensory field.

Notice any grasping in the mind to any mental construct—holding on to any sense of self or framework of thought—and let that feeling of holding on relax deep within. Let the mind settle back a bit inwardly and come to rest in the background of its awareness, which is naturally wide open and luminous, like the sky. In this way, let the mind relax into the spacious backdrop of its awareness beyond reference points—wide open, limitless, and radiant. Let this natural openness of awareness meditate you, unifying you with it more and more, by letting everything be. Let any thoughts and feelings that arise just metabolize themselves and release within this sky-like expanse of openness and lucidity, by letting all be.

When the mind closes up again, holding on to a narrow sense of self or frame of thought, let the mind again settle back into the spaciousness and clarity in the background of its awareness, naturally wide open and radiant. Let patterns of thought and feeling that arise just unwind and release within this limitless expanse of lucid openness.

Processing the Meditation

After practicing the Letting Be meditation multiple times in retreats, a number of meditators have described these effects of the meditation:

1. By letting the mind release its grip on narrow frameworks of thought and settle back a bit inwardly, we access a welcoming background of total openness, deep acceptance, wisdom, and peace that is always available, like when we spontaneously experience a moment of deep peace when relaxing in nature.

2. This is a level of awareness that lies beyond patterns of reaction to self and others, in which we can find deepening inner rest, calm, equanimity, discernment, and replenishment.

3. Stressful patterns of thought and reaction can begin to heal themselves within the unconditional openness and acceptance of this level of our being.

4. From this place, we can also start to become a more healing and unconditional presence to others.

TRANQUIL ABIDING, NO NEED TO STRUGGLE

The Letting Be of Body, Breath, and Mind meditation draws on the spirit of Tibetan Dzogchen and Mahāmudrā practice in its emphasis on naturalness. In this understanding, the body, breath, and mind have a natural capacity to settle, on their own, without the effort of a self that is performing the meditation. The first two "letting bes" let the natural power of body and breath draw us progressively into unity with them in somatic experience. This signals the mind, at the start of the third letting be, to let the underlying openness and clarity of awareness draw the mind toward unity with it, so the meditation can become increasingly effortless—powered by the natural openness of awareness that is prior to mental construction, activity, and effort.

We are usually focused outwardly on objects of thought and perception that are located within mentally created frameworks of self and world. That external focus is what the mind is habitually used to constructing and inhabiting. In the letting be of mind, the panoramic gaze of the eyes and expansive openness through all senses helps the mind sense and acknowledge a pervasive openness that is also available to it in the background of its awareness. In the third letting be, then, we let the mind settle back a little internally, like retracting a zoom lens on a camera, so the mind comes to rest in its own spacious background of awareness, which is naturally wide open, luminous, and all-encompassing, beyond all familiar mental frameworks.[31] The mind thus relaxes into the utter openness and clarity that has been in the background of its experience all along, previously unnoticed; an openness and clarity that also pervades all aspects of one's experience. There is a sense of reuniting with the intrinsic openness that was already here, vast as space, all pervasive. We experience that reuniting as like a gentle force that draws us into pervasive openness naturally, beyond any attempt to create openness.

In this way, the third letting be of mind can bring us into a meditative state referred to in Tibetan Buddhist traditions as "tranquil abiding without support" (*zhi gnas rten med*). "Tranquil abiding" translates the Sanskrit term śamatha. In that state, we are not focusing on any particular object or support for our attention—such as an image, sound, or feeling—but settling directly into the openness and pure cognizance present in the background of our consciousness, no matter what perceptions arise in the foreground. That backdrop of simple openness and cognizance is inherently stable and unwavering, and it pervades all the sense perceptions that occur in the foreground—sights, sounds, and so forth—even as those perceptions shift and change. In tranquil abiding without support, the mind settles into the stability of that cognizant background, naturally wide open and radiant. In Tibetan traditions, this is sometimes called "letting the mind settle into itself" (*sems rang la bzhag pa*).[32] It is also called "resting in nowness" (*da lta ba nyid du gnas*), because the mind is abiding in the freshness of cognizant openness in the present, here and now, without being drawn into thinking about past or future.[33]

With all senses open, perceptions are certainly occurring—feeling a breeze, seeing leaves blown by wind, hearing a car drive by. All such sense perceptions are shifting and changing, but the backdrop of openness and cognizance that takes expression in those perceptions is not changing. And the mind is resting in that backdrop. To help understand this, try to remember a time when you were in a movie theater. Did you ever turn around during the movie to look back at the stable flow of light that was coming from the movie projector, the light that transforms into changing images when it hits the movie screen? To settle into the stable openness and cognizance in the background of experience while perceptions shift and change in the foreground is like settling into the stable flow of light from the film projector that becomes changing images on the movie screen in the foreground. In tranquil-abiding meditation, we rest in the stable backdrop of cognizance and openness rather than being caught up in the shifting perceptions of the foreground, even as those perceptions continue to appear and change.

In the meditation session, as the letting be of mind helps us settle into such a state of tranquil abiding, discrete thoughts may also continue to arise. For example, if you hear the honk of a car, the thought "car" may occur. Thoughts and emotions may also begin to form into patterns in their usual way—starting to form a chain of thought or an emotional reaction, like "I don't like that honking sound."

But the meditation instruction reminds us to let the spacious backdrop of awareness increasingly unveil itself by letting things be. When we settle into that spacious dimension of awareness in the background, we can let patterns of thought and feeling that start to form in the foreground of awareness just unwind and release by themselves. Or we can let thoughts, as they arise, just rest in their own arising. In this way, the mind does not become fully identified with or caught up in its thoughts. Thoughts and reactions that arise have all the space they need to dissolve back into the openness and cognizance from which they have come. The mind is not identified with and caught up in them since it is resting in the stable, spacious background of awareness from which they arise. Instead, let thoughts and feelings that arise just subside by themselves, as the mind relaxes into the simplicity of natural openness and clarity.[34]

While tranquilly abiding in this way, there is no need to struggle to avoid generating chains of thought or reaction in order to become more settled, present, and spacious. As the natural spaciousness in the background of our awareness increasingly draws us into unity with it, thoughts and feelings that arise in the foreground of awareness are unable to fully form into chains of thought and reaction and can just unwind or release as they form. Like ocean water freely allows its waves to arise from and subside back into the watery source from which they emerge, we can allow waves of thought and emotion to arise and subside naturally back into the union of openness and cognizance, the source from which they emerge. As mental patterns are allowed to resolve themselves, by themselves, the natural spaciousness and radiant clarity of mind that is logically prior to all such mental activity can unveil itself more and more, as instructed in the meditation, by letting everything be.

A traditional metaphor for this process is the intrinsic purity of water that reveals itself naturally by letting the muddiness that had clouded the water settle gradually on its own. Another metaphor is the radiant clarity and openness of the sky that reveals itself naturally as the clouds that had obscured the sky dissipate. The intrinsic openness and clarity of the mind, and the underlying purity of water and sky, have always been present—within all our experiences, within all the muddy water, within all the cloudiness, but are not recognized until what obscured them begins to dissipate. The Letting Be meditation helps the mind release its identification with its reified thoughts and reactions so it can sense its underlying expansive, pure nature and begin to reunite with it.

Soon, though, from long habit, the mind tends to resurrect its familiar reference points of self and world and to close up, clinging to narrow, self-concerned frameworks of thought and reaction. When you notice the mind doing that, as the meditation instructs, let the mind again relax, settle back a little, reunite with the natural spaciousness and clarity that is always available in the background of its awareness, and let all be.

Relaxing Goals

The phrase *letting be* that is used within this meditation carries special significance. According to emerging perspectives in cognitive science, the mind organizes its categories around goals.[35] A small hollow object becomes a "mug" to us when our goal is to drink hot liquids from it. The same object becomes an office "penholder" when our goal for it is to store pens. Not just the object but also our corresponding sense of self is partly constructed in relation to the goal—as a connoisseur of coffee, as an organized office person. Over time such conceptualizations are repeated, yielding labels for objects and corresponding senses of self that are associated with familiar goals.

This focus on goals has practical implications for contemplative practice. Adhering to goals supports the conceptual processes that tend to hide qualities of our buddha nature. Relaxing such goals releases those processes so underlying qualities of our buddha nature can more freely emerge. During the Letting Be of Body, Breath, and Mind meditation, in any moment that we experience an emotional pull or pattern of thought, try to notice the goal that is operating in that experience. For example, when we notice the desire to have a good meditation, we can let that goal relax and notice how that starts to release the conceptual processing that maintains a subject-object structure of experience. As the tight conceptual construction of a narrow self that is focused on its goals releases, underlying qualities of openness, warmth, simplicity, equanimity, and so forth from our buddha nature naturally manifest more fully.

Please now repeat the Letting Be of Body, Breath, and Mind meditation on page 91 informed by the points above, including the notion of relaxing goals. Let those points help you more fully engage the meditation.

When the Mind Becomes Dull or Distracted

If the mind becomes *dull, foggy, or drowsy* during the Letting Be meditation, you can sit up straighter, take a deep breath into the abdomen, then allow a long slow outbreath, resting briefly after the exhale before inhaling again. Raise your gaze and let it become fully panoramic. Let that wide-open gaze help clear your mind, so the mind becomes open, vivid, and fresh. Settle back again into the naturally spacious background of awareness and let that unity of openness and lucidity increasingly unveil itself by relaxing all goals and letting things be. Becoming too warm will also promote drowsiness. In that case, you can open a window or shed some clothing.

Lack of motivation for meditation practice may be another reason that the mind becomes recurrently dull or drowsy. In that case, reconnect with your motivation and enthusiasm to awaken your best capacities for the sake of all. Within the meditation process, we are also cultivating a gentle alertness to notice when the lucid quality of tranquil abiding is becoming dull, hazy, or foggy. When we notice that, we apply methods to heighten attention like those just suggested.

If the mind becomes *distracted or agitated* in the meditation during the letting be of mind, caught up in chains of thought and feeling, you can reconnect for a little while with either the Field of Care Meditation or the Compassionate Presence to Feelings Meditation to become a spacious healing environment for those feelings and thoughts, letting them settle in their time, in their own way. When they settle, let the releasing phase of that meditation return you to the letting be of mind, to relax again into the pervasive openness and cognizance available in the background of your awareness, relaxing all goals and letting any thoughts and feelings that occur just arise and subside on their own. Within this process, we are also cultivating gentle alertness to notice when the mind is becoming distracted or agitated. When we notice that, we apply the methods suggested to help the mind return to tranquil abiding—naturally settled, spacious, and luminous.[36]

As we practice the letting be of mind repeatedly over time with alertness, we learn to settle into that backdrop of openness and clarity more often with greater ease and fullness, relaxing all goals and letting that state of tranquil abiding maintain itself for slightly longer periods of time. As the mind rests in the cognizant background of experience that takes expression in the perceptions and thoughts of the foreground, the usual sense of duality between subject and object is reduced. That which is perceiving or thinking, and that which is being perceived or thought of, are newly sensed as poles of an undivided continuum of awareness, not as absolutely separate things.

As we settle into deepening states of such tranquil abiding with repeated practice, the mind becomes more transparent to underlying capacities of its awareness—powers of spaciousness, presence, steadiness, clarity, inner peace, equanimity, ease of being, a sense of wholeness, and joy. When the mind is abiding in its stable background of cognizance and openness, it is not caught up in shifting patterns of self-focused reaction, so there is a fuller sense of presence to others as a basis to connect heart to heart with them and to respond to what is happening.[37]

Pleasant Meditation Experiences

With further practice of tranquil abiding in meditation sessions, at some point, other very pleasant kinds of experience tend to emerge from it—experiences of physical and mental bliss, brightness of awareness, and deeply peaceful states of meditative absorption that are not caught up in patterns of thinking. Such contemplative experiences, called *nyams* in Tibetan, are positive signs that the meditation process is deepening. We can take encouragement from those signs that our practice is progressing. But all such experiences are impermanent. And because they can be so pleasant, the mind tends to become attached, clinging to them—trying to get them to continue or wanting them to return. Just like any other habit of distraction, such grasping at temporary experiences can prevent us from further progressing in the meditation. We may even mistakenly think that such pleasant experiences are the very purpose for doing meditation. But of course they are not. We don't practice just to bliss out or endlessly chase after temporary pleasant feelings. We practice to become more fully present and responsive to ourselves and others, by re-uniting with the source of love, compassion, and wisdom in the depth of our being, for the sake of all. So when experiences of bliss, clarity, or deep peace occur, we can acknowledge them as good signs of meditation, renew our deepest motivation for practice, and settle back into the spacious background of experience from which all such experiences emerge.

It can be helpful in this context to recall what was said above about relaxing goals. As pleasant qualities emerge in meditation, we might notice various goal-oriented thoughts arise with them, such as "What can I do to hold on to this?," "I'm afraid this will not last," "How can I experience this again?," which foster various anxieties. However, the emphasis on relaxing goals within the letting be practice can be supportive here. We can remember to notice the goals that underlie these thoughts, relax the goal, and let that help the mind naturally settle, open, and reconnect with its spacious background. Even the thought of letting be itself might become a goal. Then simply notice that thought, relax that goal, and let the mind naturally settle into its spacious background.

Like ocean water allows its waves to subside naturally back into their wateriness, we let waves of pleasant experience and goal-oriented reactions arise and subside naturally into the spaciousness and clarity from which they emerge. Then instead of entangling us, pleasant meditative experiences and reactions, upon releasing, can further vivify the experience of openness and lucidity within tranquil abiding.

If You Have Difficulty Settling into Tranquil Abiding with the Letting Be Meditation

Within the Letting Be of Body, Breath, and Mind meditation, during the letting be of mind part, if you have difficulty settling into the stable backdrop of openness and awareness described above and find yourself struggling with the meditation, just recall and reinhabit your field of care or reconnect to the Compassionate Presence to Feelings Meditation. Each of those meditations help the mind experience the loving, healing qualities of its underlying expansive nature. This helps the mind learn to trust that nature, so it is willing to release its grip on itself in the releasing phase of those meditations, and then also in the Letting Be meditation. This frees the mind to settle into the expansive background of its experience that transcends its familiar goals and points of reference. Trust, then, is crucial to this process of meditative deepening. It can take time for the mind to trust what it is settling into, beyond its familiar frameworks of thinking and reaction. The Field of Care and Compassionate Presence to Feelings meditations inculcate that kind of trust, so the mind, in the Letting Be meditation, can trust its spacious cognizant nature enough to relax more and more fully into it.

FROM TRANQUIL ABIDING INTO NONDUAL
RECOGNITION OF BUDDHA NATURE—
THE EMPTY, LUCID NATURE OF MIND

When a practitioner is tranquilly abiding in the spacious backdrop of aware-ness described above, the experience of subject-object duality is much at-tenuated, since the mind is resting in itself, in its own backdrop of spacious awareness, which is in continuity with all the perceptions, feelings, and thoughts that arise from that spacious backdrop. But there still remains a subtle, subconscious framework of duality—a sense of someone who is maintaining a framework of meditation, someone meditating on or resting in cognizant openness, and some effort to continue to abide in that way.[38]

As noted at the start of this chapter, drawing from Buddhist psychology, the mind is in the habit of constructing, reifying, and identifying with nar-row senses of self that seem to stand apart from the mind's constructions of others and the world. The mind then mistakes those dualistic mental constructs for reality as such. Caught up in its own constructions, projec-tions, and reactions, the mind loses touch with its fuller, more expansive power of awareness that is primordially nondual and logically prior to all such constructions. In essence, all of us have been imprisoned, more than we have been conscious, in the socially conditioned habit of mistaking our own familiar thoughts of everyone (including ourselves) for the actual beings. From a Buddhist perspective, that delusion is the root cause of human-made suffering. We are endlessly reacting to our own empty, reductive mental constructs of self and others, unaware. If the mind's tendency to mistake its own dualistic constructs of beings for the actual beings, and to react to them from there, is *not* uprooted, the inmost cause of suffering remains intact. That impedes our underlying capacity to become more fully present to ourselves and others with the qualities and discernment that come from our innate nondual nature, our fundamental awareness, our buddha nature.

Settling into deepening states of tranquil abiding in cognizant openness helps us become more transparent to life-giving qualities of our fundamen-tal awareness. But because tranquil abiding per se is a conditioned state of mind that retains a subtle degree of dualism, it does not uproot the uncon-scious tendency to grasp on to dualistic frameworks of mind that underlie our habits of reaction. Therefore, tranquil abiding in itself does not uproot the inmost cause of suffering from a Buddhist perspective. When the mind abides tranquilly in its background of cognizant openness, it settles into a profound peacefulness. But at other times, when we are not settled in such a state, our conditioned tendencies to react to our dualistically constructed images of self and others with narrow self-clinging goals, aversion, possessiveness, anger, frustration, and so forth tend to return.

In time, though, with lots of practice supported by experienced teachers and community, a practitioner may settle so profoundly into further levels of tranquil abiding that they are taken beyond the subtle dualism of tranquil abiding itself. As the practitioner deepens in stages of tranquil abiding, they increasingly reunify with the qualities available in the deep nature of their mind, such as pervasive openness, simplicity, peace, stability of attention, wholeness, clarity, joy, ease, readiness to care, and so forth. Empowered by the Letting Be meditation, tranquil abiding lets those qualities draw the mind increasingly into unity with them, and through that, with their source in the nondual nature of mind—buddha nature.

Relaxing goals is a key part of this process. Practice instructions use phrases like "not doing," "not trying to cultivate anything," "letting everything be," and "not meditating" to help practitioners release the goal-based conceptual processing that maintains the self-oriented subject-object structure that hides the fuller reality of oneself and the world. Zen traditions similarly emphasize "beginner's mind" and "don't-know mind" to encourage a release of the conceptual activity that constantly seeks to carve up experience into narrow, dualistic, goal-oriented ways. As the subject-object structure releases, various aspects of conceptualization dissipate, including projection of a self into the future and past, reification of thoughts as objective realities, and effortful construction of experience.[39]

At some point in the process of tranquil abiding, the practitioner may settle so profoundly into, and reunify so fully with, the cognizant openness in which they are resting that their mind releases its grip on itself completely, at least for a moment, and the dualistic, goal-oriented structure of experience that the mind had always maintained just collapses. In that moment, the infinite unconditioned nature of mind—buddha nature—dawns spontaneously. The mind has a thoroughly nondual glimpse of its essential nature experienced as a unity of unconditioned emptiness, pure cognizance, and compassionate capacity—beyond all frames of reference, beyond all dualistic construction, beyond conditioning, beyond all effort or doing. "Emptiness" here refers to the totally insubstantial nature of all aspects of experience. The experience of emptiness in this context is like a basic space (Tib. *dbyings*) in and through all that is appearing and felt, which transcends all conceptual parameters that usually frame experience, such as frameworks of subject and object, space and time.

In the moment that the mind comes into nondual recognition of its empty nature, it reverts spontaneously to its most natural and primordial state—the cognizant aspect of the mind undivided from the emptiness of all that is appearing. From a Buddhist perspective, it is a moment of freedom from habits of reification, self-concerned goals, dualistic grasping, and reaction that had constituted the inmost causes of suffering. In that moment, all such mental patterns find no footing in the essential emptiness of all that the mind had previously been reifying, identifying with, grasping, and reacting to. Instead of identifying with shifting states of mind, the practitioner is unified with the unchanging space and clarity that pervade all such states of mind. That space and clarity harbor innate energies of love and compassion that can now unfold within the freedom of that space.[40]

In Tibetan traditions of Dzogchen and Mahāmudrā, this glimpse of the mind's empty nature is called "the view" (*lta ba*), a thoroughly nondual recognition of cognizant emptiness as the unchanging, unconditioned ground of all changing, conditioned experiences. This constitutes the dawning of liberating insight (Tib. *lhag mthong*; Skt. *vipaśyanā*), which frees the practitioner from the bondage of being identified with and caught up in conditioned states of mind.

To elaborate on this a little more: in that moment of nondual recognition, the mind spontaneously reverts to its primordial state (Tib. *gnas lugs*), which is experienced as a unity of basic space and pure cognizance (Tib. *dbyings rig dyer med*) that is unobstructed (Tib. *zang mthal*), all-pervasive (Tib. *phyal ba*), unconditioned (Tib. *ma byas*), self-knowing (Tib. *rang rig*), and self-manifesting (Tib. *rang byung*). In this state of primal awareness, the cognizant aspect of experience now recognizes its own emptiness within all facets of experience in a direct, fully nondual way, beyond all mental construction (Tib. *sphrod bral*). As Chokyi Nyima states it, "Thought-free wakefulness blows up the grammar of ordinary consciousness."[41] When this fully nondual nature of mind dawns, all aspects of experience are now sensed as conditioned expressions of unconditioned empty awareness (Tib. *rig pa'i rtsal*). Like patterns on water that arise and self-dissolve naturally back into their watery bed, all patterns of perception, thought, and feeling that arise in the mind naturally self-release and self-dissolve back into their empty cognizant nature. Rather than drawing the mind into identification with them, thoughts and feelings "self-liberate" upon arising (Tib. *rang grol*).[42]

To recall one of our metaphors, ocean waves arise and dissolve according to changing conditions of temperature, wind, and currents, but the wateriness of all the waves is not affected by any of those conditions—the waves' watery essence is not changing. Similarly, perceptions, thoughts, and feelings arise according to shifting conditions of mind, body, and world, but the cognizant space from which they arise, and which is the essence of them all, is unconditioned, not changing. In this way, to recognize the primordial unity of space and cognizance as the essence of all one's experience provides unconditioned freedom from identification with conditioned, self-clinging patterns of thought and reaction. This frees up compassionate capacities of awareness that had been impeded by such identification to unfold with greater ease, spontaneity, and inclusiveness.

Within the Letting Be of Body, Breath, and Mind meditation, the letting be of *mind* can support the process just described of deepening through stages of tranquil abiding into nondual recognition of primordial awareness. But for that depth of practice to unfold well, it needs support and input from experienced teachers and a practice community that practice at that depth, as well as ongoing engagement with the field of care receptive-mode practice.

Through the lens of attachment theory, the refuge embodied by experienced teachers, practice communities, and field of care practices serve two critical functions related to the deepening mode of practice. First, as a field of care, they help evoke inner capacities of spacious acceptance, warmth, and compassion that provide a healing environment in which self-clinging emotions and thought patterns can metabolize themselves and release, so the groundless dimension of the mind is permitted to dawn. Second, experienced teachers and practitioners, as an outer secure base, evoke our inner secure base of loving qualities and discernment, which empowers us to venture into an uncertain world with the wisdom and compassion to hold many others in care. In that way, we become an extension of the field of refuge that our benefactors have embodied for us.

A classic study on infants' visual systems illustrates how such refuge practices can be a basis for awakening to groundless spaciousness. In the 1960s, experimenters placed an infant on a clothed table. At the edge of the cloth, in between the infant and their mother, was a glass plate, giving the appearance of a drop-off—that is, a *visual cliff*. Most infants crawled up to the edge and stopped just before the "cliff." If the mother expressed joy and interest, the infant continued crawling onto the glass plane, but they avoided it when the mother expressed fear.[43] This is a great metaphor for coming into relation with the nature of our own mind: there is some natural fear of crossing into the groundless plane of our mind. In meditation, encounters with emptiness—the groundless ground of awareness—can be frightening as it challenges our familiar senses of self that we've relied upon as sources of comfort throughout our lives.[44]

Tsoknyi Rinpoche teaches that it is best to have some uncertainty when thinking about emptiness because any such conceptual understanding cannot capture the nonconceptual emptiness of our minds. To let go into the uncertainty of emptiness (beyond all our familiar ways of thinking) is akin to crawling past the visual cliff. We have more confidence to completely release goals and let go into the groundless space of awareness when there are others that embody that possibility, thereby inspiring in us the trust, curiosity, and courage to do the same. Accomplished spiritual teachers, spiritual ancestors, practice lineages, and supportive community serve this function, inviting us to join them in the empty nature of mind where they abide. With the support of experienced practitioners on which to scaffold, we learn to join them in that groundless ground of experience, just as an infant crawls onto the glass plane to join their mother. A sense of deep connection with the natural world, beyond all our anthropocentric ways of thinking about it, can also serve this function.

Dzogchen and Mahāmudrā provide additional methods to empower the possibility of going beyond subtly dualistic, conditioned states of tranquil abiding into a more fully nondual recognition of the unconditioned, empty nature of mind. Since, typically, the mind is externally focused, constantly reacting to its objects of perception and thought, various methods are provided to turn the mind's attention inward to the empty nature of the awareness that is generating those thoughts and perceptions, in ways that cut through the mind's habitual patterns of dualistic construction, reification, and reaction. In this way, thoughts, perceptions, and feelings can come to be experienced as the empty radiant expressions of primordial awareness (Tib. *rig pa'i rtsal*), like the radiance of a rainbow in the sky. That way of experiencing thoughts, feelings, and perceptions frees the mind from its long habit of reifying, fixating upon, identifying with, and reacting to all aspects of its experience. Such methods are passed down in living practice traditions from Tibet and are explained in the relevant texts of those traditions.[45]

When nondual recognition of the empty, unconditioned nature of the mind dawns, there is typically a very short time before dualistic, reified structures of conceptuality and self-representation with their familiar goals again draw the mind into identification with them from conditioned habit. Meditation training then becomes the instruction to reconnect with nondual recognition repeatedly in short moments, many times. Each time that the cognizant aspect of mind comes into recognition of its emptiness, we let that mode of awareness maintain itself for as long as it lasts. Any attempt to improve or alter this unconditioned, nondual dimension of awareness with dualistic, conditioned efforts of mind would only disrupt its natural continuity. Instead, we let this unconditioned cognizant emptiness unveil itself and maintain its own continuity under its own power, without interfering (Tib. *ma bcos*). We do that by relaxing goals and letting everything be, as instructed at the end of the Letting Be meditation.

With repetition of such practice over time, there can come a growing ability to reconnect with nondual recognition of the mind's empty nature, to let that way of being extend its own continuity for longer periods, and to come from that depth of awareness into relationships and action more often, with increasing freedom to respond compassionately and creatively to the need or situation of the moment.

To release our goals in meditation and become more unified with qualities of our buddha nature can, ironically, empower us in daily life to take up goals and activities again, but now in a more flexible way that is infused with those qualities. Such practice can help us become less rigidly caught up in one narrow sense of self and its goals, more open and flexibly responsive to others in diverse contexts. Then there is greater freedom to be who or what is needed in different situations with greater discernment and compassion for all involved.[46] In that way, the nature of mind itself becomes the *ultimate secure base*, an unconditioned dimension of being from which to become a more unconditionally loving and compassionate presence to others. This is the greatest depth of the deepening mode, from which to engage the inclusive mode explained in the next chapter, which holds others inclusively and unconditionally in love and compassion.

OUTER, INNER, AND ULTIMATE SECURE BASES

We are now in a position to point out three levels of secure base that the meditation practices of SCT help establish and strengthen, a deepening core of security from which to become more fully present to all parts of ourselves and to others. The field of care employed in receptive-mode meditations comprises an *outer secure base* (outer refuge), with the sense that you are being held in qualities and energies of love, compassion, and wisdom by your field of care. There is a felt sense of being seen in your deep worth and being embraced in those unconditional qualities by caring figures, beyond any attempt autonomously to cultivate those qualities on your own.

That outer secure base connects you to your *inner secure base* (inner refuge)—the qualities and loving energies that are evoked from your awareness when you bring to mind your field of care. In repeated practice, those qualities and energies are increasingly sensed as powers of love, compassion, and wisdom that are available not just from outside of yourself but from within your own being, from within your fundamental awareness. This *inner secure base* also includes your ability to access, settle into, and be transformed by those loving qualities into a healing environment for all parts of yourself, shifting your identity from one part of the mind (one self-identity) to the fuller awareness that can hold any such part in spacious care. After becoming familiar with field of care practice in that way, the Compassionate

Presence to Feelings Meditation helps you access those empowering qualities of awareness and become a healing environment for all your feelings, without even envisioning a separate field of care, which further strengthens your inner secure base in those qualities.

Drawing from Tibetan Dzogchen and Mahāmudrā traditions, practitioners use the Letting Be meditation to help them settle into increasingly nondual states of tranquil abiding, which further strengthen and stabilize the *inner secure base* that is needed by practitioners from all parties of interest who engage SCT. *People who work in roles of care, service, or activism* need a secure core of warmth, compassion, and awareness in which to heal their painful feelings and from which to become a reliably caring and stable presence to others. That inner secure base is strengthened by deepening states of tranquil abiding. *For those who seek reunification with the deepest nature of their minds*, meditations of tranquil abiding can deepen so much that the mind reverts to its most primordial state—a fully nondual, nonconceptual recognition of its cognizant emptiness. In Buddhist terms, this unconditioned dimension of awareness—a unity of infinite emptiness, clarity, and vast capacity—is the ultimate source of unconditional love, compassion, and wisdom—buddha nature itself as the *ultimate secure base* (ultimate refuge). This is what many Buddhists ultimately seek—to reunify with their buddha nature in order to awaken as fully as possible to underlying capacities of compassion and wisdom for the sake of all. *For people who practice in other spiritual traditions*, deepening states of tranquil abiding and nondual awareness can help them explore analogously profound levels of settling, centeredness, and inner freedom to love that are understood within their own traditions.

Whichever goal is most prominent for the individual practitioner, all of these practices continue to be relevant and important to continue to explore. Receptive-mode meditations continue to serve a supportive purpose, even if practitioners' main focus of practice shifts to a different mode. To repeatedly reinhabit your field of care is to continue to strengthen the inner secure base that supports all other practices.

SYNERGY OF LOVE AND WISDOM

The qualities of love and compassion evoked in the field of care and compassionate presence practices help the mind, at the releasing phase of those meditations, to settle with those qualities into its deep nature. As the mind feels safe enough to relax its defensive posture of clinging to self-grasping frames of mind, it can progressively settle into the source of the love and compassion—the openness and clarity, beyond reference points, that is the mind's innate wisdom. As the mind settles into its cognizant openness, beyond confinement, in deepening stages of letting be, tranquil abiding, and nondual awareness, its innate capacities of love and compassion are further freed up so they can unfold more spontaneously and unreservedly. In this way, love and compassion empower increasing wisdom of openness and nonduality. That wisdom, in turn, empowers the fuller emergence of love and compassion. We will further explore this synergy of love and wisdom in the next chapters.

3

INCLUSIVE MODE

Unconditional Love and Wisdom

IN THE MID-1980S, John spent time in northern India studying texts on aspects of Buddhist enlightenment with the learned Tibetan scholar Geshe Thupten Tsering, one of the most popular professors at the Institute of Higher Tibetan Studies. Geshe Tsering became one of John's main teachers there. As John describes, Geshe Tsering lived in a small hut, with few belongings. Each morning he made offerings of milk tea to the enlightened beings whose images were on the altar, which plump little mice slurped up throughout the day. Geshe Tsering was so popular with students and in such demand that they crammed into his hovel for his teachings the whole day. Yet somehow he made time for us all. In his hut we felt welcomed, safe, blessed, like we'd entered a sacred world of warmth and grace. Geshe Tsering's presence was also profoundly compassionate, as if he could sense subliminal levels of suffering in all of us that we were not yet conscious of. As he patiently responded to our questions, it also seemed like he knew us at a greater depth than we knew ourselves—as beings worthy of his reverence and loving regard. In retrospect, John realized, he taught us about enlightenment not just in the way John had expected, through intellectual studies, but also by means of the enlightened qualities that he spontaneously embodied. It felt as if, from the depth of his being, he knew us in the depth of our being while generating a stable, loving environment of unconditional care and wisdom that encompassed us all.

As we familiarize ourselves with the receptive and deepening modes of meditation that we learned in prior chapters, they empower us to engage the inclusive-mode meditation that holds others in love and compassion from the depth of our being, which can draw us toward Geshe Tsering's way of being. In prior meditations—Field of Care, Compassionate Presence to Feelings and Letting Be of Body, Breath, and Mind—we learned to become a loving environment of warmth, acceptance, and compassion for all parts of ourselves and for all of our feelings. As a natural extension of that, in the inclusive mode of meditation, we can become a loving environment of warmth and acceptance for all others, as if they were parts of our greater self.[1]

We also learned in the prior meditations to settle into the source of those loving qualities in the depth of our awareness—the infinite openness, clarity, and vast compassionate capacity of our buddha nature. We thereby discover a depth in ourselves from which, in the inclusive mode, we can sense others in their depth, their buddha nature, as worthy of reverence and care, beyond superficial judgments. This process of inner healing and deepening also makes us newly aware of parts of us that have been caught up in suffering patterns of reaction to our world. From there, in the inclusive mode of practice, we can be conscious of similar layers of suffering in others that likewise drive their reactions, which evokes an empathetic compassion for them all. In these ways, the receptive- and deepening-mode meditations strengthen inner levels of secure base in us from which to include many others in powers of love, compassion, and wisdom. This becomes the inclusive mode of meditation that is the focus of this chapter.

RECONNECTING WITH ASPECTS OF FIELD OF CARE MEDITATION THAT EMPOWER THE INCLUSIVE MODE

Let's revisit the receptive-mode Field of Care of Meditation, this time concentrating on the features of it noted just above, which directly empower the inclusive mode. The Field of Care Meditation is embedded in the inclusive meditation for that purpose.

First, recall the three options for generating a field of care—reinhabiting a caring moment, invoking a benefactor, or invoking a spiritual field—and identify which option is most connecting for you right now, so you feel the uplifting quality of it as you bring it to mind. Also remember the three principles of the Field of Care Meditation:

1. *Accessing:* Letting the field of care bring out loving qualities from your underlying awareness—a felt sense of warmth, acceptance, being seen, inner rest, tenderness, well-being, and so forth. Let those qualities permeate your whole being.
2. *Noticing:* Notice any sense of self (any part of you) that arises, with its patterns of thought and feeling.
3. *Including:* Let that part of you and its feelings be naturally included in this loving environment of warmth and acceptance.

As you do the Field of Care Meditation below, please focus now especially on the three features of it specified above, which we'll take into the inclusive mode when we introduce it later: (1) Sense how the loving qualities evoked by the field of care make you into a healing environment for all aspects of your experience. (2) Sense how you are seen by the field of care in the depth of your being as worthy of love, and in the releasing phase, how you settle further into that depth—the expansive openness, lucidity, and warmth of your underlying awareness. (3) Sense how these healing and deepening aspects of the meditation also make you newly conscious of painful parts of yourself and their feelings as you notice and gently include them in its healing environment. (An audio option is available at shambhala.com /howcompassionworksmeditations.)

FIELD OF CARE MEDITATION
AS BASIS OF INCLUSIVE MODE

STEP 1. ABDOMINAL BREATHING (3 MINUTES OR SO) Sit in a relaxed, comfortable way with back straight, eyes gazing gently downward. Come down from the thinking mind into the body. Take a slow, deep breath, inhaling from the abdomen so it expands, then exhaling slowly and completely, letting go of all your concerns with the exhale. Relax for a moment before inhaling again. Repeat several times. Then, while still breathing from the abdomen, let the breath settle into its own natural flow. Feel the belly expand and contract with each breath. Let that feeling draw you into it more and more, breath by breath.

STEP 2. RECONNECTING WITH LOVE (7 TO 10 MINUTES) Bring to mind your field of care—a caring moment, your benefactor, or your spiritual field—and experience it as present here now (not just a memory). You are being seen and held in deep care, compassion, acceptance, and warmth beyond judgments. (*Pause*) Relax into this experience, steeping in its loving energies, feeling its tender qualities, and letting them spaciously infuse your whole being. Accept these loving energies and qualities into your whole body and mind—every part of you loved in its very being. (*Pause*) Let these loving qualities unify you with them more and more. (*Pause*)

If part of you starts to have difficulty with this practice or to draw your attention away, *notice* that part of you and what it's feeling in a completely accepting way, deeply allowing it to be here. Let it be gently *included* in the warmth and acceptance of this loving environment. Let it have all the space it needs to relax, find its own place in its own time, and metabolize itself in its own way.

If you lose the feeling of the loving qualities, freshly recall your field of care as present here now and let its power draw you back into the felt sense of it.

STEP 3. RELEASING (3 TO 5 MINUTES) Now let this loving environment of warmth and acceptance help your mind to relax deeply and release all its frameworks of meditation and concern. Let the mind settle back a bit inwardly and come to rest in the background of its awareness, which is naturally wide open and luminous, like a sunlit sky. As thoughts and feelings arise, let them just metabolize themselves and release within this sky-like openness of awareness, by letting everything be.

When you finish the meditation, let the felt sense of it continue to resonate.

Processing the Meditation

Did you notice all three features of the Field of Care Meditation we had noted above? Let's review them in light of the meditation you just did: (1) In this meditation, we let the loving energies and qualities evoked by the field of care make us into a loving, healing environment for all parts of ourselves. That becomes the basis, in the inclusive mode, for us to become a loving, healing environment for others. (2) In the second and third steps of the Field of Care Meditation, we settle into those loving qualities and their source in the depth of our being: the expansive openness, lucidity, and vast capacity of our buddha nature. From that depth in us, in the inclusive mode, we can begin to sense and uphold others in the *depth of their being*, the great dignity and vast capacity of their buddha nature. (3) As we explored in chapter 1, those healing and deepening aspects of the Field of Care Meditation also make us newly conscious of reactive, often painful parts of ourselves that harbor feelings of anxiety, fear, struggle, resentment, and so forth; parts of us that have impeded fuller access to our depth and its qualities. This increasing awareness of our own painful layers of reaction becomes the basis, in inclusive mode, to hold others in compassion, conscious of similar painful layers in them that hide their depth, with which they too struggle and from which they also react.

The Field of Care Meditation is included at the beginning of the Inclusive-Mode Meditation in order to empower it in those three ways.

So, take a break now if you'd like. When you feel ready, you can read about and proceed to do the Inclusive-Mode Meditation on page 114.

THE INCLUSIVE MODE OF MEDITATION

The inclusive meditation always begins with reconnecting to our field of care, to reestablish our secure base of unconditional love and compassion. Then we let that environment of loving energies, warmth, and acceptance, which embraces all parts of us, become a loving environment for others, as if they were parts of our greater self. We let that help us *commune* with others in a caring way—to sense them not just as objects of our wants and needs but as fully dimensioned subjects—persons with whole lives, deep worth, and vast underlying capacities that transcend our superficial impressions of them. To commune with others in this way is thus to sense them in the depth of their being—their buddha nature, to resonate with them in their profound dignity and hidden layers of suffering, and to wish them deepest well-being—the wish of love.[2]

We will begin this process of extending warmth and love to others with just one person or being that you would like to include in this way, and then gradually include others as instructed. If you are part of a group or community of people that need deep healing, you can consciously include them all. For example, if your ancestors have experienced much trauma, you can include them all in this unconditional holding environment of loving energy, spacious acceptance, and healing warmth.[3]

If a part of the mind has trouble including some other persons or draws your attention away, just settle back into your field of care, reunite with its healing environment, and become compassionately aware of that part of you (that sense of self) with spacious acceptance and warmth. When that part of you settles and your mind unblends from it, you can return to the practice of extending warmth and love. If your mind becomes tired or tight at any point, you can take a short break, rest your heart and mind, and begin afresh.

(An audio option is available at shambhala.com/howcompassionworks meditations.)

INCLUSIVE-MODE MEDITATION

STEP 1. ABDOMINAL BREATHING (2 TO 3 MINUTES) Sit in a relaxed, comfortable way with back straight, eyes gazing gently downward. Come down from the thinking mind into the body. Take a slow, deep breath, inhaling from the abdomen so it expands, then exhaling slowly and completely, letting go of all your concerns with the exhale. Relax for a moment before inhaling again. Repeat several times. Then, while still breathing from the abdomen, let the breath settle into its own natural flow. Feel the belly expand and contract with each breath. Let that feeling draw you into it more and more, breath by breath.

STEP 2. RECONNECTING WITH LOVE (3 TO 5 MINUTES) Now bring to mind your field of care—your caring moment, benefactor, or spiritual field—and experience it as present here now (not as just a memory). You are being seen and held in deep care, compassion, acceptance, and warmth beyond judgments. Relax into this experience, steeping in its loving energies, feeling its tender qualities, and letting them spaciously infuse your whole being. (*Pause*) Accept this loving energy and its qualities into your whole body and mind—

every part of you loved in its very being. (*Pause*) Let any thoughts, feelings, or parts of yourself that arise be included in this healing environment of loving energies, warmth, and acceptance. Let them find their own place and settle in their own time, by letting them all be.

STEP 3. INCLUDING OTHERS (10 MINUTES) Now think of someone dear to you that you'd like to include in this same loving environment and let them also be included in this field of loving energies, warmth, and acceptance. Let these loving energies and qualities permeate their whole being. Let this help you to commune with them in the depth of their being, to resonate with them in their hidden layers of suffering, and to wish them deepest well-being. (*Pause*)

Now let a few more beings come to mind that you'd also like to include in this field of loving energies and warmth, and let them also be included, along with the first person. Let these loving energies and qualities permeate their whole being. Let this help you sense them in the depth of their being and hidden layers of suffering, and to wish them deepest well-being. (*Pause*) Now let this practice expand to include larger circles of beings that come to mind, including them all in this field of loving energies and warmth, sensing them all in their depth and hidden sufferings while wishing them deepest well-being.

If part of you has trouble with this or draws your attention away, settle back into your field of care, reunite with its healing environment, and become compassionately aware of that part of you, that sense of self and what it's feeling, with acceptance and warmth. When it settles, you can return to extending love to beings.

Finally, you can let the vast underlying capacity of warmth and compassion from your basic awareness expand much more fully to include all beings—human, animal, all creatures—or imagine this is happening. Let this help you commune with them all in the depth of their being and hidden sufferings while wishing them all deeply well.

STEP 4. RELEASING (3 TO 5 MINUTES) Now, let this pervasive environment of loving warmth and acceptance help your mind to relax deeply and release all its frameworks of meditation or concern. Let the mind settle back a bit inwardly and come to rest in the background of its awareness, which is naturally wide open and luminous, like a sunlit sky. Let any thoughts and feelings that arise just metabolize themselves and release within this sky-like openness of awareness by letting everything be.

When you finish the meditation, let the felt sense of it continue to resonate.

Processing the Meditation

Again, the love and compassion that can spaciously hold all parts of our mind can also hold all other beings, as if they were parts of our larger self. That means that we don't have to struggle to send love to others; we can let them be naturally included in the loving space generated by our field of care and let that help us commune and resonate with them in their great worth and wish them deeply well. This helps us increasingly access a vast capacity of openness, warmth, and compassion in our buddha nature, which helps us resonate with the same underlying capacity in others in their buddha nature, with reverence for them in that depth of their being. From there, we can also sense how all of us have been largely lost from that depth, caught up in reactive and struggling parts of ourselves, which can evoke a sense of compassion for us all. (We'll further explore the cultivation of compassion in chapter 4.)

During the Inclusive-Mode Meditation, if it feels effortful or stressful to commune and wish well to others, then your mind might be identified with a caretaking role—a sense of self that is in the habit of trying, on its own, to provide what it thinks others need, divorced from the empowering qualities of your buddha nature. Or the mind might be identified with a different pattern of thought and feeling that struggles with the practice. That's a sign, again, to settle back into your field of care, reunify with its loving environment, and unblend from that part of you by holding it in healing warmth and compassion. As the mind naturally unblends from that caretaking sense of self (or any other sense of self), the healing space of awareness that holds that part of the mind is again freed to hold many other beings as well.

This practice is intuitive—learning to commune with others at a pre-verbal level, below the field of socially conditioned judgments and reactions.[4] We experience ourselves as an extension of the field of care in which we are held. We learn to hold as we are held, love as we are loved, know as we are known. This inclusive meditation thus generates powers of wisdom, love, and compassion that would exclude no one—since all are being known and embraced both in their depth and in their hidden sufferings, beyond superficial labels and judgments. Our buddha nature is more fully enacted when we consciously relate it in this way to many others, which allows its expansive nature to manifest.

During an intensive retreat, Paul recalled a memory of a research study that has crucial implications for compassion training. Researchers have shown that sharing experiences with others intensifies the experience and makes it more memorable.[5] In that study, sharing the experience of eating a chocolate bar with another person made it more memorable and enjoyable. Although a chocolate bar seems like a mundane example, it points out the possibility of expanding qualities of our buddha nature by sharing those qualities with others as we commune with them in the inclusive mode. In this way, we allow our buddha nature to express its all-inclusive nature. The memory of that study helped Paul to understand this possibility.

The Thoroughness of the Love We Cultivate

Recall the instruction in step 3 above as you include others in the same loving environment that holds you: "Let these loving energies and qualities permeate their whole being. Let this help you to commune with them in the depth of their being, to resonate with them in their hidden layers of suffering, and to wish them deepest well-being." Notice how thorough is the permeation of others with the energy and wish of love in this practice. In the receptive phase of step 2, we accept loving energies and qualities into our whole being. When extending those same energies and qualities to others, we imagine them pervading their entire being. Indeed, we may have never consciously accepted and extended love in such a thoroughgoing way.

Part of the power of the practice comes from that thoroughness. Ultimately, to make that wish of love for others' deepest well-being is to wish for them to actualize their fullest capacities of goodness, love, compassion, freedom, wisdom, creative responsiveness, flourishing, and joy—in Buddhist terms, to actualize the vast positive potential of their buddha nature.

At the same time, with this meditation we are also wishing each being every other kind of temporal relief and well-being: healing, wholeness, nourishing relationships, needed resources, support, consolation when overwhelmed, a beautiful and life-giving environment, fulfillment, and happiness. We are also wishing them the smallest delights: a cool breeze on a hot day, delicious food in a moment of hunger, and many moments of fun, playfulness, and humor.

To have that full depth and scope of well-being in mind when repeating that wish of love in the meditation can orient and motivate our activity in the world, for everyone to have access to such things, and also for the well-being and welfare of animals.

The Vastness of the Love We Cultivate

Besides its thoroughness, notice how vast the scope of love becomes in the final stage of extending it, literally encompassing all beings. Part of the power of the practice comes from that great scope, so vast it is beyond the comprehension of self-centered thought. It opens our heart and mind to their fullest capacity, stretching us past all ego-centered frames of mind. Such boundless love harmonizes us with the infinite openness and limitless loving capacity of the mind's deep nature, its buddha nature. The meditation instruction helps us to release our narrow frames of reference to allow the infinitely inclusive power of that nature to extend itself. We may not feel that initially, but even just imagining that all beings are included helps harmonize us with the all-encompassing power of love available in the depth of our awareness.

Many people, after they have long familiarized themselves with that all-inclusive aspect of the Inclusive-Mode Meditation, find that the receptive mode of meditation with a field of care then also becomes more meaningful and powerful. Why? The fact that many other persons have been holding us and our whole world in unconditional love and compassion becomes more real to us as we regularly experience *ourselves* holding all others in that way within this inclusive meditation. In traditional terms, such persons have been referred to as buddhas, bodhisattvas, saints, spiritual ancestors, and such—beings who have so fully realized the qualities of enlightenment or become so transparent to the divine that they've become conduits of limitlessly inclusive, unconditional powers of love, compassion, and wisdom that embraces all others, including all of us. In Buddhist terms, the actualized buddha nature of the buddhas and bodhisattvas resonates with our own buddha nature—the energies of their love and wisdom empowering our buddha nature to awaken. To newly realize, in light of this inclusive meditation, that we have been held in love, compassion, and wisdom long before we realized it and then to become receptive to that pervasive, unconditional, and unchanging power of love greatly empowers our own practice of extending love, literally, to all others. It is to become newly conscious, in our own experience, of a vast spiritual field of love, compassion, and wisdom and to learn to rely on it to empower our practice. Ultimately, through this inclusive-mode practice, we are learning to become an extension of that spiritual field by joining the buddhas, bodhisattvas, saints, or spiritual ancestors in holding the whole world in unconditional powers of care.

In this way, we begin to sense the unity of the receptive mode and inclusive modes of meditation. By engaging both modes of practice, we experience qualities of buddha nature through different lenses that refract and intensify each other. When extending love, we are also becoming more receptive to it; when receiving love, we are also learning to more fully extend it. Each practice strengthens the other by drawing on the nondual ground of buddha nature that underlies both.

The Synergy of Love and Wisdom in This Meditation

The powers of love, warmth, and compassion evoked in steps 2 and 3 of the Inclusive-Mode Meditation help the mind, in the releasing phase of step 4, to trust, relax, and release its narrow frames of reference so it can settle increasingly into the source of the love and compassion: the infinite emptiness, all-pervasive openness, and lucidity of its buddha nature, which is the mind's innate wisdom. This wisdom is nondual, beyond any division or boundary. Step 4, the releasing phase, is thus a brief form of the Letting Be meditation, the deepening mode of practice we explored in the last chapter. As the mind thus settles back into its empty nature, its basic openness beyond limitation, its innate capacities of love and compassion are freed to manifest more fully, ultimately beyond limitation—to encompass all beings, beyond any distinctions between who seems to matter and who does not. Such all-pervasive love, in turn, further empowers the mind, in the releasing phase, to release its narrow self-referential patterns of thought, to settle more fully into the expansive openness of its deep nature. With repetition of practice, the unlimited power of love and unlimited openness of nondual wisdom help each other to emerge more and more.

From a Tibetan Buddhist perspective, deep within us is an underlying yearning, from our buddha nature, to realize our innate powers of love and wisdom in a completely unconditional, all-pervasive, unchangeable way, not only for all parts of ourselves (as we explored in chapter 1) but also, literally, for all other beings. When, through deepening practice, that liminal desire becomes more fully conscious to the practitioner, it takes form in the unwavering commitment to awaken fully to all such powers of one's buddha nature for the sake of all, the vow of the bodhisattva, which Geshe Tsering reconfirmed every morning in his daily ritual practices.

REPEATING THE INCLUSIVE-MODE MEDITATION

Please do the Inclusive-Mode Meditation on page 114 again now with the points above freshly in mind. Explore the possibility, empowered by this meditation, of unleashing a vast capacity of love and warmth from the depth of your being that blesses and upholds all others in the depth of their being. Even just to imagine that is happening attunes us to that underlying capacity.

When you finish the meditation, let the felt sense of it continue to resonate.

Processing the Meditation

To extend love ultimately to all beings gives us a glimpse into the limitless capacity of love that has been hidden in our being all along. But that is only a glimpse of our potential, not yet a stable realization of such love. In our daily lives, our minds are typically habituated to far more limited ways of perceiving and reacting to others, which impede that vast, underlying potential. So we turn next to that issue.

INCLUDING STRANGERS AND
PEOPLE WE HAVE AVERSION FOR

We may have a relatively easy time extending loving energy and wishes to those who feel dear to us and then broadly to many beings in general. Yet we have greater difficulty extending love specifically to individuals whom we dislike or hold grudges against, or to those we consider strangers—people we haven't met who feel less important to us than those we know personally. So when first introduced to this inclusive mode of meditation, it is probably not just a free and easy flow of love. Indeed, this meditation often evokes parts of us (senses of self) that object to the notion of extending love equally to dear ones, strangers, and those we dislike. After all, someone who looks like just a stranger to me doesn't seem as intrinsically worthy of love as those who are close to me. And people I strongly dislike evoke aversion in me that makes them seem totally unworthy of care.

Because our ego-centered thoughts reduce others to such limited images of them, we tend to treat others in precisely the ways we don't want to be treated—for example, with callousness, partiality, or self-righteous anger (though we may not be conscious of it at the time). Like us, others also have sometimes seen us as merely strangers or unlikable and treated us in callous ways. When they do so, we tend to react to them, in turn, as just contemptible. Even as we misperceive and react to each other mutually in such negative ways, our own mind tends to ascribe all such negativity to the other person, not to ourselves. For example, do you remember a time when you were upset that someone had treated you with disrespect as just unlikable or as merely a stranger who is not worth any caring attention? At that moment, did you also remember times in the past when you had similarly seen and reacted to others as just a stranger or just unlikable? Probably not. In this kind of destructive framework of perceiving and reacting, we keep mistaking our own reductive thoughts and fractured images of each other for the actual persons, triggering painful senses of self in each other that react automatically, without ever seeing each other more deeply or fully.

As noted in chapter 2, drawing from Buddhist psychology, the mind is in the habit of constructing, reifying, and identifying with narrow senses of self that seem to stand apart from the mind's constructions of other persons and beings. The mind then mistakes its own thoughts of self and others for reality as such.[6] Others don't experience themselves in the superficial ways that our ego-centered thoughts label them, but we tend in the moment not to notice that—as if the unknown person passing us on the street is really just a "stranger" in their own right, not a multidimensional human being of depth and potential who is worthy of caring attention. Or as if, when we are very angry at someone, that person is nothing more than they appear through the lens of our anger—worthy only of hostility or blame—not a fuller person who, like us, is trying to find well-being for themselves and their loved ones while caught up in all the struggles of living and dying here. Our minds, identified with their own limiting thoughts and reactions, lose touch with the fuller, more expansive power of our awareness to sense much more in others and in ourselves.

In this way, we have all been imprisoned, more than we've been conscious, in the socially conditioned habit of mistaking our own limited thoughts of everyone (including ourselves) for the actual persons. We keep endlessly reacting to our own empty mental constructs of self and others, unaware. How can we break free of this conditioned habit of mutual reaction, to access our underlying capacity for more discerning, unconditional, and inclusive love? How can we come to know others in the depth of their being from our own depth as intrinsically worthy of care, as always more than what our superficial reactions make of them?

Empowering Care and Empathy for Others by Recognizing a Deep Sameness in All

From a Buddhist perspective, all beings are profoundly the same as ourselves in three basic ways: (1) Everyone has a tremendous positive potential like what we are now discovering in ourselves—a great underlying capacity for warmth, openness, care, compassion, clarity, wisdom, calm, joy, and so forth (buddha nature). (2) Everyone often gets caught up in self-centered perceptions and reactions that mistake others for their own limited thoughts of them, which obstructs the positive potential of their buddha nature and causes themselves and others endless suffering. (3) Everyone wants to be well, happy, free of suffering, and wishes the same for their loved ones.

As the practices we've been exploring make us more conscious of all three of those dimensions of our own being, we can sense the same in others. Then when we see or think of anyone, if we take a moment to recall their profound sameness with us in those three ways, we become less fully captivated by our self-protective habits of reaction to them. Our underlying capacities of care and empathy can naturally emerge. We become freer, then, to sense them in their deep dignity and worth, join them in their wish to be well, and have compassion for them in the suffering we are all undergoing when we react only to our superficial impressions of each other.

Try now to think of a stranger—someone you've seen but don't know personally, for example a store clerk or other people in the store who are waiting in line. First notice how they look and feel to you as merely a "stranger," not worth loving or hating since you don't know them well enough to care. Try to be very honest about this—really notice how they appear to you as merely strangers. Then reflect on those three deep aspects of sameness with them. Notice how that affects your perception of them. Now do the same with someone you have disliked. We can recall those three samenesses frequently in order to open our perception of others and give more access to our innate capacities of discernment, empathy, care, and compassion.

TAKING PARTS OF US THAT CONSTRICT OUR PERCEPTION OF OTHERS INTO THE PRACTICE OF EXTENDING LOVE

There are also some psychological principles from Buddhism and modern psychology that can significantly empower our Inclusive-Mode Meditation, giving us more freedom from our limiting habits of reaction so we can access more of the depth and potential in ourselves and others.

When the mind is largely identified with one protective part of the mind and what it wants from others in that moment (its goals for others), our perception of others becomes narrow and reductive, and our capacities of care, compassion, and wisdom get impeded. For example, when John's mind is identified with a narrow sense of self whose primary goal—what it wants from others—is that they stop obstructing him from getting somewhere in a hurry, other people tend to be perceived in that moment as just something in his way. Try to remember a moment when you were trying to get somewhere quickly—perhaps a time when you were waiting impatiently to get through a checkout line at a store. How did the people in front of you, who were moving more slowly, look to you then? Another example: Paul has noticed that when he only focuses on his personal needs and goals in a work meeting, he may experience others in that moment as competing with those goals rather than as human beings with their own needs or as part of a collective with a larger need and purpose. John has noticed that when part of himself is really angry at another person for thwarting his needs or something he wanted, the other is viewed in that moment as only worthy of anger—just bad. Try to think of your own examples when part of your mind was mainly focused on a goal or perceived need of the moment (something that you wanted from the other person) that kept you from seeing more fully what others needed or were bringing to that moment.

But recall that the field of care practice, which is the second step of the inclusive meditation above, can shift our identity from any one narrow part of the mind to a much more inclusive awareness that is not caught up in that part. How so? The field of care practice makes us into a loving, healing environment for all aspects of our experience—including all of our senses of self, all of our feelings, and all of our goals. That shifts our identity from any narrow sense of self and its goals to the fuller awareness that holds that part of the mind in unconditional warmth and care. As the mind thus starts to relax, heal, and unblend from any part or narrow goal it has been caught up in, we begin to settle into the unconditional depth of our awareness from which to sense others more in their depth and fuller being, beyond superficial reactions, beyond what we want from them in the moment. Then our perception of others can naturally start to open, so we sense more of their humanity and positive potential—e.g., perceiving them now not just as objects of management or anger, not just in terms of what we want from them, but as fuller human beings with great dignity, worth, and many facets of experience and possibility. With this opening of perception, our capacities of discernment, love, and compassion become less impeded, so we can be more fully present and responsive to them.

So, for example, when John enters a classroom and notices that he is seeing students mainly through his goal for them of covering all class discussion topics on time, if he mentally settles back into his field of care and reunites with its loving environment, then as his mind unblends from that narrow part of himself and what it wants from the students at the moment, he begins to see them more fully as beings with great capacities, beauty, and mystery. Then John can again take up the goal of covering class topics, but now while holding that goal more loosely, so he is more present to student strengths and needs in the moment—their own distinctive ways of learning. As you might imagine, that supports a much more energized, responsive, creative, and enjoyable class period for the students and the teacher.

Therefore, as you extend love to others in the third step of the Inclusive-Mode Meditation, when part of the mind is having difficulty or holding back from including someone in the energy and wish of love, try to notice that sense of self and what it is wanting from that other person. Then settle back into your field of care, reunite with its loving environment, and become compassionately aware of that part of you with spacious acceptance and warmth. Let that part of you and its goals and feelings relax in that healing space and settle in their own time. As they settle, notice how your perspective on the other person opens, so you now sense more of their depth, potential, and suffering, beyond what you had wanted from them. You are better able, then, to include them in warmth and care, and to let that help you commune with them in their fuller being and wish them well. In this way, we reengage the three principles of the field of care practice (accessing, noticing, including) within the inclusive mode, but in a different order: (1) *noticing* any part of the mind that is having trouble including some others in warmth and care, (2) settling back into your field of care to further *access* loving qualities from your basic awareness, and (3) *including* that part of the mind and its feelings and goals in the loving environment of those qualities.

As your mind begins to relax, heal, and unblend from that part of you by holding that part in warmth and acceptance, your mind is freed to sense the fuller persons beyond the labels, beyond just what you want from them—sensing them now as beings who also wish to be well and happy; who are facing all the sufferings of living, loss, and dying; and who are endowed with great dignity in the depth of their being—the infinite openness, lucidity, and vast capacity of their buddha nature—the three samenesses.

Let's now apply the points in the section above to the Inclusive-Mode Meditation on page 126 by redoing that meditation with an adjustment in the instruction. This time the meditation will also specifically include one or more strangers. The inclusive step of the meditation begins, as earlier, by extending love to one being who is dear to you, then to further beings you find easy to include. Later, when the practice expands to include larger circles of beings, try now specifically to include at least one person that you have seen but haven't personally met, who feels like a stranger to you. If part of the mind has difficulty extending love to them in the same way as to the others, or if you notice a goal (something you want from them) that impedes the extending of love, apply the principles in the paragraph above: settle back into your field of care, reunite with its healing environment, and become compassionately aware of that part or goal with acceptance and warmth. When it settles, notice your perception of the "stranger" open to sense more of their humanity and depth of being beyond what you wanted from them. Then continue with the meditation extending love to beings, including that person.

After doing the meditation in that way, take a break and relax. Then when you feel refreshed and ready, do the inclusive meditation below again. This time, after including strangers among the expanding circles of inclusion, try also to include someone you have felt some aversion for. If part of you has trouble with that, again apply the principles from above: settle back into your field of care, reunite with its healing environment, and become compassionately aware of that part of you and its goals with acceptance and warmth. When it settles, see if your perception of the other person starts to open, and if so, return to the practice of extending love to beings, including that person. If not, continue to be compassionately aware of the part of you that is maintaining aversion toward the other person (as in Compassionate Presence to Feelings Meditation), to let it find its own place in its own time; to let it metabolize itself and begin to heal in the loving qualities of your basic awareness.

(An audio option is available at shambhala.com/howcompassionworks meditations.)

INCLUSIVE-MODE MEDITATION: WITH STRANGERS, DISLIKED ONES

STEP 1. ABDOMINAL BREATHING (2 TO 3 MINUTES) Sit in a relaxed, comfortable way with back straight, eyes gazing gently downward. Come down from the thinking mind into the body. Take a slow, deep breath, inhaling from the abdomen so it expands, then exhaling slowly and completely, letting go of all your concerns with the exhale. Relax for a moment before inhaling again. Repeat several times. Then, while still breathing from the abdomen, let the breath settle into its own natural flow. Feel the belly expand and contract with each breath. Let that feeling draw you into it more and more, breath by breath.

STEP 2. RECONNECTING WITH LOVE (3 TO 5 MINUTES) Now bring to mind your field of care—your caring moment, benefactor, or spiritual field—and experience it as present here now (not as just a memory). You are being seen and held in deep care, compassion, acceptance, and warmth beyond judgments. Relax into this experience, steeping in its loving energies, feeling its tender qualities, and letting them spaciously infuse your whole being. (*Pause*) Accept this loving energy and its qualities into your whole body and mind—every part of you loved in its very being. (*Pause*) Let any thoughts, feelings, or parts of yourself that arise be included in this healing environment of loving energies, warmth, and acceptance. Let them find their own place and settle in their own time, by letting them all be.

STEP 3. INCLUDING OTHERS (7 TO 10 MINUTES OR MORE) Now think of someone dear to you that you'd like to include in this same loving environment and let them also be included in this field of loving energies, warmth, and compassion. Let these loving energies and qualities permeate their whole being. Let this help you to commune with them in the depth of their being, resonate with them in their hidden layers of suffering, and wish them deepest well-being. (*Pause*)

Now let a few more beings come to mind who you'd also like to include in this field of loving energies and warmth, and let them also be included, along with the first person. Let these loving energies and qualities permeate their whole being. Let this help you sense them in the depth of their being and hidden layers of suffering, and to wish them deepest well-being. (*Pause*) Now let this practice expand to include larger circles of beings that come to mind, including them all in this field of loving energies and warmth, sensing them in their depth and hidden sufferings, while wishing them deepest well-being. Let one or more strangers also be specifically included among them now (and, in a later session, also one or more persons you've disliked).

If part of you has trouble with this or draws your attention away, settle back into your field of care, reunite with its healing environment, and become compassionately aware of that part of you and its goals with acceptance and warmth. As that sense of self and its goals starts to relax, notice your lens on others begin to open, to let you include them in this same loving environment.

Finally, you can let the vast underlying capacity of warmth and compassion from your basic awareness expand much more fully to include all beings—human, animal, all creatures—or imagine this is happening. Let this help you commune with them all in the depth of their being and hidden sufferings while wishing them all deeply well.

STEP 4. RELEASING (3 TO 5 MINUTES) Now let this inclusive environment of warmth and acceptance help your mind to relax deeply and release all its frameworks of meditation and concern. Let the mind settle back a bit inwardly and come to rest in the background of its awareness, which is naturally wide open and luminous, like a sunlit sky. As thoughts and feelings arise, let them just metabolize themselves and release within this sky-like openness of awareness, by letting everything be.

When you finish the meditation, let the felt sense of it continue to resonate.

Processing the Meditation

This meditation does two basic things: (1) It makes us aware of the limiting labels that we'd mistaken for other persons, and (2) it brings out the inclusive power of love and care in us that had been obstructed by our reactions to those labels. This meditation introduces a new degree of freedom to choose whether to continue to relate mainly to our ego-centered limiting thoughts of others or to the actual persons beyond those thoughts. We experience what it is like to connect with the deep worth of other persons more than to our own limiting impressions of them, as just "strangers" or "dislikable ones" or even as just "my friends." This does not involve putting on "rose-colored glasses" to try to pretend that all others are worthy of care. Rather, the meditation helps us take off the distorted glasses of the socially conditioned, reductive labels that have hidden everyone's fuller humanity. As reactive patterns of mind settle and heal in the loving environment generated by our field of care, the "spell" of our conditioning is broken; our mind gains more freedom to commune with the fuller persons beyond the limiting labels. So we can sense the deep humanity that we share with them—their fuller life experience beyond superficial images of them; their sufferings of living, loss, and dying; their wish for themselves and their loved ones to flourish; their depth of being. This shared humanity represents an underlying unity more fundamental than the seeming divisions of in-groups and out-groups. This meditation helps us bring the recognition, voice, and healing power of that unity into our life and work with others.

Within this meditation, we might notice some resistance to release the grip of our familiar labels of self and others as well as our ordinary goals. However, with time, we can begin to notice how it can be joyful to integrate these patterns with the practice and thereby realize the newfound freedom that is made possible. When we relax our identification with narrow goals, we can more fully participate in the present moment, enjoy whatever experience is occurring and then take up more informed goals with greater flexibility. As a teacher at a university, Paul has noticed that his classes seem to go much better when he lets go of his narrow goal to give the ideal lecture or teach a perfect class. By noticing and relaxing that goal, there is more space to listen to the class and respond to whatever needs or organic process might emerge from the group dialogue, which becomes the new goal. Although it might feel difficult to release our identification with a sense of self and relax our goals, we can approach this process with some curiosity and see what becomes newly possible.

DEVELOPING GRANULARITY TO TRANSFORM OUR REDUCTIVE IMAGES OF OTHERS AND THE PARTS OF US THAT HOLD THEM

In light of the meditation we just did, let's review one aspect of it. In step 3 of the meditation, if you have difficulty seeing another person as more than a reductive impression ("But they're just a stranger," "They're just unlikable," or "I can't include them"), then your mind is identified with a part of you and what it wants from the other that sees the other just through that narrow lens. Notice that sense of self and what it wants from others, then settle back into your field of care, reunify with its healing environment, and become compassionately aware of that part of you and its reactions. As that part of the mind begins to feel safer and relax, notice your lens on the other person begin to open, so you can sense more of their life, dignity, and potential beyond what you had wanted from them. With that, you have more ability to include them in the loving space of the meditation and wish them well. (If, when beginning this inclusive practice, the mind moves toward thinking of others who have caused much harm or trauma to you, it may be best to revert to the Field of Care Meditation or to focus the practice just on others for whom it is easier to extend care for now. With more familiarity, the practice can extend to more difficult places in its own time. It is important that you discern your best path forward with the practice, exercising your choice and agency.)

In chapter 1 we cultivated granularity with regard to loving qualities and parts of the mind that were surfaced by the Field of Care Meditation. We thus increased our ability to distinguish more and more loving qualities and senses of self so we could take them into practice. Now, in the Inclusive-Mode Meditation, we cultivate granularity also with regard to our reductive images of others that are associated with various parts of us. How so? When we experience difficulty extending love to someone, not wanting to wish them deep well-being, it shows us that we are seeing that person only through a reductive image of them (e.g., as just a stranger or unlikable) or a narrow goal (e.g., wanting something from them). Then we can notice that this limiting image of them is just our own mental *image* of them, *not actually them*, which points us to the part of ourselves or goal that is seeing in that restricted way. Then we can hold that part of the mind and its corresponding goals for others in compassionate awareness, so it has the loving space it needs to relax, settle, and heal in its own time. Then our perception of the other person can start to open beyond the previous narrow image, to sense more facets of them beyond just what we had wanted from them, and to commune with them in their fuller being.

In chapter 1 we also noted that the Field of Care Meditation raises up senses of self and associated reactions that obstruct our practice, but as we learned to take them all into the meditation, they helped empower it. Instead of reacting to those parts of us as obstacles, we welcomed them as supports for practice by embracing them in warmth and acceptance, which brought out our innate capacities of care and inner healing. In that process, we learned to *reappraise* what at first seemed negative (reactive parts of us) as positive (supports for bringing out healing qualities of our buddha nature). Similarly here, the Inclusive-Mode Meditation makes us more aware of our own limiting images of others, and through that, parts of the mind that are seeing in that limited way. As we learn to take those images of others and parts of us into the meditation as explained above, they help us access more of our capacity for warmth, healing, love, compassion, and wisdom for ourselves and for others. As we become newly aware in that way of more parts of our mind from which we have habitually reacted to others, it shows us what others are also struggling with and why they, like us, often react in less-than-ideal ways. This profoundly undercuts our tendency to judge others as simply bad or good, empowering us to see more facets of them with wisdom and compassion. In these ways, what had seemed as just an obstacle—our limiting images of others—is now functioning as an ally for deepening practice of love and compassion for all parts of ourselves and for all others.

Further effects of this Inclusive-Mode Meditation unfold from this process. As we hold protective parts of the mind in care and our mind unblends from them, we begin to inhabit our fuller awareness, our buddha nature, which can spaciously embrace any part of us in warmth and kindness. From that fuller awareness in us, we also sense that others have a fuller awareness beyond any one part of them, their buddha nature, with which we can also resonate. This helps us see them in their depth, beyond any one part of them, from our depth, even when their minds are identified with just one part of themselves.

Having said all that, we may still need to acknowledge that there might be parts of us that have tremendous difficulty letting go of their aversion for certain other people, for whom we hold a strong grudge, purportedly because of what they've done to us or to someone we care about. We will speak to this challenge in the section on page 135 on the possibility of extending love to those we have hated.

HOW THE INCLUSIVE MEDITATION BUILDS PROGRESSIVELY OVER WEEKS AND MONTHS

In the explanations and meditations above, we introduced the possibility of extending love to strangers, and even to beings we have disliked or hated, to learn the principles of practice that empower that possibility. But every meditator opens to such possibilities in their own time, which cannot be forced into any presumed timeline. The practice process of inner healing, opening, deepening, and extending love to more kinds of beings unfolds in different ways and time frames for different individuals, and cannot be rushed. Since the foundation of the inclusive mode is the receptive-mode field of care and the deepening-mode practices of the prior two chapters, regular practice of those modes supports the further unfolding of the inclusive mode.

In the Inclusive-Mode Meditation, when you feel the energy and wish of love for others to be strong and stable at one stage of extending love, you are ready to explore the next stage. You can spend many weeks or months first extending the wish and energy of love just to dear ones and expanding circles of beings that feel easy for you to include. After weeks or months of such practice, as you grow more stable in it and feel an urge to extend love further to strangers, you can also include a stranger, then more strangers, within the circles of inclusion. After weeks or months of such practice, when you grow confident in extending to dear ones and strangers, and you begin to feel an urge to explore extending further even to someone you have disliked or hated, you can spend weeks also including them within expanding circles of inclusion, then also others you have disliked, and so forth. Until gradually it begins to feel more natural to extend to all such categories within the widening circles of inclusion.

If you get stuck or have too much difficulty at any of those stages (from those easy to include, to strangers, to disliked ones), just back up and spend more time familiarizing yourself with the prior stage in daily practice. However far you take the meditation in these progressive stages, always complete the meditation by finally extending love literally to all beings as instructed (or imagine that is happening), in order to let your fullest innate capacity of love to express itself, followed by the releasing phase.

Some practitioners find that the final stage of inclusion in the meditation—extending the energy, warmth, and wish of love literally to all beings—provides the broad perspective and expansive scope of care within which to become increasingly conscious of strangers and disliked ones as already included in that scope. That is another way that the Inclusive-Mode Meditation can progressively build.

INTEGRATING THE INCLUSIVE-MODE MEDITATION WITH OUR DAILY LIFE AS A WAY OF BEING

We progress in this inclusive-mode practice by doing the meditation for a little while first thing in the morning as the anchor of our day, then repeatedly reengaging it many times in the day, even for brief periods—reuniting with the loving environment generated by our field of care, noticing whoever is around us or whoever we think of, sensing their threefold sameness with us, including them in that loving space, and communing and wishing them well, as instructed in the meditation. In that way, within ordinary life, we more frequently discern the difference between our limiting impressions of everyone and the actual persons. We reconnect with the loving wish and energy we've come to know in meditation often in the day, with growing familiarity and ease. Gradually we learn to abide at this level of caring connection for longer periods, to settle into loving connection as a way of being, communing with those around us, in touch with their deep worth and potential, rather than living at the level of shifting reactions to our own reductive impressions of everyone. This process is also supported by continuing regular practice of the Compassionate Presence to Feelings Meditation, which we can alternate with the Inclusive-Mode Meditation.

The process of unblending from self-clinging parts of ourself and reunifying with the openness, warmth, and broad perspective of our larger awareness further unfolds with such repeated practice, helping us sense more in others beyond the narrow lens of just one part of the mind. This larger perspective on others is further empowered by the releasing phase of the Inclusive-Mode Meditation, where we settle into the depth of our being and inhabit our expansive underlying awareness more fully, instead of being sucked into one or another narrow self-identity and associated reactions. From that depth of being we can sense and respond to others in the depth of their being, beyond limiting perceptions and judgments that hide their fuller dignity and worth. From that place of depth, we have greater freedom to take up whatever role, sense of self-identity, or goal is needed, but now without being so fully identified with it and without losing the positive qualities of our basic awareness in that identity. There is greater openness in the mind to be who or what is needed in each situation. We can learn to hold any needed identity lightly, with greater resilience, humor, compassion, appreciation of others, and creative responsiveness to them.[7]

In the bustle of daily life, we all tend to perceive and react to others in reductive ways as a conditioned habit, more than we have all been conscious. This meditation makes us newly conscious of that habit, so we notice better when it is happening in daily life. When we notice it, we can let that make us newly aware of whatever sense of self is viewing the other in that narrow way. Then we can take that sense of self into practice on the spot as described above, which opens our lens on others, so we can commune with them and wish them well. When we practice this meditation often, first in the morning and then connecting with it repeatedly in the day with whoever we see or think of, it becomes naturally more inclusive and expansive. It helps us grow into the way of being we most deeply intend.

A New York City Cabdriver's Encounter with an Enraged Man

A friend of ours shared this true story about a taxi driver in New York City. The driver, originally from Haiti, was driving slowly while searching for his destination when he accidentally ran a stop sign. Suddenly he noticed a man walking rapidly toward his vehicle, furiously waving his fist at him. The taxi driver stopped his vehicle and rolled down the window for the man. Red in the face and cursing, the enraged man put his face to the window and shouted a series of abusive expletives at the cabdriver for having run the stop sign. To the angry man's surprise, the cabdriver replied in a slow, measured tone, "I am sorry! You're right! I *should* have stopped." The man looked stunned, unable to speak for a moment. Then he said, "Everything I just said to you—I take it all back!"[8]

The angry man, outraged at the driver for his misstep, viewing him just through that irate part of himself, saw the cabdriver as worth nothing but abuse. The driver, in turn, spoke not to that angry part of the man but to his fuller being, including his underlying capacity to recognize the profound sameness of both men in their dignity and worth, their tendency sometimes to make mistakes, to suffer for them, to want to do better. Being seen and addressed at that level of depth made it impossible for the angry man to continue identifying with his enraged concepts of self and other. His reductive perception of the cabdriver as just contemptible fell away. The cabdriver, by speaking not to the man's irate sense of self but to the depth of his being, evoked the fuller person, eliciting his final response, an apology for not having seen the one at whom he had shouted. The cabdriver's way of being and responding exemplifies what is possible when we learn to live at that level of depth—communicating from the depth of our being to others in the depth of their being rather than living at the level of superficial impressions and reactions.

Take a break now if you'd like, and when you feel ready, go ahead and do the Inclusive-Mode Meditation on page 114 again, now freshly informed by the points above about granularity, integration with daily life, and the story of the cabdriver. When you have difficulty extending love to someone, notice your limiting image of that being. Let that image of them point your attention back to the part of your mind that is holding that image of the other. Then take that part of you into practice as instructed above. When you finish the meditation, let the felt sense of it continue to resonate.

LEARNING TO EXTEND LOVE TO THOSE WE ESPECIALLY HATE OR HOLD A GRUDGE AGAINST

People that we really hate, fear, or hold a grudge against can be especially difficult to see as more than our negative image of them. As the philosopher Martin Buber noted, when we love another being as a subject, we love them as a whole person, endowed with great dignity and worth. But when we hate someone, feeling hostility and aversion for them, we hate only a partial image of them that we mistake for the whole person.[9] We may feel justified in our rage at them for a harm they have caused us or someone we care about. But we should ask, what contributed to their harmful behavior? One likely factor is their tendency to get caught up in a part of their mind that mistakes other people for their own reductive thought of them, as just unworthy or contemptible, and treats them as such. Just as the person we are hating has not seen some others as anything more than their negative image of them, we are not seeing the one we hate as anything more than our negative image of them. In that light, we can begin to recognize how their hurtful behavior has been conditioned by mental tendencies much like our own, and that our conditioned reactions to their behavior—seeing them as inherently unworthy of care—imitates the harmful pattern that they have also been caught in. To hate or hold a grudge against someone for harm they've done, then, is not to oppose their harmful way of being but to join them in the destructive habits of misperception and misreaction in which we've all been participating.

As Martin Luther King Jr. wrote, "Far from being the pious injunction of a utopian dreamer, the command to love one's enemy is an absolute necessity for our survival. Love, even for enemies, is the key to the solution of the problems of the world. . . . Let us be practical and ask the question, 'How do we love our enemies?' . . . We must recognize that the evil deed of the enemy neighbor, the thing that hurts, never quite expresses all that he is. An element of goodness may be found even in our worst enemy. Each of us is something of a schizophrenic personality, tragically divided against ourselves. . . . This means that there is some good in the worst of us and some evil in the best of us. When we discover this, we are less prone to hate our enemies. When we look beneath the surface, beneath the impulsive evil deed, we see within our enemy-neighbor a measure of goodness and know that the viciousness and evil of his acts are not quite representative of all that he is."[10]

When someone you hate or hold a grudge against comes to mind in this meditation of extending love, rather than struggling to make yourself love *the negative image of them that your mind is holding,* use your field of care (or compassionate presence) practice to help you become a healing environment for the part of you that sees them as *just that one image.* As that sense of self and its feelings begin to relax and settle, you will be able to sense more facets of the person beyond that one image, and more of their depth. By practicing in this way, we learn increasingly to sense the three samenesses of self and others experientially: the other's underlying wish to be well and happy (like our own); their deep nature endowed with many positive capacities (like our own); and their tendency to mistake their own partial images of others for the persons, to misreact from that place, and to suffer endlessly for it (like our own tendency).

Our own reactions to those we hate intensely reveal to us the kinds of reactions that drive others to act hatefully. Our reactions show us the sorts of "inner demons" that drive everyone's harmful behaviors. By taking our own hateful reactions into the practices of compassion and wisdom described above, we access more of the qualities of our buddha nature—that is, more of our depth, which thereby reveals the hidden depth of anyone we may hate, even when it is concealed from them (and us) by their habits of reaction. In this way, those who have harmed us empower our practice by surfacing the reactions in us that, taken into practice, help us further access the awakening powers of our buddha nature. Increasingly, through this practice, we can feel compassion for those who have hurt us, for being caught in deep causes of suffering that are very difficult to notice and address, causes in which we have all been participating far more than we have *all* been conscious.[11]

AUTHENTIC LOVE BOTH CONFIRMS AND CONFRONTS

Extending love inclusively does not involve accepting anyone's harmful thoughts or actions. It puts us in touch with their fuller humanity, dignity, and potential. By learning to connect to that dignity and potential in them, we can challenge people's harmful ways of thinking and acting on behalf of that potential—on *their* behalf, not just on behalf of others whom their actions may harm.

The words of Martin Luther King Jr.—on examining the good and evil in oneself and uncovering the fuller humanity of our "enemy"—resonates with our practice here. The practice of the Inclusive-Mode Meditation taken into daily life can help us learn to reject a person's harmful behaviors or ways of thinking, not out of hatred for the person and not just to protect others but also to uphold the fuller humanity of the person, whether they are close to us or not. Such a stable power of care can be far more effective in working for change in institutions and societies. When others sense that our motivation for challenging some of their actions includes our deep care for them (as well as others), their response is frequently not the same as if they sensed only an uncaring hostility from us toward them. Indeed, this was often Dr. King's experience. Authentic love confronts what needs to be confronted in others as a way to confirm what is good in them—upholding their capacity to be more than any potentially harmful part of themselves.

CULTIVATING THE STRONG MOTIVATION NEEDED TO EMPOWER INCREASING REALIZATION AND FREEDOM

Please recall now the story of Geshe Thupten Tsering from the start of this chapter. Every morning as a preliminary part of his meditation practices, Geshe Tsering recommitted himself to a responsibility that he had taken up as a young man: to practice assiduously to fully realize all the capacities of his buddha nature, to embody them, and to apply them for the sake of all beings—the vow of a bodhisattva to awaken fully for the sake of all. Dr. King took up a similar responsibility, to actualize as fully as possible the image of God in himself through God's grace, in order to uphold the deep dignity and worth of all people (also in the image of God), by confronting harmful social systems and norms for the sake of *everyone* involved in those systems.

The challenges to realizing our fullest capacities of love and wisdom, summarized in this chapter, are daunting. When we begin practicing as described, we see, far more than we had before, that we have been caught up in patterns of mind that misperceive ourselves and others in fragmented ways. We also become more conscious of how much we have been acting largely from our own self-concerns, even when we thought or said that we were acting on behalf of others. We newly see how often we have mistaken our own reductive images of everyone for the persons, and mis-reacted to them from there. Because those around us are captivated by similar habits of misknowing and mis-reacting, we condition one another to remain caught up in them—for example, in the reductive ways that we tend to speak with other people about those that we mutually despise. When first hearing this, some part of us may want to deny it—to think of ourselves as the nice people, unlike other people who are the not-nice ones (ironically, since in this mode of thinking, we are already not so nice). But as we engage these forms of meditation in all three modes, we see more of the positive capacities and negative tendencies in ourselves and others than we had seen before. Then we can recognize when the mind is identified with a defensive reaction that wants to deny those negative tendencies in ourselves, or to avoid relying more fully on the positive capacities. To become increasingly conscious of those capacities and tendencies, and to take them into practice in the ways described above, is challenging. And we cannot meet that challenge unless we have a strong enough motivation to do so—we have to really want to.

But the more we practice, the more we access the positive capacities and experience little moments of relative freedom from the negative tendencies, which strengthens our motivation for reconnecting with the practice more often and more fully. As we do the practice frequently and progress with it, we experience more of our positive capacity and more moments of freedom from what's impeded it. That deepening process increasingly empowers our determination, like Geshe Tsering's, to realize our awakened potential as fully as possible for the sake of all other beings who, like ourselves, want to be well and happy; are undergoing the many sufferings of living, loss, and dying; and are endowed with tremendous dignity in the depth of their being—the infinite openness, lucidity, and immense positive capacity of their buddha nature.

Take a break now if you'd like, and when you feel ready, go ahead and do the Inclusive-Mode Meditation on page 114, now freshly informed by the discussions above about going beyond hatred, confirming and confronting, and cultivating strong motivation for practice. When you finish the meditation, let the felt sense of it continue to resonate.

FURTHER REFLECTIONS THAT HELP EMPOWER THE PRACTICE OF INCLUDING ALL BEINGS IN LOVE

In addition to the considerations above, several other reflections adapted from Tibetan Buddhism can elevate our perspective on our relationship to others, supporting our practice of extending love more inclusively and unconditionally. These reflections strengthen our appreciation for all other beings, for contributing as they have to the web of life that supports all that we are. And they help us feel a natural concern for all beings in the struggles of living and dying that we all share.

Recalling Interdependence

Every aspect of our lives that we value is dependent on countless beings who support our survival and ability to flourish. For example, try to think of an ability you have that you take pride in. John has sometimes taken pride in his abilities to speak and to write reasonably well. In the individualistic society in which he grew up, it seems natural for him to think of these abilities as simply his own. But where do they come from? Those abilities depended on countless moments of input in infancy and young childhood from parents, relatives, neighbors—an entire linguistic community. In school, his teachers exerted so much effort and attention to inform his learning of language and writing; and all the authors that he read in school, starting in first grade, offered themselves to his learning through the hard work that went into their writing. When he speaks and writes now, therefore, he is never just exercising his own personal abilities. He is always also expressing the outcome of efforts by a vast community of caring attention.[12]

Or think of anything that makes you happy to possess. For example, it seems natural for me to think of a beautiful shirt in my closet as a delightful object of *my* possession, nothing more. But where did it come from? The cotton in the shirt came from an ecosystem including many creatures who aerated and fertilized the soil, and from many human beings who labored to bring the crop to maturity, harvested the cotton, invented the machinery, processed the cotton, wove the cotton into fabric, made a shirt of it, drove the trucks that carried the shirts to market, created marketplaces in which cotton can be sold, and on and on. The cotton infrastructure behind this shirt also includes a long history of enslaved peoples who labored under intolerable conditions to make cotton goods available. Indeed, if we look deeply into the causes and conditions of anything we think of as our own— whether a material thing, a skill, or an ability—we find that every facet of our lives has been supported by innumerable other beings who have made the world in which that thing or ability could come into existence and into our lives.

Please take a moment now to think of one thing in your life that you depend on and appreciate, or of an ability or accomplishment that you think of as your own. Consider what this thing (like the water you drink, or one of the foods you ate today, or the vehicle you ride in to work, or your ability to do something well) depends on—where it comes from to support your life. Reflect on all the beings involved in making this possible for you. If we reflect in this way regularly, with many examples of things or abilities we had thought of as "mine," it shifts our perspective on ourself and our world, making us more inclined to think of all others, including "strangers," as the matrix of every aspect of our own lives, with appreciation, gratitude, wonder, and care for them. To become newly conscious of how every single aspect of our lives has been supported by so many others enhances our sense of closeness and affection with beings far beyond a conception of any narrow "in-group."

Recalling the Struggles and Sufferings That We All Share

As discussed earlier, when we see someone as just a stranger or just worthy of blame, our mind in that moment sees them through one narrow image of them that it has constructed, hiding most of their existence from us. In addition to the practices above, another practice that can open our lens on others is to reflect on the struggles and sufferings that we all share. As the Buddha taught, given the impermanence of all phenomena, and everyone's fear of dying, all beings are shadowed by subconscious fears of loss, illness, pain, affliction, and the unknown. Everyone, like us, must eventually face the loss of all who are dear to them and all that they have known in this life. Everyone, like us, harbors numerous subconscious layers of anxiety and fear as they undergo the many struggles of living and dying on this earth. Think of someone dear to you and reflect on all they've gone through and will go through unto death. Then consider the same with regard to a "stranger" and someone you have disliked. This reflection on universal impermanence and suffering profoundly undercuts our tendency to view others in merely reductive ways.

Please reflect in these ways on universal interdependence and suffering now, then redo the Inclusive-Mode Meditation on page 114 as instructed above (extending in circles that include dear ones, then expanding circles that include strangers, disliked ones, and finally all beings).

Did these reflections affect how you experienced that meditation? You can return to these reflections often over time to see how they can progressively empower this practice.

BLESSING YOUR PRESENT, YOUR PAST, AND YOUR PRESENT WORLD

When you do the Inclusive-Mode Meditation in daily morning practice, you include expanding circles of beings, "blessing" them all with the loving perspective, energy, and wish of the meditation. At that time, you can also consciously include within this blessing all the people you are likely to see later in the day and all the places that you will go—your home, workplace, the roads you will travel, the places you will visit, and so forth. This process of visualizing and pre-blessing your world parallels the practice of high-performing musicians and athletes, many of whom visualize success in their upcoming performances down to minute detail. By visualizing loving qualities blessing beings and places, we are simulating those qualities in a fully embodied experience that prepares the mind and body to reenact them in the future. Then as you see and meet people in those places throughout the day, even if they appear to you out of habit mainly as just a "stranger" or "dislikable" or "my friend," your contact with them can draw you back into the perspective and energy of your meditation session, on the spot, to sense them as beings of great dignity and worth beyond such reductive labels. In this way, the morning meditation can increasingly reveal your daily life as a kind of sacred realm, sensing others as basically holy. As you see or think of anyone during your day, you can commune with them again in the basic goodness of their being, beyond limiting labels, making it increasingly natural to respond to each with a degree of reverence and care. It is as if your morning meditation pre-blesses your day, so when you arrive anywhere, you receive its blessing.

Similarly, you could use your morning meditation to bless all beings who have ever been part of your life from its beginning up to now, from your earliest memories as a child, to each stage of your schooling, to all the later stages of your life—recalling progressively more of the people who played a part in your life, whether or not they seemed important to you at the time, and blessing everyone you recall with the energy and wish of love as you think of them. Then you can let the circles of inclusion in the meditation expand as instructed to include many other beings of this world—human, animal, and finally all creatures.

NOTICING HOW DAILY PRACTICE OF THIS INCLUSIVE MEDITATION SHIFTS YOUR PERCEPTION OF THINGS

As you touch in repeatedly on the Inclusive-Mode Meditation in your days, what are you newly noticing in light of it? What does this meditation raise up or highlight for you in your relationships with others and with those you work with or serve? How is it affecting your ways of being with others and their ways of being with you? Is it making anything newly possible? Responding to those prompts, or to others that you think of, write in your journal what you freshly notice day by day.

THE THREE MODES OF SUSTAINABLE COMPASSION TRAINING SYNERGISTICALLY EMPOWER EACH OTHER

Throughout the arc of contemplative practice in this book, we discover new facets of each meditation in light of the others, every time we circle back to a meditation we've previously learned after having done the others. In this way, each of the three modes of practice empowers the other two modes. To be seen in our deep worth and held in unconditional acceptance and love in the receptive mode empowers us to see others in their deep worth and to hold them in love, in the inclusive mode. Both those modes of practice, in their releasing phase, help us settle into the source of that love: the infinite openness, warmth, and wisdom in the depth of our awareness—the deepening mode. As we gradually learn through this deepening process more fully to trust the limitless openness that we are settling into, self-clinging habits of hesitancy and anxiety that have held back our capacity of love can further release, so the capacity for more un-conditional and all-inclusive love can unfold more freely into the receptive and inclusive modes of our practice. In this way, each mode of meditation is engaged more deeply as we train in the other two modes. As we continue to practice each of these three modes over time, they establish the basis for further training in practices of compassion, which are the subject of the next chapter.

4

GENERATING ALL-INCLUSIVE
COMPASSION AND WISDOM

ASIAN BUDDHISTS OFTEN communicate their understandings of compassion and wisdom through stories, many of which center on encounters with the Buddha or other enlightened figures. One such story, well known throughout Asia, concerns a young woman who became a leader in the Buddha's spiritual community after finding great compassion and wisdom through her own suffering.

Kisā Gotamī was a poor village woman who longed desperately for a child. When she finally gave birth to a baby boy, she was overjoyed. But as a toddler, the child became ill and quickly died. Gotamī was completely overwhelmed by grief. Unable to accept what had happened, she carried the body of her child on her hip as if he were still alive and wandered from home to home throughout her town, desperately pleading, "Please, give me medicine for my son!" At first astonished by her behavior, some people began mocking her, asking, "What medicine can there possibly be for the dead, Gotamī?" But a wise man, who had sympathy for Gotamī, told her that the greatest of sages, the Buddha, was teaching near their town. "Go to him to ask for your medicine," he advised. Filled with hope, still carrying her son's body on her hip, Gotamī rushed to the place that the Buddha was teaching amid a gathering of monks and nuns.

Moving through the crowd, she came before the Buddha and beseeched him, "Please, Blessed One, give me medicine for my son!" Recognizing Gotamī's spiritual potential, the Buddha replied, "You did well, Gotamī, in coming here for medicine. But first, return to your town and visit every single home there, leaving none out. At each home where nobody grieves for the dead, fetch a pinch of mustard seed. Then return to me with all those mustard seeds."

Thinking the Buddha planned to use the mustard seeds to conjure a cure for her son, Gotamī enthusiastically returned to the town. At the first house she said, "The Buddha has told me to get mustard seeds from every home where no one grieves for the dead. Please give me mustard seeds for my son's medicine." But the householder replied, "Alas, Gotamī, we grieve for our little daughter who died last year." Gotamī went to the next house, "Please tell me no one here grieves for the dead so that I may gather mustard seeds." The man there said, "Alas, Gotamī, we grieve over our dear son who died months ago." At the next house she was told, "Alas, Gotamī, we grieve for our beloved parents."

So her fruitless search continued until she had canvassed the entire town. She was unable to collect a single mustard seed! And then it struck her: "*Everyone* in this town—indeed, every being in the world—undergoes grief like my own!" In that moment her intense personal grief was transformed into intense empathy and compassion for all beings who suffer, like her, by trying to keep what they must inevitably lose. It suddenly dawned on her, "*This* is what the Buddha, in his compassion for all of us, has seen!" She was now ready to offer her son's body to the funeral pyre and return to the Buddha.

Upon her return, the Buddha asked, "Gotamī, did you get the mustard seeds?" "O Blessed One," she replied, "I am done with mustard seeds. Just give me refuge." And so she was entered into the early Buddhist community.[1]

In Asian Buddhist cultures, Gotamī's story illustrates not only the Buddha's skill in teaching but also the progressive development of deep compassion and wisdom. At first Gotamī was utterly absorbed in her own grief, to the brink of madness. But the practice she received from the Buddha made her own intense grief a doorway to empathy with all others in their grief. For Gotamī to realize the profound significance of her suffering, she had first to experience it in its full intensity, then to recognize in her own suffering of loss what all others similarly undergo in their own time. So she exclaimed, "This is what the Buddha has seen!" for she had now begun to share in the Buddha's awakened vision of universal compassion and wisdom that embraces all beings in their shared suffering and potential for awakening. At the end of Gotamī's story, the Buddha welcomed her into his monastic community, where she quickly traversed the stages of the Buddha's path and became an enlightened teacher. In this chapter, we will learn practices that take us into a process of awakening analogous to Gotamī's—by rediscovering our own layers of suffering as gateways to empathy and compassion for others.

CULTIVATING FOUR FACTORS OF COMPASSION

In this chapter, we will focus on the development of strong, sustainable compassion that can extend to anyone and everyone. As we explored in the last chapter, drawing both on understandings from Buddhism and areas of psychology, authentic love does not accept our limiting impressions of other persons but relates to them in their fuller being. Love is the power to commune with persons (including animals) in the depth of their being, in their profound dignity and worth, while wishing them deeply well beyond discriminations of in- or out-group. Compassion is a form of love; it is the form that love takes when we are resonating with someone in their suffering and wishing for them to be free of the suffering and its causes so they *can* be deeply well, which motivates responsive action. As the contemplative scholar Matthieu Ricard has said, "When altruistic love passes through the prism of empathy, it becomes compassion."[2]

Compassion, as defined here, has four aspects: (1) deep loving care for beings, (2) empathic concern for them in their suffering, (3) a strong wish that wills their freedom from the causes of the suffering as a basis for action, and (4) wisdom. When we cultivate all four of these factors, they give rise to a compassionate orientation and attitude to remedy suffering that is energizing and replenishing rather than emotionally exhausting or depleting.[3] The practices in this manual cultivate all four of those factors of compassion. We'll say a few things about the first three factors, then discuss the fourth factor, wisdom:

1. *Loving care* senses all persons as fundamentally dear and worthy of unconditional care, so we root for them and wish them deeply well.

2. *Empathy:* When we feel such care for persons and are aware that they are suffering, we tend to resonate with them in their suffering, sensing and imagining what it must feel like for them, which gives rise to a caring *empathy* for them.[4]

3. *Compassionate will:* From that empathic care comes the wish for them to be free of the suffering so they can be deeply well. When this compassionate wish and attitude becomes strong, it becomes a *compassionate will* to alleviate the suffering, embodied in responsive action.[5]

Three restrictive tendencies prevent those first three factors of compassion from becoming more all-inclusive, unconditional, powerful, and sustainable. (1) The first such tendency restricts our loving care, hence, our compassion, just to our in-group—to those that appear to us as the only ones that really matter.[6] (2) The second such tendency restricts our ability to empathize with others just to those undergoing obvious forms of suffering, like severe physical or mental pain. Of course, caring empathy is important then. But a more fully aware empathy doesn't stop just at obvious layers of suffering; it is also conscious of hidden layers in everyone—fears, struggles, grief, and stress that may not even be fully conscious to them. Such caring empathy can encompass everyone we meet or think of, aware that each being is undergoing much inner suffering beyond the obvious. (3) The third restrictive tendency is the tendency to be overwhelmed by suffering in ourselves or others, preventing us from becoming more fully and compassionately present to those in distress.[7] These restrictions on our compassion are undercut by three kinds of wisdom, which comprise the fourth factor of compassion.

4. *Wisdom:* The fourth factor of compassion—wisdom—empowers the other three factors of compassion by undercutting those three tendencies that restrict compassion.

Three kinds of wisdom do this:
(1) To have all-inclusive loving care (the first factor of compassion noted above), we need the wisdom that sees through limiting labels of other persons as merely "strangers," "merely annoying," "the unimportant ones," and so forth; the wisdom that is aware of everyone's *fuller personhood, depth, and*

worthiness to be loved. So one's loving care is not restricted to any perceived in-group (the first restrictive tendency noted above). People in all kinds of caring roles and professions need a power of care that extends to whoever comes to us—every member of the community; every patient, student, client; not just those in our in-groups. Such inclusive loving care is also what the world desperately needs: a concern for all who are suffering, not just for those in our own ethnic, religious, racial, social class, sexual identity, or other in-group.

(2) Empathy for others in the layers of their suffering (the second factor of compassion above) needs to be informed by the wisdom that is aware of *inner layers of suffering within all of us,* beyond the obvious. So our empathy and compassion is not restricted just to those undergoing the most obvious sufferings (the second restrictive tendency) but can encompass everyone, aware that each being is undergoing more suffering than would appear on the surface.

(3) For the will of compassion (the third factor of compassion above) to become powerful and stable, it must contain the wisdom that knows, when we experience sufferings of self or others, that *suffering is never the entire reality* but can be experienced within a fuller reality of unconditional openness and caring awareness that permits the suffering to heal and transform. With that wisdom, our compassion is less subject to the third restrictive tendency of getting overwhelmed by the sufferings we encounter. These three aspects of wisdom help make compassion all-inclusive, strong, and sustaining, instead of being narrowly biased or devolving into empathic distress and emotional depletion.[8]

The three modes of meditation we learned in the prior three chapters of this manual are already contributing to all four of these factors of compassion: loving care, empathy, compassionate will, and the wisdom that empowers them. We cultivated *loving care* for persons, beyond discrimination, through the inclusive mode of practice. That practice, supported by the deepening mode, brings out the *wisdom* that discerns the difference between our limiting labels of people and the actual people, so we can commune with them beyond such labels in the depth of their being with loving care and reverence. We began cultivating *empathy* with others with the help of all three modes of meditation. The receptive and deepening modes of practice made us conscious of painful parts of ourselves with which we have struggled, providing the *wisdom* to recognize analogous layers of struggle in others as we commune with them empathetically in the inclusive mode. Finally, we cultivated the basis for a *compassionate will* in the face of suffering with the help of the receptive and deepening modes, which showed us how to become a loving environment for all painful feelings, embracing them in acceptance, warmth, and openness in which they could reveal their empty nature, start to heal, and release. That process brings out the *wisdom* in the inclusive mode that holds all the suffering parts of ourselves and others within unconditional openness and compassionate awareness.

In these ways, we've already started cultivating all four factors of compassion, but we need now to go further, especially into practices to deepen the factors of caring empathy and compassionate will for service and action. This chapter will introduce meditations for that purpose. Such meditations further empower *empathy* by making us more fully aware of layers of the suffering in ourselves and others. And they further empower a strong *will of compassion* by evoking a heartfelt sense of connection to others who are suffering that is not subject to empathic distress or emotional depletion.

INSIGHT INTO THE NATURE OF SUFFERING
THAT SUPPORTS ALL-INCLUSIVE COMPASSION

According to the Dalai Lama, the cultivation of an all-inclusive and unconditional power of compassion (like Kisā Gotamī's) requires deep insight into the nature of suffering that all beings are undergoing. The Buddha explained three levels of suffering: obvious suffering, the suffering of changeableness, and the suffering of conditioned reactions. *Obvious suffering* includes the agonies that commonly come to mind when we hear the word *suffering*: grave illnesses and injuries, disabling grief and despair, the anguish of dying, and so forth. Societies tend to think of compassion for others only when their suffering is of this obvious kind. We tend not to view others with compassion as they experience moments of happiness in pleasant circumstances. But clinging to such temporal happiness is an example of what the Buddha identified as the second level of suffering: the misery inherent in relying on changeable circumstances as a source for stable happiness and well-being.

The Buddha declared, "All accumulations end in depletion; all rising in falling; all meetings in partings; all life in death."[9] Within the usual stance of self-grasping, the very things that we cling to for our happiness—wealth, loved ones, pleasurable possessions, and personal power—all transform into conditions of suffering as we lose them throughout life and approach our death. Although such things may trigger transient feelings of happiness, they are not its source. The *suffering of changeableness* is the futile attempt to have and hold on to such things as if they were the very source of our well-being, when deep down we know we will lose every one of them. A college student reacted to the Buddhist teaching of suffering by asserting that he was *not* suffering—since he very much enjoyed his beer, his playful times with friends, and being with his family. His professor replied, "Then you will be very sad when you lose each of those things, won't you?" From a Buddhist perspective, the actual source of our well-being is authentic love, compassion, and wisdom, whose capacities are always available in the deep nature of our minds—our buddha nature. The transient happiness of changeable suffering comes and goes with changing circumstances. But love, compassion, and wisdom can be cultivated to enduring power through practice, a power that can be drawn upon in all circumstances.

The third level of suffering, the *suffering of ego-conditioning*, is the basis of the other two levels. This level of suffering refers to the subtle anxiety and dissatisfaction that is endemic to the ego-centered conditioning of our minds. From this perspective, our minds' habitual tendencies to identify fully with shifting constructs of self and their reactions of self-clinging and aversion are forms of suffering *in themselves*, afflicting our minds and bodies even before anything else happens. By motivating narrowly self-centered actions, those tendencies also contribute to innumerable individual and social forms of suffering.

It is because the Buddha had insight into all three of these levels of suffering, it is taught, that he had equal compassion for all beings. Not just for those who are undergoing severe sufferings right now but for all beings, including those now enjoying passing moments of happiness and those who ignorantly seek their well-being by hurting others. He understood how all are caught in layers of misery and afflictive ego-conditioning beyond what they see. When someone becomes enlightened, it is taught, just to *see* a sentient being is to have spontaneous compassion arise from the depth of awareness that senses the layers of suffering operative in that being. The meditation below helps us gain insight into those three levels of suffering, so our own vision of beings may be brought closer to the Buddha's.[10]

Becoming More Conscious of Suffering in Ourselves as a Doorway to Compassion for Others

The Dalai Lama recommends a clear progression in the cultivation of compassion: "One thing specific to the contemplation of suffering [as a basis of compassion] is that it tends to be more powerful and effective if we focus on our own suffering and then extend that recognition to the suffering of others."[11] Dzogchen Ponlop Rinpoche reiterates that progression from self to other: "Compassion must start by sensing our own suffering. If it does not, then seeing the suffering of others will be merely conceptual."[12]

To connect with what others are undergoing, we have to become more fully aware of what we ourselves are going through in all the layers of our being. If we don't have enough awareness of our own layers of struggle, fear, and suffering, we can't establish a deep connection to what others are experiencing at those levels of their being. To empathize deeply with others, we must be able to sense from within the layers of suffering that all share in our basic humanity. Not just in terms of what we are currently feeling but also on more subtle levels: our personal struggles to hold on to what is dear, to maintain security, to avoid loss and death, to protect our loved ones from loss and death.

We saw this progression of self-awareness in Kisā Gotamī's story. It was the final acknowledgment of her own grief as a deep connection to others that transformed the grief into compassion for them all. But Gotamī was not so self-aware when her quest began. Although, in the receptive and deepening modes of practice, we have begun to notice painful parts of ourselves with which we have struggled, many aspects of our own suffering probably still remain largely hidden from our view. There are layers of fear, anxiety, pain, grief, and struggle that get suppressed or lost from our conscious awareness because of our aversion to such feelings. Until we become more conscious of all three levels of suffering in ourselves, we can't sense them in others with empathy and compassion.

Embracing All Layers of Suffering in Compassion

By holding Gotamī in his unconditional compassion and assigning her the "mustard seed" quest, the Buddha helped her find a safe way to become newly conscious of the depth of her suffering from which to empathize with others at that depth of suffering in them. Analogously, by learning in the receptive and deepening modes of our practice how to become a loving holding environment for all of our feelings, we've established a safe way to become more fully conscious of layers of our own suffering, at all three levels of suffering noted above, as a basis of compassion for beings with similar layers.

In the meditation on page 155, we become an unconditional, compassionate holding environment for all those levels of suffering. As we sense the similarity of ourselves and others in such deepening layers, it becomes natural to think of them all with care and compassion, further undercutting the tendency to reduce others in our minds just to familiar superficial labels for them (as just a stranger, just a clerk who should be serving me faster, just my relative, just a jerk, and so forth). Through this practice we learn to sense the underlying traces of insecurity, anxiety, distress, and grief that shadow everyone, even in their moments of happiness, and to hold them all in compassion that wills their deep freedom and well-being, as Kisā Gotamī learned to do.

INTRODUCING THE FIRST COMPASSION MEDITATION BY STARTING WITH OUR OWN LAYERS OF SUFFERING

To develop a more sustaining, unconditional, and all-inclusive compassion, we need to become more conscious of underlying layers of suffering in ourselves that correspond to analogous layers in others as part of our shared human condition: feelings of distress, grief, loss, loneliness, trauma, despair, unworthiness, brokenness, fear of physical danger, fear of dying, fears for loved ones, and so forth. Then we can empathize with others in their analogous hidden layers of suffering, which further undercuts our limiting impressions of them all.

To develop such awareness, we need an effective way to become more conscious of our own painful inner feelings. Ordinarily such an exploration might feel unsafe. After all, we all want to avoid distressing feelings. However, we have now trained in the Field of Care Meditation, Compassionate Presence to Feelings Meditation, and Letting Be meditation. The next meditation draws on the secure base we've cultivated in those meditations, particularly the Field of Care, to experience all of our feelings, including painful ones, within a loving, healing environment of warmth and compassion. This provides the inner sense of safety we need to be present to our most difficult feelings, which can inform our empathy for others who experience analogous feelings. In this way, we can experience our sufferings as *connecting* instead of isolating, as a way to know others sympathetically from inside, drawing us into compassionate solidarity with them right through our feelings. This meditation can become a joyful discovery because it provides a way to experience our own suffering feelings not as disconnecting and meaningless but as profoundly meaningful and deeply connecting. Just as we have learned to reappraise challenging emotions as opportunities for practice in the Compassionate Presence to Feelings Meditation, here too we can reappraise all our layers of suffering as opportunities for empathic connection with others.

In the next meditation, then, we need to more consciously experience a feeling of struggle, stress, or suffering that is familiar to us as human beings in order to explore how it can become a point of empathetic connection to many others who share such feelings as part of the human condition. To access the feeling, we can recall a situation that evokes it. The aim is not to ruminate about the situation but to let it trigger the feeling so we can explore it as instructed in the meditation. A sample list of such feelings is provided below. Please select one such feeling with which to begin this meditation. As you become familiar with this meditation through repetition, you can explore further feelings on the list, and let this practice help you develop your own fuller list of feelings to explore over time. Take a moment now to select one feeling from the list that is familiar to you:

- Become conscious of a feeling of physical pain anywhere.
- Recall an anxiety you have about your body or health; or a fear you have of severe illness, injury, or violence.
- Recall a feeling of fear you have over obtaining enough security for yourself or your family; or of meeting all your obligations, responsibilities, or debts.

- Bring to mind grief that you feel at the loss of a relationship, a job, or a part of your life.
- Recall a feeling of not being seen; of being looked down upon, silenced, humiliated, marginalized, or excluded.
- Recall a feeling of failure, hopelessness, or despair.
- Recall a feeling of intense longing, incompleteness, or addiction.
- Recall feeling very lonely, abandoned, or cut off.
- Bring to mind fears you have for a loved one in their vulnerability and mortality.
- Bring to mind grief that you feel at the loss of a loved one who has died.
- Bring to mind fears you have for your own impending death.
- Sense the exhaustion you feel from identifying with brittle senses of self that are endlessly reacting to other parts of yourself, to narrow impressions of others, and to your world.

Do you have a feeling you can bring to mind now for the meditation? Do you have a field of care to recall that helps you access loving qualities of your awareness? Then you are ready to begin.

Please note: If you have too much difficulty at any stage of this meditation being with the feeling you've chosen, just settle back and reunite with your field of care, let that feeling of difficulty be embraced in its loving qualities, and rest thus. Then return to the meditation instruction when you feel ready. *You can do that repeatedly as needed.*

(An audio option is available at shambhala.com/howcompassionworks meditations.)

COMPASSION MEDITATION 1, SUPPORTED BY A FIELD OF CARE: TURNING OUR SUFFERING FEELINGS INTO COMPASSION FOR OTHERS

STEP 1. SETTLING INTO BODY AND BREATH (2 TO 3 MINUTES) Sit in a relaxed way, with the back comfortably straight, eyes gazing gently downward. Come down from the thinking mind into the body and settle into the grounded feeling of the body on your seat. (*Pause*) Let the breath flow naturally while breathing from the abdomen, so you feel the belly expand and contract with each breath. Let that feeling draw you into it more and more, breath by breath.

STEP 2. RECONNECTING WITH LOVE AND COMPASSION (3 TO 5 MINUTES) Now bring to mind your field of care as present here with you now. You are being seen and held in deep care, compassion, acceptance, and warmth beyond judgments. Relax into the felt sense of this experience, steeping in its loving energy and tender qualities, and letting them infuse your whole being. Accept these loving qualities into your whole body, heart, and mind—every part of you loved in its very being.

STEP 3. EXPERIENCING A SUFFERING FEELING AS A DOORWAY TO EMPATHY (5 MINUTES OR SO) Now, with this loving environment as support, bring to mind the distressing feeling that you selected for this meditation. Take time to sense what it's like for someone to experience this feeling: How does it feel in your heart, mind, and body? What other feelings arise in association with it? Let the loving environment of your field of care support you in sensing those things.

If a part of you starts to have too much difficulty with this, just settle back and reunite with your field of care. Let that feeling of difficulty be embraced in its loving qualities and rest there. Then when you feel ready, again freshly recall the distressing feeling you chose for this meditation to sense what it's like for someone to experience it.

After a little while, recall that many other people experience feelings like this in their own ways. So now, while supported by your field of care, sense right through your feeling what others feel. Feel, through your feeling, what they feel. In this way, sense this feeling as not just your own, but as your deep connection to many others.

STEP 4. ACCEPTING COMPASSION FOR ALL (5 TO 7 MINUTES) After exploring in this way for a little while, recall that your whole being is held in the unconditional love and compassion evoked by your field of care and consciously allow all of your feelings to be embraced in that compassionate energy, every part of you loved in its very being. By accepting this loving energy into your own suffering feelings, imagine you are accepting it into everyone who has similar feelings. Let the radiance of this energy extend through you to them all while wishing them deeply well and free of suffering. As this radiance permeates them all, imagine they are becoming free of the suffering, each in their own best way, and let yourself take joy in their relief and joy.

STEP 5. RELEASING (3 TO 5 MINUTES) After some time, let this loving environment of warmth and compassion help your mind to relax, settle back a bit inwardly, release all its frameworks of meditation and concern, and come to rest in the background of its awareness, which is naturally wide open and luminous like a sunlit sky. As thoughts and feelings arise, let them just metabolize themselves and release within this sky-like openness of awareness by letting everything be.

When you finish the meditation, let the felt sense of it continue to resonate.

Processing the Meditation

Part of the reason we get overwhelmed by suffering is that we tend to experience the suffering as if it were the only reality here. In this practice, we experience our suffering feelings not as the entire reality but as embraced in a larger reality of compassion and wisdom—a larger awareness of openness, loving energy, and spacious acceptance that is profoundly healing, in which we can feel safe enough to become newly conscious of layers of suffering in ourselves that we share with others as a basis of compassion for them all.

Often our suffering makes us feel terribly isolated from others, alone in our pain. In this practice, we experience our painful feelings not as isolating us from others but as deeply *connecting* us to them—as a basis of compassionate solidarity with all others. As one practitioner responded to this practice: "Recognizing that we share the same burden feels like an unburdening." In this way, the meditation enacts the psychological capacity of reappraisal. We reappraise our distress and pain as resources, not just as difficulties. Suffering experiences help us sense more of what others are going through.

By sensing hidden layers of suffering in all others as part of our shared human condition, no matter how they appear to us, this practice much further breaks down the in-group boundaries and superficial judgments of others that impede the freer flow of care and compassion and deepening discernment.

Some people react to teachings about this meditation practice by saying that they are afraid to pay so much attention to their own suffering. But that may be because they are focusing on the suffering alone, apart from the compassion in which it is held in the meditation. There is no need to rush the process. We are enabled to become more conscious of feelings of pain, fear, and despair as we sense the safe, healing power of the unconditional care in which they are always held. By gradually sensing more layers of suffering in that way, with increasing granularity, we are sensing similar layers in others, which empowers deep empathy for them.[13] By receiving compassion into each aspect of our suffering as instructed, we become increasingly aware of all three levels of suffering that were explained above, in ourselves and in others, as a basis of compassion for all.

Through progressive practice, then, we discover that our suffering is not just a personal problem. It need not isolate us from others into narrow confines of personal pain. We can rediscover the meaning of our own suffering as a profound connection to countless others and to the dignity and sacredness of all our lives. Practicing this Compassion Meditation repeatedly over time provides a way for us to become familiar with more kinds of suffering feelings. Then, increasingly, as we experience our own difficulties in life, they become a bridge of empathy and compassion for what many others are undergoing, evoking a basic attitude of care for others that can beneficially empower and inform every part of our lives and work with people.

In chapter 2 we noted that with repetition of the Compassionate Presence to Feelings Meditation, the qualities of warmth, acceptance, and openness that encompass each emotion in the meditation can become part of the experience of that emotion. Such qualities can get associated with the emotion, so the next time you experience the emotion, some degree of warmth, acceptance, and openness spontaneously occurs with that feeling state. Analogously, as we repeat the first Compassion Meditation in this chapter more and more, the qualities of empathy and compassion for others that we associate with our own layers of suffering can become part of our experience of those layers. In this way, with repeated practice, difficulties of life themselves can spontaneously start to generate empathy and compassion for others even as you are experiencing those difficulties. Difficulties, in this way, become resources of awakening, not just through intellectual reflection but in this deeply embodied way.

This meditation can be adapted for and informed by the experiences and difficulties of people in various social locations or identities (e.g., according to race, gender, sexuality, physical disabilities, class, ethnicity, and so forth). For people in marginalized groups, this Compassion Meditation can empower deepening solidarity with others in your group in the kinds of suffering that you share, including ancestors over generations, with a strengthening wish and energy of compassion that pervades them all. This can be deeply healing and support caring action. Then over time, you can let this same meditation also empower growing solidarity with all other persons in the broader types and hidden layers of suffering that all share as part of their human condition—such as the three types of suffering noted earlier, including fear of loss, fear of dying, fear for loved ones, and so forth. That can support and empower any work you may do in the world, in service or work for change.[14] We will discuss this further in chapter 5, which focuses on compassion and wisdom as powers of service, activism, and work in the world.

Compassion Meditation 1 Can Also Be Supported by Compassionate Presence to Feelings

Again, to become newly aware of subliminal layers of suffering in all others, we need to become newly conscious of similar layers of suffering in ourselves. But we probably won't feel safe enough to do that unless we have a secure base to become newly conscious of our own layers of suffering without getting overwhelmed by them. In the prior meditation of compassion, we relied on our field of care to generate the loving environment toward all our feelings that could allow us to become increasingly conscious of them as a bridge of empathy and care for others. Whenever we had too much difficulty staying with a painful feeling, we could reconnect with the holding environment generated by the field of care and let that feeling of difficulty relax in that healing space. Then, when ready, we could return to the instruction to sense the painful feeling as an empathic link to others.

Some people find the Compassionate Presence to Feelings Meditation more effective than a field of care for establishing a healing environment for difficult reactions that may arise during Compassion Meditation 1. For them, Compassion Meditation 1 can be done with the support of compassionate presence to feelings instead of with a field of care. Other practitioners may prefer to alternate these two ways of doing Compassion Meditation 1, sometimes with a field of care, other times with compassionate presence to feelings, letting each inform and empower the other.

Let's try Compassion Meditation 1 again now with compassionate presence to feelings as support. First, review the list of common painful feelings in the introduction to Compassion Meditation 1 on pages 154 and 155, and select one of those as a focus for step 3 in the meditation below.

(An audio option is available at shambhala.com/howcompassionworks meditations.)

COMPASSION MEDITATION 1, SUPPORTED BY COMPASSIONATE PRESENCE TO FEELINGS

STEP 1. SETTLING INTO THE BODY (2 TO 3 MINUTES) Sit in a relaxed way, with back comfortably straight, eyes gazing gently downward. Come down from the thinking mind into the body, feeling the body as a whole, and letting the breath settle into its own natural flow.

STEP 2. BECOMING A COMPASSIONATE HOLDING ENVIRONMENT FOR FEELINGS (3 TO 5 MINUTES) Now sense whatever emotional feeling is present within you, from within your body. This may be a subtle emotional feeling such as a little anxiety or unease, or liking or disliking a little how things are. Or you may feel a stronger emotion, like fear, frustration, or joy. Become aware of that feeling within you while fully allowing it to be here—letting it have all the space it needs to find its own place. Like a friend sympathetically present to a friend, let this feeling have all the space it needs to find its own place and to settle or heal in its own time. Without trying to do anything to the feeling, just spaciously rest with it and let it metabolize itself.

STEP 3. EXPERIENCING A SUFFERING FEELING AS A DOORWAY TO EMPATHY (3 TO 5 MINUTES) Now, supported by this compassionate holding environment, bring to mind the distressing feeling that you selected for this meditation. Take time to sense what it's like for someone to experience that feeling through your own experience of it (pausing after each question to explore): How does it feel in your heart and mind? How does it feel in the body? What other feelings come up in association with this feeling?

If a part of you starts to have too much difficulty with this, become compassionately present to that feeling of difficulty, letting that feeling have all the space it needs to find its own place and settle, heal, or metabolize itself in its own time. Then when you feel ready, again recall the painful feeling you selected for this meditation, sensing what it's like for someone to experience it.

After a little while, recall: Many other people experience painful feelings like this in their own ways. So now, sense right through your own painful feeling what others feel. Feel, through your feeling, what they feel. In this way, sense this feeling as not just your own, but as your deep connection to many others.

STEP 4. BECOMING A COMPASSIONATE HOLDING ENVIRONMENT FOR ALL (5 MINUTES OR MORE) Now fully become a compassionate holding environment for this distressing feeling, and for any other suffering feelings at all levels of your being, letting all such feelings have the space they need to feel safe, to find their own place, settle, heal, or metabolize themselves in their own time. Remember now that many other beings experience layers of suffering analogous to yours. Think of your own layers of suffering now as one with theirs. By providing this spacious, compassionate environment for your feelings, you are now providing it also for all the others, while wishing them deeply free and well. By spaciously aerating your feelings with acceptance and warmth, you are aerating them in all who experience such feelings. Imagine they all become free of the suffering, each in their own best way, and let yourself take joy in their relief and joy.

STEP 5. RELEASING (3 TO 5 MINUTES) After some time, let this spacious environment of warmth, acceptance, and compassion help your mind to relax, settle back a bit inwardly, release all its frameworks of meditation and concern, and come to rest in the background of its awareness, which is naturally wide open and luminous, like a sunlit sky. As thoughts and feelings arise, let them just metabolize themselves and release within this sky-like openness of awareness by letting everything be.

When you finish the meditation, let the felt sense of it continue to resonate.

Processing the Meditation

Compassion takes expression in many forms of action, certainly actions that respond to others' intense needs but also in quiet ways: in the quality of our attention to others, in our sensitivity to them as subjects worthy of care, in how deeply we listen.[15] This practice helps us sense into the feelings of others behind their words, to respond from there with compassion, much like when we are compassionately present to our own feelings. To listen so deeply, in turn, can inform all of our work and action with others.

RETURNING TO THE INCLUSIVE-MODE MEDITATION, NOW WITH AN INCREASED FOCUS ON COMPASSION

As you will recall, in our practice of Inclusive-Mode Meditation in the previous chapter, we learned to hold others in warmth and care from the depth of our being while resonating with them in the depth of their being (their buddha nature). As we did so, we also became aware of how much time we have spent lost from that depth and caught up in struggling parts of ourselves, which generated a sense of compassion for all others in their analogous layers of lostness, struggle, and suffering.

The meditation we just explored, Compassion Meditation 1, helps us become more fully conscious of layers of stress, struggle, fear, and pain that we share with other beings as part of our human condition, which can much further inform the compassionate component of the inclusive mode. So after familiarizing ourselves with Compassion Meditation 1, becoming conscious of further layers of our own suffering, we can return to the Inclusive-Mode Meditation with a further depth of compassion for all others who have analogous inner layers of suffering.

In the next meditation, then, we again take up the inclusive mode. But this time further exploring in it how our own experiences of pain, anxiety, and woundedness connect us to others rather than isolating us from them. Our painful experiences become a bridge of empathy to others. Indeed, if we are not conscious of these feelings in ourselves, we cannot know them deeply in others. Furthermore, as we learn in the next meditation to let these stressful patterns release and be healed by the power of openness and compassion, we can more deeply notice what cries for healing in others.

Let's explore this now. We will do the Inclusive-Mode Meditation with this further focus on compassion, supported by a field of care.

(An audio option is available at shambhala.com/howcompassionworks meditations.)

INCLUSIVE-MODE MEDITATION WITH A FOCUS ON COMPASSION

STEP 1. SETTLING INTO BODY AND BREATH (2 TO 3 MINUTES) Sit in a relaxed way, with back comfortably straight, eyes gazing gently downward. Come down from thinking mind into the body and settle into the grounded feeling of the body on your seat. (*Pause*) Let the breath flow naturally while breathing from the abdomen, so you feel the belly expand and contract with each breath. Let that feeling draw you into it more and more, breath by breath.

STEP 2. RECONNECTING WITH LOVE AND COMPASSION (3 TO 5 MINUTES) Now bring to mind your field of care as present here with you now. You are being seen and held in deep care, compassion, acceptance, and warmth beyond judgments. Relax into the felt sense of this experience, steeping in its loving energy and tender qualities, and letting them infuse your whole being. Accept these loving qualities into your whole body, heart, and mind—every part of you embraced in unconditional love and compassion. Let yourself also become aware of inner layers of stress, pain, suffering, and struggle within you, and let them all be embraced in this loving, healing, holding environment.

STEP 3. INCLUDING OTHERS (5 TO 10 MINUTES) Now think of someone dear to you that you'd like to include in this same loving environment and let them also be included in this field of loving energies, compassionate warmth, and acceptance. Let these energies and qualities permeate their whole being. Let this help you to commune with them in the depth of their being; to sense them in their inner layers of stress, struggle, and pain; and to wish them deeply well and free of suffering. (*Pause*)

Now let a few more beings come to mind that you'd also like to include in this field of loving energies and compassionate warmth, and let them also be included, along with the first person. Let these energies and qualities permeate their whole being. Let this help you commune with them in the depth of their being and inner layers of struggle and pain and to wish them deeply well and free of suffering. (*Pause*) Now let this practice expand to include larger circles of beings that come to mind, including them all in this field of loving energies and compassion, communing with them in their depth and hidden layers of stress and pain, while wishing them deeply well and free of suffering. Let one or more strangers be included among them and, as you can, one or more persons you've disliked—sensing them all in the depth of their being and in their inner layers of suffering, wishing them deeply well and free.

If part of you has trouble with this or draws your attention away, settle back into your field of care, reunite with its healing environment, and become compassionately aware of that part of you with acceptance and warmth. When it settles, you can return to extending love and compassion to beings.

Finally, you can let the vast underlying capacity of warmth and compassion from your basic awareness expand much more fully to include all beings—human, animal, all creatures—or imagine this is happening. Let this help you commune with them all in the depth of their being and hidden sufferings while wishing them all deepest well-being and freedom.

STEP 4. RELEASING (3 TO 5 MINUTES) Now let this inclusive environment of warmth and acceptance help your mind to relax deeply and release all its frameworks of meditation and concern. Let the mind settle back a bit inwardly and come to rest in the background of its awareness, which is naturally wide open and luminous, like a sunlit sky. As thoughts and feelings arise, let them just metabolize themselves and release within this sky-like openness of awareness by letting everything be.

When you finish the meditation, let the felt sense of it continue to resonate.

Processing the Meditation

The Inclusive-Mode Meditation above differs from the one taught in chapter 3 not so much in its instruction but in the background from which we engage it, one that is informed by Compassion Meditation 1 as we continue to familiarize ourselves with it. People all over the world experience hidden layers of suffering like those we explore in the latter meditation, though they do so in their own ways in their own contexts and cultures. Compassion Meditation 1 thus prepares us to reengage the practice of Inclusive-Mode Meditation, to sense further all those around us in inner layers of suffering that we share as human beings, which empowers deepening compassion for all.

As we become familiar with Compassion Meditation 1 and reengage the inclusive mode in its wake, through repetition of practice, we can increasingly recognize—even as we experience feelings of fear, grief, frustration, and so forth—that such feelings are not just our own but shared with many others. We can learn to hold all such feelings and in turn hold others in deep care. We learn to become more stable sources of courage and compassion for all parts of ourselves and others.

We could alternate Compassion Meditation 1 with the Inclusive-Mode Meditation as informed by it, doing the former daily for one week and the latter daily the next. We could do either practice in the morning as an anchor for the day and reconnect with it throughout the day in many moments. As we do so, we increasingly sense everyone around us as possessed of hidden layers of stress and suffering analogous to our own. By sensing those hidden layers in others, including seeming strangers and those we have disliked, the practice further breaks down limiting impressions and biases that impede more inclusive and unconditional love and compassion.

COMPASSION AND SOCIAL LOCATION

These meditations can also empower us to be less self-defended—more ready to listen and learn from others whose cultural, social, racial, ethnic, sexual, or political identities differ from our own—by staying attuned to the deep dignity and inner layers of suffering that we all share as human beings across those real differences.[16]

Can you remember a time when you had an altercation with someone who lashed out at you in ways you felt were totally unreasonable, making you extremely angry with them, later feeling enraged whenever you thought of them? Then, after the incident, someone tells you about something terrible that person is undergoing, such as the death of their child or a recent eviction from their home with nowhere to go, and you realize how terribly unhappy, afraid, and alone they must feel. What happened to your angry perception of them then? To become conscious of someone's hidden layers of suffering can completely demolish our reduction of a person to just one image or story. Our limiting impressions of others are much further undercut by a vivid awareness of their hidden sufferings.

These meditations thus help us become more conscious of underlying layers of suffering in ourselves that correspond to analogous layers in others, empowering compassion for all that is not restricted to superficial perceptions of them, but senses them from the inside—in their parallel layers of distress, fear, grief, and so forth. At the same time, as mentioned, people have different kinds of life experience and difficulty that are conditioned by very different backgrounds and physical, social, and economic contexts. So beyond meditation, we also need other ways to educate our empathy within those differences, that help us become more aware of what others are going through in their own particularities—by building relationships with others whose lives differ from our own, getting to know them, working with them, studying history, and regularly exposing ourselves to news, journalism, literature, film, art, theater, and so forth.[17] (See the appendix for a short list of books we have found helpful in educating ourselves about the lives of people from parts of society different from our own.)

The meditations of this chapter can also help expose and undercut ways that we tend to turn away from others' difficult lives to avoid becoming more aware of how our own lives intersect with theirs. The theologian Paul Knitter succinctly states the problem, regarding those in more advantaged parts of societies: "The tendency to ignore the poor and marginalized comes not just from inattention, but from fear of confronting how we are complicit in their difficulties, insofar as we may be part of oppressive economic, social or political systems. We ignore those who suffer differently from us in order to avoid critically inquiring into the systems that bring us so much benefit."[18]

Those of us with more advantages may tend to avoid noticing or confronting others' difficult conditions because we benefit from those conditions. For example, we may resist looking into alternative ways of funding school systems because we live in a community whose funding for education is well resourced, much greater than what is available in poorer communities. Or we may resist the economic and social changes we would have to undergo to prevent further environmental damage and its impact on the poorest communities, by denying the extent of that environmental damage. Or those with generationally inherited wealth may resist tax policies designed to support those who lack such wealth because of generations of discrimination. To be willing to see how conditions that make our own lives relatively comfortable may be connected to conditions that make others' lives uncomfortable, we need a strong empathetic awareness of others' lives as they experience them.

So, besides cutting through limiting impressions of others, the compassion meditations of this chapter can also help us cultivate the deepening empathy that is needed to undercut our tendencies to avoid seeing more of what others are undergoing. In the meditations we've engaged so far in this chapter, we do this by sensing layers of suffering shared by human beings, layers we can fellow-feel with them—fears for the security and safety of loved ones; fear for one's life; sufferings of loss, grief, humiliation, feeling invisible, demeaned, the seemingly endless repetitiveness of our own painful emotions; and so forth. In what follows, as we introduce Compassion Meditation 2, we will generate empathy and compassion by working to sense, feel, and picture what others' painful experiences are like from their own perspective, which must also be informed by getting to know others whose living conditions and histories are different from our own.

INTRODUCING COMPASSION MEDITATION 2: GENERATING A STRONG WILL OF COMPASSION FOR ACTION

In Compassion Meditation 1, we become more conscious of our own layers of stress and suffering, which helps us sense from inside similar feelings that others experience in their own ways, including feelings of fear, distress, grief, frustration, loneliness, despair, and so forth. That meditation helps us make an empathetic connection to others from *inside* our own experience, so it can become natural to wish them free of suffering as we would for ourselves.

In Compassion Meditation 2, after reconnecting with the power of love and compassion in which we are held, we turn our attention *outward* to someone or some group whose suffering has deeply touched our hearts. We take time to put ourselves in their shoes, imagining how it must feel for them to experience such suffering. As our empathy for them intensifies, we let it become an intensifying wish and radiant energy of compassion for those beings. The energy of that compassionate wish then extends through them to all who suffer similarly and finally to all who undergo all the sufferings of living and dying.

In this way, Compassion Meditation 2 helps us become more conscious of how others experience their sufferings, sufferings that we may have avoided dwelling on from fear of being overwhelmed by the pain of our empathy for them. Practice of this meditation cultivates skill at converting even powerful feelings of empathy into compassion responsive to others' suffering, instead of empathic distress or empathy fatigue.[19] Then as we encounter suffering around us in our lives and the world, our compassion can become stronger, more sustainable, and proactive.

The spiritual writer Henri Nouwen tells the story of a priest he knew who told Nouwen he had stopped reading newspapers and listening to the news. When Nouwen asked him why, he said that the terrible events reported in the news disturbed his heart, making it too difficult for him to practice spiritual contemplation. Nouwen, a deep contemplative himself, was appalled. If our awareness of suffering is not taken deeply into our contemplative life, Nouwen argued, contemplation becomes a means to avoid reality rather than to more deeply engage it.[20] But to be fair to that priest, it sounds like he may have been suffering from empathic distress—that is, he was overwhelmed by his own pain of empathy for others who are suffering.

Compassion Meditation 2 Guards Against Empathic Distress

As noted, compassion *empathizes* with others in their suffering and wishes them free of it. The empathy of compassion resonates with others in their adversity, sensing and imagining what it must feel like for them to experience that. *Empathic distress* occurs when we turn *inward* and get caught up in the pain of our own empathy for others who are suffering. Can you remember a time like that, when it felt too painful for you to stay in touch with someone else's pain? Repeated empathic distress in caregivers and activists can lead to emotional exhaustion and burnout. Empathic distress often causes us to turn away from others' suffering because it feels too painful to stay connected to it, preventing us from being compassionately present to them.[21] Some people avoid the news for this reason. Or, when experiencing empathic distress, we may try to "help" a person in pain more from a desire to get rid of our own painful feelings than from a genuine concern that is focused on them.

Empathy for others who are in pain is also painful for us, but it doesn't have to devolve into an empathic distress that would prevent compassion. Instead, the pain of empathy can energize compassion. In Compassion Meditation 2, we learn to avoid empathic distress, not by avoiding others' suffering or avoiding empathy but by letting the power of love and compassion evoked by our field of care guide our empathic attention caringly *outward* toward others. This prevents us from internalizing the pain as empathic distress as our own. Instead, we generate a powerful energy and attitude of compassion that is directed *outwardly* toward others, making us more fully present to them and ready to respond. In other words, the meditation instruction specifically directs the energy of our own empathy into compassion instead of empathic distress. A further protection from empathic distress is the wisdom we have cultivated in all prior meditations of SCT and with our field of care—the awareness that suffering is never the only reality here but is embraced in a much larger reality of openness, warmth, and care in which it can transform and deeply heal.[22]

Two key purposes of Compassion Meditation 2, then, are (1) to develop skill at channeling empathy into compassion instead of empathic distress, and (2) to bring out a strong willpower of compassion for action. First, with your field of care, you reestablish your secure core of love and compassion. Then you bring to mind someone or some group whose suffering deeply touches your heart—like you can't bear that they have to experience that. You may think of someone in your family or community in that way. Or you may think of someone or a group you have heard of anywhere in the world whose suffering moves you.

The meditation instruction asks us to sense and imagine the suffering feelings that others are experiencing. But to avoid getting stuck in the pain of our strengthening empathy, we direct its energy outward as a radiant energy of compassion that wishes them deeply free and well. The principle of this practice is like the martial art of judo. When an opponent charges at a judo practitioner, the practitioner doesn't push back against the force of the other but draws on their force to throw them. Similarly, in this meditation, we don't push away or avoid the pain of our intensifying empathy but transform its energy into a strengthening energy of compassion. This skill also builds on the skill of reappraisal that we developed in prior meditations—we reappraise our empathic connection with others' pain as fuel for the energy of compassion.

Please read through Compassion Meditation 2 on page 171 now, taking special note of the instruction in step 3, which reminds us not to turn inward and get stuck in the pain of our empathy for others but to let its energy become a force of compassion that radiates to others, infusing them with its healing power. Then during the meditation, once strong empathy for others has emerged, *don't dwell on that empathy alone for very long*—let it become a powerful radiant energy and wish of compassion that radiates outward to others.

To prepare for the next meditation, please be ready in step 2 to bring to mind a field of care that gives you effective access to loving capacities of your basic awareness. In step 3, you will then be asked to bring to mind someone or some group whose suffering deeply touches your heart—like you can't bear that they have to experience that. Please be ready to do that.

(An audio option is available at shambhala.com/howcompassionworks meditations.)

COMPASSION MEDITATION 2: GENERATING A STRONG WILL OF COMPASSION FOR ACTION

STEP 1. ABDOMINAL BREATHING (2 TO 3 MINUTES) Sit in a relaxed way with back straight, eyes gazing gently downward. Come down from the thinking mind into the body. (*Pause*) Take a slow, deep breath, inhaling from the abdomen so it expands, then exhaling slowly and completely. Relax for a moment before inhaling again. Repeat several times. Now, while still breathing from the abdomen, let the breath settle into its own natural flow. Feel the belly expand and contract with each breath. Let that feeling draw you into it more and more, breath by breath. (*Pause*)

STEP 2. RECONNECTING WITH LOVE AND COMPASSION (3 TO 5 MINUTES) Now bring to mind your field of care as present here with you now. You are being seen and held in deep care, compassion, acceptance, and warmth beyond judgments. Relax into the felt sense of this experience, steeping in its loving energy and tender qualities, and letting them infuse your whole being. Accept these loving qualities into your whole body, heart, and mind—every part of you loved in its very being.

STEP 3. LETTING WHAT TOUCHES YOUR HEART EVOKE STRONG CARE AND COMPASSION (10 TO 15 MINUTES OR MORE) Now, with this loving environment as support, bring to mind a person or group whose suffering deeply touches your heart, sensing the suffering they must be experiencing. How must it feel for them in body, heart, and mind? What other feelings may be arising for them? Take some time to deepen your empathy in this way.

But don't get stuck in the pain of this empathy. Instead, supported by your field of care, let your empathy for those beings become a powerful energy of compassion that wishes them free of the suffering and deeply well. Let this intense energy and wish of compassion radiate powerfully outward from your heart as light to that person or group, infusing their whole being and world in the healing power of compassion. Imagine that this radiance supports them in their process of becoming free of distress and suffering, each in their own best way, and let yourself take joy in their relief and joy.

After a little while, let this strong, compassionate wish and energy radiate now to all others who undergo similar kinds of suffering, infusing their whole being and world in its healing power. Imagine that this radiance supports them in their process of becoming free of distress and suffering, each in their own best way, and let yourself take joy in their relief and joy.

After a little while, let this compassionate wish and energy extend to all beings who experience the sufferings of living and dying in this world, infusing their whole being and world in its healing power. Imagine that this radiance supports them in their process of becoming free of distress and suffering, and let yourself take joy in their relief and joy

STEP 4. RELEASING (3 TO 5 MINUTES) After some time, let this radiant environment of warmth and compassion help your mind to relax, settle back a bit inwardly, release all its frameworks of meditation and concern, and come to rest in the background of its awareness, which is naturally wide open and luminous, like a sunlit sky. As thoughts and feelings arise, let them just metabolize themselves and release within this sky-like openness of awareness by letting everything be.

When you finish the meditation, let the felt sense of it continue to resonate.

Processing the Meditation

Let's review key principles of this meditation now in light of having just done it. Again, empathic distress occurs when our attention turns inward on ourselves, so we get caught up in our own feelings of pain from empathizing with others. In contrast, the power of love and compassion in Compassion Meditation 2 converts our empathic pain into an energy of compassion that radiates outward to others, holding them in its healing power. In that way, we don't internalize or confuse others' suffering as our own empathic distress. The more intense our empathy for beings who are suffering, the more intense is the force of our compassion that is directed outward to them. We imagine that the radiance of this compassion supports them in their process of becoming free of distress and suffering, and we let ourselves take joy in their relief and joy. This cultivates our innate capacities and energies of care, compassion, and sympathetic joy. To become present to others with those qualities can be empowering and supportive for them, even at subliminal levels of everyone's awareness.

A further protection from empathic distress is the wisdom we have cultivated in all the prior meditations of this book—the awareness that suffering is never the only reality here but is embraced in a much larger reality of openness, warmth, and care in which it can transform and deeply heal. That larger reality is the deep nature of mind, buddha nature, whose qualities are accessed at the start, when we evoke our field of care and reunify with its healing environment. Compassion Meditation 2 also points us in a direction of creative responsiveness for action by turning our attention to others' best ways of becoming free from suffering, encouraging us to deepen our learning in support of their liberative process.

In the last step of the meditation, the "releasing phase," we let the radiant energies and qualities of love and compassion that have been generated in the meditation help the mind release its narrow frameworks of self-clinging and begin to settle into the source of those qualities—the utter openness, lucidity, and warmth of its buddha nature. Some may think of that releasing phase as a letting go of compassion, but that would be inaccurate. In the earlier steps of the meditation, we connected with qualities of compassion within a dualistic framework of self and others. In the final releasing step, we start to reunite with the very source of compassion in the lucid empty nature of the mind, in which we are undivided from others. At that ultimate level, to abide in the very ground of compassion—the empty, sky-like nature of mind—is to commune with others in a space of deep inner freedom, beyond dualism, beyond thinking, subliminally evoking their potential to awaken similarly to the deep nature of their minds beyond suffering. It is to resonate with them in their inmost nature of freedom, blessing that nature in them to come to self-recognition. It is to touch them at the depth of their being. From a Tibetan Buddhist perspective, this is what our spiritual benefactors, enlightened beings, have been doing for us long before we had noticed. Their awakened buddha nature has communed with our own, blessing it to awaken similarly—to actualize itself in compassionate energy and service to others. Our earlier stories of Nechung Rinpoche (chapter 1), Geshe Thupten Tsering (chapter 3), and the Buddha (chapter 4) exemplified this way of being.

Notice how all those principles are embedded in the instruction of this short meditation.

Letting Compassion Meditation 2
Inform Our Lives and Actions

Often in life, the suffering of someone we know or hear about (on the news, via social media, or elsewhere) stirs powerful feelings of empathy that can be disturbing to us. Perhaps most of the time, we don't know what to do with those feelings other than to turn away, suppress the feelings, or be overcome by empathic distress. In contrast, this meditation converts even our most painful feelings of empathy into compassion—the stronger our empathy for beings who are suffering, the more powerful is the energy of our compassion for them that radiates to them and wishes them deeply free and well.

Part of the meditation instructs us to imagine that the radiance of compassion supports others in their process of becoming free of distress and suffering, each in their own best way. That instruction points us in a direction of creative responsiveness for action by turning our attention to others' best ways of becoming free from suffering, encouraging us to deepen our learning from them in support of that process.

Such compassionate action can take many forms according to circumstance and need: paying fuller attention to someone who is little cared for by others; providing a smile of encouragement or appreciation; listening deeply to someone who needs to be heard, in ways that help them discern their hidden strengths; joining with others to address an urgent need in the community; helping to address systemic problems in education, health, housing, or the environment; supporting initiatives to meet pressing needs of those who suffer from violence, hunger, discrimination, neglect, disastrous effects of climate change, and so forth.

As we engage in such activities, we learn from others and become more familiar with causes and aspects of suffering that we would not have known without having gotten involved. This fuller, engaged knowledge of suffering and its causes can then inform our meditations of compassion, which empower further forms of action, which further inform our meditations.

According to Buddhist psychology, the energy and will of compassion, in itself, even before doing anything else, is also considered an action—a powerful action of intentionality and presence. You are willing to be compassionately present with another in their suffering rather than immediately trying to fix them to assuage your own discomfort with their suffering. Perhaps you can recall a time when you were willing to be present to someone who was in pain without turning away—willing to listen deeply to them with empathy and care—and they experienced that, in itself, as deeply supportive and healing. Or recall a time when someone was present to you in that way. Such a power of care and presence, willing to be with others who are in pain, is itself an action that can profoundly affect peoples' well-being, and it can then take shape in many further kinds of action.[23]

In sum, Compassion Meditation 2 provides a safe way to stop hiding from painful feelings of empathy that are triggered by others' sufferings, empowering us to notice more of the suffering around us with a growing strength and courage of compassion. The increasing power of compassion from this practice can become a force to pay fuller attention to the suffering in our communities and world, making us more present to others in ways that support them in meeting individual and systemic needs.

When you feel ready, you can do Compassion Meditation 2 in daily practice, connecting with it each morning and touching in on it as you can throughout the day, letting it freshly inform and affect your life in the ways noted above. Both Compassionate Meditation 1 and 2 can also be taken into daily life in the form of tong-len, which we will discuss.

FORMS OF JOY EVOKED BY THESE
PRACTICES OF COMPASSION

Many people are surprised at how quietly joyful renowned meditation teachers can be, like those mentioned in prior chapters, despite their focus on compassion and suffering. Tibetan Buddhism holds that compassion practices over time naturally produce various experiences of joy. Some of the forms of joy evoked by these practices include:

The joy of discovering that our own sufferings and struggles are connecting rather than isolating; that they are a door of empathy and compassion for others.

The joy of becoming more fully aware of and present to the sufferings of others that are different from our own, which opens a doorway to new connections and relationships.

The joy of getting real; of not having to hide from the fears, griefs, pain, and struggles of ourselves or others.

The joy of discovering a power of compassion that can embrace such sufferings unconditionally in a healing, transformative way.

The joy of participating in compassionate activity, not only admiring others who have done good for others but learning to become what we admire in them. Taking the growing confidence of compassion from these meditation practices into our activities—our ways of being and working with others.

TONG-LEN AS A WAY TO TAKE DAILY EXPERIENCE
INTO COMPASSION AND WISDOM

Tong-len has been a widespread form of practice in Tibetan Buddhism for transforming ordinary experiences into qualities of awakening. Tong-len expresses a profound form of reappraisal at the heart of Tibetan Buddhism. It involves reevaluating our ordinary, day-to-day experience as an opportunity for awakening and reengaging it in ways designed to bring out powers of love, compassion, and wisdom from our buddha nature in an increasingly sustainable and unconditional way. Instead of viewing difficulties of self and others as just miserable, we reframe them and practice with them as allies of awakening. Instead of viewing moments of happiness as just our own, we mentally share them with many others. The practice involves exchanging our usual sense of concern, focused narrowly on ourselves, for a concern expansively focused on others. We *accept* the difficulties (Tib. *len*) and *offer* our well-being (Tib. *tong*). Such repeated practice increasingly cuts through the self-grasping patterns of mind that have been impeding our buddha nature and holding back its qualities.[24]

We will learn two forms of tong-len here. Tong-len Meditation 1 builds on Compassion Meditation 1 and takes it into our daily life by noticing our feelings of distress and suffering as they arise in our day, and letting those feelings become a basis of empathy and compassion for all who harbor similar feelings. Tong-len Meditation 2 builds on Compassion Meditation 2, evoking compassion in our daily life by letting the sufferings of others touch our hearts and open them to the subliminal power of compassion that they hold.

Both forms of tong-len thus provide ways to practice in daily life that can transform our experience of suffering in ourselves and others into powers of compassion and wisdom for action, and to empower the awakening mind of *bodhicitta*—the will to fully awaken our innate positive capacities for the sake of all beings.

INTRODUCTION TO TONG-LEN
MEDITATION 1 WITH TWO OPTIONS

Tong-len meditation 1 can be done with the support of either your field of care or your practice of compassionate presence to feelings, whichever is most effective for you. Both of those approaches are guided. In both cases, the meditation begins with your own feelings of distress and suffering, which become a basis of empathy and compassion for others who experience analogous feelings. In this form of tong-len, supported by your field of care or compassionate presence to feelings, you become a spacious healing environment for your own painful feelings, which then becomes a healing environment for all others with analogous feelings. Then, in the final step, you let the loving qualities that have been evoked by the practice help your mind to settle back into the source of those qualities—the emptiness, lucidity, and compassionate capacity of the mind's deep nature, buddha nature.

(An audio option is available at shambhala.com/howcompassionworks meditations.)

TONG-LEN MEDITATION 1, SUPPORTED BY A FIELD OF CARE: TAKING YOUR OWN PAINFUL FEELINGS INTO COMPASSION

STEP 1. FINDING A PAINFUL FEELING WITH WHICH TO PRACTICE Bring to mind something you've been worrying about, struggling with, or suffering through recently so that you experience the difficult emotional feeling that comes with that—for example, a feeling of fear, anxiety, loneliness, sadness, frustration, anger, longing, fear for a loved one, a painful reacting to pain or illness, and the like. Then drop the situation or person who triggered the emotion and give your attention just to the feeling of it—how it feels in your body and mind.

STEP 2. BECOMING A HEALING ENVIRONMENT FOR THAT FEELING (5 MINUTES) Bring to mind your field of care as present here with you now. Relax into the felt sense of this field, steeping in its loving energies and tender qualities, and letting them infuse your whole being. Let the suffering feeling you brought to mind also be embraced in this spacious warmth, acceptance, and loving energy. Rest with this feeling spaciously in that way, without rejecting it, without trying to solve or change anything in it. Like a sympathetic friend with a troubled friend, let the feeling have all the space it needs to feel welcome, relax, metabolize itself, and begin to heal in its own time. (*Pause*) By aerating the feeling in this way with spacious acceptance and warmth, the feeling may even begin to reveal inner qualities of well-being, spaciousness, and peace from deep within it.

STEP 3. BECOMING A HEALING ENVIRONMENT FOR OTHERS (5 MINUTES) Now remember that many other beings experience suffering feelings like this one of yours. Think of your own suffering feeling now as one with theirs and that by providing this healing environment for your feeling, you are providing it also for others. Imagine that by aerating this feeling with spacious acceptance and warmth from your field of care, you are aerating it in all the others, through which they become free of the suffering and deeply well. Let yourself take joy in their relief and joy.

STEP 4. RELEASING (3 TO 5 MINUTES) Now drop the visualization, let your mind relax deeply, settle back a bit inwardly, and come to rest in the background of its awareness, which is naturally wide open and luminous, like a sunlit sky. As thoughts and feelings arise, let them just metabolize themselves and release within this sky-like openness of awareness by letting everything be.

After a little while, when your mind begins to feel troubled or upset about anything, take that feeling into the same four steps of this practice. Steps 1, 2, and 3 bring out qualities of warmth, empathy, compassion, and sympathetic joy from our buddha nature. Step 4 brings out qualities of deepening equanimity and discernment.

TONG-LEN MEDITATION 1, SUPPORTED BY COMPASSIONATE PRESENCE TO FEELINGS: TAKING YOUR OWN PAINFUL FEELINGS INTO COMPASSION

STEP 1. BECOMING A HEALING ENVIRONMENT FOR A PAINFUL FEELING (5 TO 10 MINUTES) Think of something you've been worrying about, struggling with, or suffering through recently so that you experience the painful emotional feeling that comes with that—for example, a feeling of fear, anxiety, loneliness, sadness, frustration, anger, longing, fear for a loved one, a feeling about illness or pain, and the like. Now drop the situation or person who triggered the emotion and give your attention just to the feeling of it—how it feels in your body and mind. Give this suffering feeling deep permission to be here, allowing it to have all the space it needs to find its own place in its own time. Rest with this feeling spaciously in that way, without rejecting it, without trying to solve or change anything in it. Like a sympathetic friend with a troubled friend, let the feeling have all the space it needs to feel safe here; to relax, metabolize itself, and begin to heal in its own time. (*Pause*) By aerating the feeling in this way with spacious acceptance and warmth, the feeling may even begin to reveal inner qualities of well-being, spaciousness, and peace from deep within it.

STEP 2. BECOMING A HEALING ENVIRONMENT FOR OTHERS (5 TO 10 MINTUES) Now remember that many other beings experience suffering feelings like this one of yours. Think of your own suffering feeling now as one with theirs and that by providing this healing environment for your feeling, you are providing it also for others. By aerating this feeling with spacious acceptance and warmth, you are aerating it in all others. Imagine, through this, that they become free of the suffering of this feeling and deeply well, and let yourself take joy in their relief and joy.

STEP 3. RELEASING (3 TO 5 MINUTES) Now drop the visualization, let your mind relax deeply, settle back a bit inwardly, and come to rest in the background of its awareness, which is naturally wide open and luminous, like a sunlit sky. As thoughts and feelings arise, let them just metabolize themselves and release within this sky-like openness of awareness by letting everything be.

After a little while, when your mind begins to feel troubled or upset about anything, take that feeling into the same three steps of this practice.

Processing the Meditation

It is good to do Tong-len Meditation 1, in either option, often, not only in formal meditation sessions but also off the cushion and frequently in our daily lives. Choose the option that works best for you. Take feelings of struggle and difficulty that arise in your day right into this practice. This becomes an ongoing discovery that our feelings are not just our own but a doorway into empathetic connection with what many other beings are going through. In this practice, we are sensing others as our larger self while transforming painful emotions we share into qualities of awakening: warmth, empathy, compassion, wisdom, sympathetic joy, and solidarity. The difficult feelings that we had not wanted are rediscovered as a valuable resource for cultivating the compassion and wisdom of the bodhisattva path. The difficulties of samsara themselves become the fuel of awakening.

As with prior practices, with repeated practice of Tong-len Meditation 1, the qualities of warmth, acceptance, and openness that encompass each emotion can become part of the experience of that emotion in our daily life. Also, the empathetic connection we make to others through our emotional feeling in the meditation can become an increasing tendency to make that connection when experiencing difficult emotions in our days. In time, our most familiar difficulties can spontaneously generate compassion for many others even as we are experiencing them.

We can also do this kind of practice with happy experiences that we have in our days, mentally sharing the joy that they bring to us with others, as a radiant offering to them all.

INTRODUCTION TO TONG-LEN MEDITATION 2: DEEPENING AND EXPANDING COMPASSION

In Tong-len Meditation 2, you bring to mind a being or group whose suffering deeply touches your heart, to evoke a deep, genuine feeling of care and empathy. You let that empathy become a strong compassion for them that cuts through the patterns of self-clinging in your mind by imagining that you take their sufferings into yourself and offer them all your care, resources, and well-being in the form of radiance, to support them in their process of becoming free from suffering. Then you extend this same radiant compassion to all beings who suffer similarly, beyond in-group and out-group categories, which brings out the fuller capacity of your buddha nature. In the last step, you let the compassionate qualities of the meditation help your mind settle back into the source of those qualities—the emptiness, lucidity, and capacity of the mind's deep nature.

This practice is done in order to strengthen and expand our innate capacities of care and compassion to greater inclusiveness and unconditionality, as a power of presence and motivation for action responsive to suffering.

(An audio option is available at shambhala.com/howcompassionworks meditations.)

TONG-LEN MEDITATION 2: DEEPENING AND EXPANDING COMPASSION

STEP 1. ACCESSING STRONG EMPATHY AND CARE Bring to mind someone or some group that you know or have heard of, whose painful experience really touches your heart; as though you can't bear that they have to experience such suffering. Let that evoke your strong empathy and care for them as a heartfelt wish for them to be able to be free of the suffering and its causes, each in their own best way, so they can be deeply well.

STEP 2. TAKING IN OTHERS' SUFFERING AND BREAKING THE SHELL OF SELF-CLINGING Let that strong wish of compassion take expression by envisioning their sufferings as a cloud, which you absorb into your heart so they can be freed from the suffering. As that cloud is absorbed into your heart, it breaks open a shell of self-clinging at your heart through which radiant light spontaneously pours out.

STEP 3. OFFERING TO OTHERS AND TAKING JOY IN THEIR RELIEF (5 OR MORE MINUTES) Imagine this radiance from your heart pervades that person's or group's whole being, offering all of your care, well-being, and resources to them through the light. Imagine that this radiance supports them in their process of becoming free of distress and suffering, each in their own best way, and let yourself feel joy in their relief and joy. (*Pause*)

Repeat steps 1 through 3 several times with that same being or group.

STEP 4. EXTENDING TO MANY OTHERS (5 OR MORE MINUTES) Now extend this practice by thinking of all others that suffer in similar ways, and imagine this radiance from your heart pervades their bodies and minds, offering all of your care, well-being, and resources to them through the light. Imagine that radiance supports them in their process of becoming free of distress and suffering, each in their own best way, and let yourself feel joy in their relief and joy. Finally, think of all beings that experience the sufferings of living and dying throughout the world and do the same.

STEP 5. RELEASING (3 TO 5 MINUTES) Now drop the visualization and let your mind relax deeply, settle back a bit inwardly, and come to rest in the background of its awareness, which is naturally wide open and radiant like a sun-lit sky. As thoughts and feelings arise, let them just metabolize themselves and release within this sky-like openness of awareness by letting everything be.

Processing the Meditation

The "shell of self-clinging at your heart" mentioned in step 2 refers to our tendency to cling to our limiting impressions of self and others and associated reactions, which impedes our underlying capacity for fuller presence. In the meditation, we imagine that our willingness, out of compassion, to take on others' suffering and offer our well-being cracks open that shell of self-clinging, which spontaneously releases energies of love and compassion that have been hidden in our being by that shell. The imagination is harnessed here in ways that help open up channels of subtle energy in our bodies and minds that support greater openness, compassion, unconditional presence, and responsiveness.

These two forms of tong-len are employed to transform our conditioned patterns of self-clinging into an increasingly all-inclusive and powerful compassion for others, to generate bodhicitta (the will to fully realize our buddha nature for the sake of all beings), and to empower action to address suffering.[25]

Taking Tong-len into Daily Life

When you have familiarized yourself with Compassion Meditation 1 and 2, you can increasingly experience their transformative power in your daily life by doing either of those meditations in the morning and then reconnecting with either of them during breaks in your day. Or, since Tong-len Meditation 1 and 2 build directly on those Compassion Meditations, you can also reconnect with the transformative power of the latter meditations by practicing the two Tong-len Meditations throughout your day.

Tong-len in Tibet was designed to be accessible and practicable in all the situations of our lives without having to establish a separate meditative environment for practice. In light of tong-len, life itself becomes the practice—every experience can be taken into it. With familiarization, whatever is encountered can increasingly come into tong-len, where it is converted into a fuel for actualizing qualities of our buddha nature, empowering compassionate presence to others, service, and action.

In daily practice, you could do either option of Compassion Meditation 1 (with a field of care or with compassionate presence to feelings) in the morning, then do either option of Tong-len Meditation 1 repeatedly throughout the day as various situations stir up difficult feelings in you. In this way, Tong-len Meditation 1 becomes a situated expression of Compassion Meditation 1. On other mornings, you could do Compassion Meditation 2, then Tong-len Meditation 2 throughout the day as a further expression of that. When you are familiar with all of these meditations, whichever Compassion Meditation you do in the morning, you can follow up by doing Tong-len Meditations throughout the day—letting moments of difficulty evoke Tong-len Meditation 1; letting moments of empathy with others evoke Tong-len Meditation 2. In moments of enjoyment and happiness, tong-len can take the simple form of imagining that your pleasure and joy takes expression as radiance from your heart that shares your joy with many others.

THE SYNERGY OF COMPASSION AND WISDOM

In the releasing phase of each meditation in this book, and in the Letting Be meditation, we let the infinite openness and lucidity of our buddha nature—our innate wisdom—increasingly unify us with it. As we learn to reunify with that depth of awareness, we also become newly conscious of ways that our mind has gotten lost from that depth—by habitually identifying with its own narrow constructs of and reactions to self and others; lost from the fuller reality of them all. This dawning wisdom thereby reveals layers of suffering in us that we share with others, strengthening our compassion for everyone in those layers. As our compassion thus deepens and expands to include all, it further empowers the mind to release its fixation on its own narrow constructs and reactions, enabling it to settle more fully into the infinite source of the compassion—the utter openness, lucidity, and capacity of its buddha nature, its innate wisdom. That wisdom senses and upholds all others in that same deep nature, which we all share. In this way, all-inclusive compassion and the all-pervasive openness and lucidity of innate wisdom increasingly empower each other as we familiarize ourselves with these meditation practices.

COMPASSION, WISDOM, AND EQUANIMITY

Several kinds of equanimity emerge as we reconnect with this synergy of compassion and wisdom in regular practice, which can stabilize and ground our ways of being and acting in the world. One kind of equanimity is the *impartiality and inclusiveness* of the compassion and wisdom we are cultivating, which cares for all beings in their layers of suffering while upholding them all in the vast positive capacity of their deep nature—their buddha nature. As we become conscious of more layers of suffering that we share with others—our painful forms of reactivity, grief of loss, fear of dying, fear for loved ones, and so forth—this knowledge opens our perception of others. We become less exclusively focused on superficial appearances or social assumptions about them and more focused on their fuller reality—not only their intrinsic dignity and worth but also their inner layers of distress and suffering. Such deepening empathy further undercuts limiting images of others as merely this or that—as "just a stranger," "just an old guy," just a kid," just someone "taking too long in line," or with regard to other species, "just an animal." The practice empowers equanimity less bound by bias, by upholding something worthy of deep care and compassion in everyone. This kind of equanimity cuts through the socially conditioned tendency in every society to care for one's in-groups while seeing many others as far less worthy of reverence or care.[26]

A second kind of equanimity that accompanies this growing synergy of compassion and wisdom is *freedom from expectations*; from clinging attachment to circumstances, goals, or outcomes. Our minds may become discouraged when we wish someone who is sick to become well but their condition worsens over time. Or our wish for an alcoholic friend to improve their life may turn into anger at them when they refuse to improve themselves. But the unity of compassion and wisdom that we are cultivating emerges from beyond our ego-based goals for others and therefore need not be significantly affected by shifting circumstances. It is a force of care that wills the inner freedom and well-being of persons no matter what happens. Learning to release our goals in the releasing phase of all our meditations helps us learn how to hold goals more lightly in post-meditation and in action. So when suffering conditions can be changed, if one way to bring benefit does not work, we can try another way. The number of tries doesn't have to matter so much. We don't have to take it personally, since the power of compassion can continue to radiate and call us back to action again and again in fresh and innovative ways. This is the sort of force of care and tenacity that has empowered the perseverance in action of figures such as Harriet Tubman, Dolores Huerta, Nelson Mandela, Fannie Lou Hamer, and Dorothy Day.[27]

The energy, perspective, and will of compassion is itself an action that can beneficially affect people and the world around us, even when the time inevitably comes for any of us to undergo kinds of illness or affliction that are not curable, even unto death. The beneficial power of compassionate presence to someone who is terribly ill or dying is palpable for all those affected, as many know from their own experience with dying loved ones.

A third kind of equanimity also emerges as this synergy of compassion and wisdom helps us experience all the sufferings of ourselves and others as encompassed in the larger reality of *unconditional compassion and openness.* This brings out a deep sense of inner safety, calm, and peace in the face of suffering, yet with a growing power of care for all who suffer, not just apathy. To experience suffering not as the only reality here but as embraced in the larger reality of infinite openness, warmth, and care also protects us from empathic distress, from being overwhelmed by the pain of our empathy for others, since we become increasingly grounded in the reality of care, compassion, and wisdom rather than in the experience of suffering alone.[28]

Above, we noted several forms of joy that emerge from compassion practice. A further type of joy emerges with these forms of equanimity. As we loosen the grip of expectations, attachments, and goals and tap into an inner dimension of unconditional openness and warmth within all experiences, we sense the possibility of engaging with suffering from a place of joy, knowing that it is compassion and wisdom, not suffering per se, that has the last word. Warmth, ease, openness, and well-being can remain steady even as we encounter and work with suffering because the suffering is embraced in compassion that holds the possibility of liberation from that suffering.

The sun doesn't get discouraged when there are clouds; it keeps radiating regardless. Similarly, the unconditional care and compassion that we are cultivating, when increasingly stabilized and endowed with all these kinds of equanimity, can keep radiating to everyone around us wherever we are, no matter what anyone may think, say, do, or not do. Such a force of care can continue to motivate action to benefit others no matter what happens. We thus learn through this practice how to reconnect with and stabilize a force of care that can protect us from burnout and empathy fatigue, from the tendency to lose our caring motivation. It is this unconditional power of compassion and wisdom, associated with these three kinds of equanimity, that is the most effective motivational power for service and action.

COMPASSION CONFIRMS THE DIGNITY OF BEINGS WHILE CONFRONTING THEIR HARMFUL TENDENCIES

In the previous chapter we noted that authentic love, because it is in touch with the deep dignity and positive capacity of beings in their buddha nature, upholds that positive potential in them even when confronting their harmful ways of thinking or acting. Indeed, to confront someone out of love is a way of confirming their positive potential—by challenging what obstructs it.

As compassion informed by wisdom becomes increasingly aware of all three levels of suffering in beings (empowered by the compassion meditations above), the power to confront people's destructive behaviors as a genuine expression of love and compassion deepens. This is because we become more conscious of the layers of suffering and self-grasping in ourselves and others that drive our harmful behaviors. At the same time, we also become more conscious of the depth of ourselves and others in our buddha nature; the unconditioned openness, lucidity, and vast capacity that is always prior to and more fundamental than our conditioned reactions and behaviors. Our increasing ability to discern both the conditioned layers of suffering and the unconditioned depth in ourselves and others empowers a growing ability to simultaneously confirm and confront—to confront what hides someone's positive capacity on behalf of that capacity in them.

Genuine compassion, therefore, does not involve condoning destructive behavior, policies, or systems. It confronts what is destructive in persons in order to uphold and confirm their fuller humanity and potential. The wisdom of compassion distinguishes between a person's harmful behaviors and the person, confronting the person's behaviors on behalf of the person. A loving parent confronts a child involved in destructive behaviors not from hatred but from love, with a deep concern for the child's well-being. A good therapist or counselor doesn't just accept their patient's habitual ways of thinking about themselves and others but often challenges them. Martin Luther King Jr. repeatedly taught his followers to confront racism in people and communities not out of hatred for them but on behalf of their fuller humanity. For confrontation to promote positive change effectively, it needs to express genuine care for those confronted.

We can test this in our own experience. When we challenge someone's actions with deep respect and care for them, what happens? When we challenge someone in a self-righteously angry way that has little real care and respect for them, what happens? All the contemplative practices we are learning empower us increasingly to maintain awareness of the dignity and potential of each person, even when it is necessary to confront harmful behaviors and systems.

This depth of discernment and responsiveness runs counter to the common social tendency to denigrate some people on behalf of others—to loathe the bad ones (the "oppressors" or "victimizers") as part of what it means to defend the good ones against them (the "oppressed" or "victims"). Although we are all subject to this socially conditioned reaction to harm, it feeds the underlying causality of harm by assuming, in any context, that some are worthy of care and others are not. To assume that, and to act on it, *is* to harm. It is the assumption operative in all of us when we become the ones who harm whoever we perceive as unworthy of any care.

Authentic compassion runs directly counter to this tendency by being aware of both the destructive tendencies and the underlying positive capacity in everyone involved in any situation. This point has been articulated and embodied by figures like Thich Nhat Hanh, Archbishop Desmond Tutu, bell hooks, the Dalai Lama, Maya Angelou, and others. Our meditations of compassion and wisdom help open a door into that kind of discernment, responsiveness, and as needed, caring confrontation.

5

INTEGRATING PRACTICES OF LOVE, COMPASSION, AND WISDOM WITH OUR LIVES

THIS CHAPTER WILL DISCUSS how all the practices we've learned in prior chapters can be integrated into our lives to inform and empower our relationships, work, service, and action in the world. All of our activities can inform our meditations, and each meditation can increasingly inform our activities and our responsiveness to others. The key to integration is repetition of practice. The meditation training we've presented involves a great amount of repetition, repeatedly reinhabiting and settling into experiences of love, compassion, communion, inner healing, openness, awareness, and responsiveness that are evoked by the meditations. Over months of practice of each meditation, a practitioner will have repeated such experiences thousands of times, a process that can gradually train the mind and body for increasing ease in accessing, deepening into, and holding others in qualities of love, compassion, and awareness.

First, a reminder about the importance of motivation for any contemplative practice. If our motivation to do the meditations is weak, we won't have a strong enough interest in the meditation instructions to keep bringing our attention back to them when distracted. For success in meditation, therefore, prior to any practice, we need to reconnect with our motivation. A basic motivation for the practices in this book is to bring out unconditional powers of love, compassion, and wisdom from the depth of our being, with which to become more fully present to others in the depth of their being for the sake of all.

The meditations introduced in the introduction of this book are excellent practices for establishing powers of attention and calm that are drawn upon in all the other meditations of this book. We recommend you choose one or two of those to do when you first sit down to meditate each day. Meditations from the introduction of abdominal breathing and settling into body or breath have also been incorporated into many of the other meditations in this book.

Long daily meditation sessions are not necessary if that doesn't fit into your life. We need one morning meditation session each day as an anchor, which we can then touch in on briefly, repeatedly, throughout the day. This is what can gradually transform the patterning of our mind and heart. If we don't meditate each day, in the morning if possible, there won't be anything to integrate into the rest of the day. But if we rest in the unconditional power of openness, warmth, and care each morning in daily meditation, we can return to that perspective and flow of energy repeatedly throughout the day in many moments. Then warmth, compassion, and wisdom can flow more freely into our relationships and interactions, even before we speak or act, and take more frequent expression in our words and actions. By recalling the perspective and attitude of morning meditation throughout the day, we learn to commune with others at the level of the heart, below the reactivity of the head, transmitting the energy of care and compassion to whomever we meet, live with, work with, or even think of.

Start by focusing on one or two of the meditations that are most connecting and inspiring for you. For many people, the Field of Care Meditation (receptive mode) becomes the main point of entry into the arc of practice in this book. For others, a meditation in deepening or inclusive mode, or a combination of two meditations—such as the Field of Care Meditation and the Letting Be of Body, Breath, and Mind meditation—may serve as their best main entry point. Practice whichever meditation is most connecting for you first thing in the morning for whatever length of time you can: twenty minutes or more if possible. If your time is limited, even ten minutes of morning meditation can give you the touchstone needed for the rest of your day. The morning meditation provides the perspective and attitude with which to reconnect many times throughout the day, even briefly. As we repeat the practice, it becomes more likely that the qualities of the practice will be reenacted and infused throughout the day.

Because each mode of practice empowers the other two modes, to repeatedly reconnect with any of the meditations prepares us to access all the others. Receptivity to loving qualities (receptive mode) empowers our ability to reunite with their source (deepening mode) from which to extend care (inclusive mode), which empowers the prior two modes in turn. If we focus on one or two meditations for weeks or months in daily practice, it prepares us to focus on the next meditation for a similar period, then on the next meditation, taking them into daily practice as described above.

Most people choose the Field of Care Meditation (receptive mode) as their starting point because the deep healing it provides feels crucial to them to bring out all other possibilities of love, compassion, and wisdom. By repeating that form of meditation many times in their days, they become increasingly skilled at accessing an inner secure base of loving qualities and awareness that supports all other meditations and empowers their lives with others. Some find the Compassionate Presence to Feelings Meditation (deepening mode) works best as their starting point for practice because it helps them become a healing environment for all their feelings in such a direct way. This helps them to embrace the feelings stirred up in their days and to become more compassionately present to others. Both of those meditations establish the inner secure base of positive qualities that help the mind settle into the source of those qualities in the Letting Be of Body, Breath, and Mind meditation (also deepening mode).

As we familiarize ourselves with those receptive and deepening modes of meditation, they empower us to take up the Inclusive-Mode Meditation and Compassion Meditations (including tong-len) in several ways. First, the receptive and deepening modes evoke qualities of love and compassion as a healing environment for all of our feelings. That same loving environment is then extended to many others in the Inclusive-Mode Meditation and Compassion Meditations. Second, the releasing phase of each meditation and the Letting Be of Body, Breath, and Mind meditation helps us settle into the source of those loving qualities in the depth of our minds, our buddha nature. There we find a depth in ourselves from which to uphold others in the depth of their being within the Inclusive-Mode Meditation and

Compassion Meditations. Third, the loving qualities and depth of our being that are accessed in the receptive and deepening modes of practice provide an inner secure base of well-being and safety that gives us confidence to become more conscious of layers of suffering in ourselves and others that meditations of compassion engage.

With increasing familiarity to all the modes of practice in this book, there comes a deepening trust in the qualities that they evoke in us—loving-kindness toward all parts of ourselves and others, compassion, healing, inner calm, courage, inner freedom, creative responsiveness, wisdom. With increasing trust, we are more willing to be given over to the instruction of each meditation.

In that spirit, when doing meditation, put yourself into it as fully as possible. During the meditation session, don't worry about trying to figure out what is happening. Instead, let the powers of warmth, acceptance, compassion, and wisdom evoked by the practice increasingly emerge in their own way. You can reflect more discursively on implications and meanings of the practice after your meditation session. But during the actual meditation, just follow its instruction, letting the qualities it evokes provide you with fresh insights and discernment.

When beginning this path of meditation practice, you may initially be drawn to a combination of two meditations. In that case you could do both meditations together in the morning session, then reconnect with one or both repeatedly throughout your day.

SETTING UP A DAILY PRACTICE

It is important to make time for a meditation session in the morning before the activities of your day unfold. For that morning session, do the meditation that's your current focus of practice as the touchstone for your day, with whatever time you can make available. Then touch in on that meditation briefly many times throughout the day, even if just for a minute or two at a time. In that way, the meditation informs your day by reconnecting you repeatedly to awakening qualities that open new perspectives and possibilities of discernment and responsiveness. Over a period of months, you will have reconnected thousands of times. Contemplative scientists and attachment theorists posit that such repetition may gradually change the patterning of our hearts and minds by strengthening neural connections that correspond to fuller awareness, care, compassion, and discernment.[1]

Many people say that they don't have time to meditate, as if meditation can only happen in long sessions that would interfere with daily responsibilities. But even a ten-minute meditation in the morning can provide the anchor to reconnect with awakening qualities in short breaks throughout the day. To reconnect so regularly with your sources of positive energy and discernment can only help you become more fully present and effective in your activities. The ability to sustain a meditation practice may require us to make choices that help foster a supportive environment for the morning meditation. Removing access to technology in the physical space, for example, can help us have fewer distracting thoughts.[2] Similarly, you can pay attention to and prioritize the situational factors in your life that help the mind and body to feel inspired, at ease, and relaxed for meditation. Paul, for example, has noticed that allowing himself breaks in his workday, even in small moments, and holding boundaries around his schedule helps his mind find a sense of ease throughout the day in which to reconnect repeated with the spirit of meditation. In a similar way, we can continue to pay attention to and prioritize the work, relationships, and activities that help us to connect with qualities of our deeper awareness.

If the Field of Care Meditation is your first focus of practice, you can then explore over time which of the other meditations it connects you to next, within your own process. For example, the experience of the field of care may empower fuller engagement with one of the practices of attention and calm that were introduced in the introductory chapter. Over time, the latter practices could become benefactors that help draw your mind into the present serving as anchors that are always available when the mind gets lost in conceptual ruminations or intense effort. Or at some point, the field of care practice, by making you into a healing environment for feelings, may inspire you to connect to the Compassionate Presence to Feelings Meditation to give even fuller attention to that way of being with feelings. At that time, in the morning session, you might touch in on the Field of Care Meditation more briefly and spend more time on the Compassionate Presence to Feelings Meditation, and then touch in on compassionate presence many times in your day.

In that example, after further months of practice, you might wish to shift your main meditation to Letting Be of Body, Breath, and Mind or to the Inclusive-Mode Meditation, whichever helps you access more of your innate capacities at that point in your own unfolding process. In that case, you might briefly touch in on the Field of Care Meditation or Compassionate Presence to Feelings Meditation in the morning session but spend more time on the Letting Be of Body, Breath, and Mind or the Inclusive-Mode Meditation as your main morning meditation. Then you would reconnect with that main meditation repeatedly in the day. And when you feel ready, you can engage the compassion meditations and tong-len as your main daily meditations.

As you become familiar with all of these meditations over months of practice, you might want to explore alternating two or more practices in many moments of your day—one that involves more effort to mentally construct and one that is less effortful. The meditations that involve less constructive effort are the meditations for cultivating attention and calm that were introduced in the introduction, Compassionate Presence to Feelings Meditation, and Letting Be Meditation. Meditations that involve a little more constructive effort are the Field of Care, Inclusive-Mode and Compassion Meditations, including tong-len.

When you are quite familiar with the various meditations, you may want to explore alternating your main meditation month by month. For example, you might focus on the Inclusive-Mode Meditation one month (as in chapter 3), then one of the Compassion Meditations the next month. Or you might alternate between the various Compassion Meditations month by month.

RECONNECTING WITH YOUR MORNING MEDITATION TO BECOME A HEALING ENVIRONMENT FOR YOURSELF AND OTHERS

If the Field of Care or Compassionate Presence to Feelings Meditation is your main practice in the morning, then in many moments throughout your day you can reconnect with that way of being, each time becoming a healing environment for all parts of yourself. Take whatever feelings and reactions arise in your day into that form of meditation even as you experience them. For example, when you notice that you are looking down on others or feeling anxious, afraid, angry, despairing, lonely, judged, and so forth, take that feeling right into field of care or compassionate presence practice on the spot, becoming a healing environment for any such feelings, letting them metabolize themselves in their own way. As you do that frequently in your day, try to notice how this way of being affects your well-being, your vision of others, the quality of your presence to them, and their ways of responding to you. From that place of groundedness and equanimity, you could also reconnect with the Inclusive-Mode Meditation, abide in its loving qualities and power of presence, and notice how that affects your presence to others and their responses to you. As you continue these practices, you may find that you can spontaneously engage in them on the spot. This allows you to participate in your activities more fully, effectively, and with a greater sense of healing and love.

For example, as a professor, John often experiences a "managing" part of himself when he is about to begin a class at the university where he teaches. If he enters class overly identified with that part of his mind, he can find himself focusing more on what class topics must be covered than on what the students need for their learning. By taking a moment before class to reconnect with his field of care and reunite with its loving environment, John finds himself listening to his students more deeply, with more responsiveness to their strengths, needs, and inner beauty. His students, in turn, seem to have more enjoyment and energy for class participation. This way of being can flow spontaneously throughout the whole class period and into the rest of his day.

When you are familiar with Compassion Meditation 1 and Tong-len Meditation 1, you can practice similarly—taking whatever troubling feelings arise in your day into that practice on the spot, then noticing how that affects your well-being, vision of others, and ways of being with them.

Blessing All Those in Your Day and in Your Life

When a meditation of extending love and compassion becomes your main morning practice, you can tap into that perspective and energy throughout your day. In morning meditation, consciously include all the people and beings in all the places you will go over the course of your day—in your home and neighborhood, when passing people along the roads you will travel, when arriving at the places you will go—the store, your workplace, and so forth. Then as you see or meet people in all those places, let that contact pull you back into the perspective and energy of your morning meditation session on the spot. Holding those beings in qualities of warmth and compassion while sensing them in the depth of their being and layers of suffering—it becomes natural to respond to each with a degree of reverence and care, nonverbally or verbally.

In your morning practice, you can also consciously include all the people and beings that have been part of your life from your earliest memories in this life to the present time—briefly scanning your life, recalling parents, siblings, relatives, schoolmates, teachers, those you have lived near and worked with, in all the settings of your life up to now. You can hold all of them in love and compassion while sensing them in their deep dignity and layers of suffering, blessing and healing your life and world from the beginning to the present, and then taking that perspective and energy into all of your encounters that day.

Reconnecting with the Basic Openness of Your Being

In the releasing phase of each meditation, and in the Letting Be of Body, Breath, and Mind meditation, you learn to relax and settle deeply into the abiding nature of the mind, the sky-like expanse of openness and awareness beyond reference points. In this way, meditation each morning familiarizes you with the natural wisdom of resting in nondual simplicity, beyond grasping to oneself or any sense of separateness from others. Then during the day, you can recall and reinhabit this wisdom when you're with others, relaxing into natural awareness wherever you are, as in morning meditation. To do so is to become more fully present to others, not lost in self-concerned worries, not clinging to yourself as separate from them. To abide like that when with others is to appreciate them in their very being and to listen deeply.

When you are outside in the natural world, gazing upon a wide-open vista or sitting by a large body of water, let that vast panorama pull your mind beyond its narrow posture of self-clinging into the expanse of natural awareness. Let the limitless spaciousness of the sky awaken the limitless "inner sky" of cognizance and openness. In this way, let the infinite spaciousness of the outer universe help draw you gently into recognition of the infinite nature of mind.

ALLOWING MEDITATION AND
ACTION TO INFORM EACH OTHER

As we touch in on these meditations repeatedly throughout the day, the care, compassion, and wisdom they evoke can take increasing expression in our ways of being with others, the quality of our presence to them, and our actions. Such activity, in turn, informs our meditations. As the meditations become familiar to us, we can access them more easily to explore how the secure base they provide shifts our perceptions and presence to others in all the settings of our lives.

An enjoyable time to integrate meditation practice is when you are out and about, surrounded by people unknown to you. At the grocery store, post office, or shopping area, notice all the people that your mind tends to label "stranger." Commune with them in the inclusive mode, sensing them in the depth of their being and hidden layers of suffering, beyond the thought of them as merely strangers. In the releasing phase, you can rest in the simplicity of the natural state, lucid openness, beyond clinging to a strong sense of sepa-ration between self and others. Practice similarly when sitting in a restaurant or theater; when shopping, taking a walk, traveling on a bus or train, waiting at the airport, driving, engaging with social media, and so forth. Over time, such practice increasingly reveals all those around us, wherever we are, as beings of depth and dignity, worthy of reverence and compassion. The label "strangers" falls away as we sense people freshly in the primal goodness of their being, cognizant of layers of suffering in all our lives.

When you are feeling upset with someone in your family, community, or workplace, if you are familiar with the field of care or compassionate pres-ence practice, take that upsetting feeling right into the practice to become a deeply accepting, healing environment for that feeling. See how that way of being with the feeling shifts your own sense of well-being, your percep-tion of the other person, and your ways of relating to them. You can do the same with the entire host of disturbing feelings and reactions that emerge in your relationships with others in every area of your life, helping you become increasingly skilled at allowing feelings deeply to heal, find their place of openness, and reveal levels of equanimity and discernment that empower a fuller perception of others that supports a better response to them.

You may feel justifiably angry at someone for something malicious they did to you. By becoming a loving holding environment for your feelings of hurt and anger, your perspective can open to reveal more of the causes and conditions that drive such people (and yourself) to do harmful things, more of the depth and capacity in all those involved, and more compassion for all involved, including yourself.

Notice more of the limiting labels for others that arise in your mind throughout the day: as merely a stranger, or unimportant, or in your way, or annoying, or off-putting, and so forth. Draw on those very perceptions as entry points into the Inclusive-Mode Meditation on the spot, by reuniting with the loving environment of your field of care, so you unblend from the part of your mind that tightly holds that perception, which naturally opens your perception of others, as we explored in chapter 3. In this way, explore settling into a deeper sense of identity in yourself and others, attuned to their mystery, beyond familiar assumptions of who everyone is, curious to hear and learn more from others, appreciating more in them, open to more creative possibilities with them. By practicing in that way, your reductive perceptions and negative reactions to others become the very fuel for deepening practice.

A situation at work may surface a tendency you have to be overly hard on yourself, which is making you hard on others which can become a fresh entry into Compassionate Presence to Feelings Meditation, and through that, to others and their feelings. Such meditations, in turn, can further empower your ways of being and working with others.

These are just examples, but all our experiences of difficulty can enter us directly into practice in such ways. They can also be taken right into Compassion Meditation 1 or Tong-len Meditation 1, empowering our empathy for all who experience similar difficulties and our solidarity with all in the layers of their suffering.

In the releasing phase of all such meditations, and in the Letting Be of Body, Breath, and Mind meditation, we can repeatedly reconnect with the natural state of total openness, simplicity, lucidity, and warmth to replenish at the deepest level of our being, from which to reengage our world again and again.

The contemplative practices in this book can also support and inform our efforts to build relationships and community, which we can then call upon as needed for emotional and practical support. At times, that kind of social support may be more helpful or necessary than only relying on meditation practices. In addition to the support from spiritual teachers, practice communities and peers can foster support for challenges that inevitably arise in life and during contemplative practice.[3] We will discuss the role of support from teachers and practitioners to inform contemplative practice toward the end of this chapter.

RESPONDING TO THE WORLD WITH NEW EYES OF COMPASSION

When we reach the point of regularly practicing the compassion meditations of chapter 4, which evoke strong empathy and compassion in broadening circles of inclusion, it can profoundly affect our perception and responsiveness to our larger world. These days we see in the news that many thousands of people throughout the world have sworn themselves to the painful death of their enemies. Millions have been heartlessly uprooted from their homes by brutal attacks, with thousands dying from violence, hunger, and disease. Many laborers, including children, work such long hours on farms and in factories for so little pay that they barely survive. Families throughout the world are overwhelmed by the need to support relatives with debilitating diseases. People in vulnerable communities across the globe—categorized primarily by race, ethnicity, religion, gender, sexuality, and so forth—are routinely despised, abused, and discriminated against. Millions suffer from mental illness, severe depression, and addiction. Each day, innumerable animals undergo unspeakable sufferings of mistreatment.

Some of us turn away from the daily news because we feel helpless in the face of so much misery and don't know what to do with the painful feelings of empathy that it evokes. But if we do so, it feels as if we are hiding from the realities of our world and therefore ultimately from ourselves as part of that world. Compassion Meditation 2 and Tong-len Meditation 2, in contrast, convert our painful feelings of empathy into compassion—the stronger our empathy, the more powerful our compassion that radiates to those who are suffering and wishes them deeply free and well. When you are familiar with those compassion meditations, pay special attention each day to people and groups you hear of whose suffering deeply touches you. Perhaps now, with the help of Compassion Meditation 2, you can let more of the pain and distress experienced by those around you evoke your empathy, so you really wish that they didn't have to go through that. When this occurs, reconnect with Compassion Meditation 2 on the spot, letting the compassionate energy from your field of care come through you to those in distress, with a wish for their deep freedom and well-being. In this way, when we become more empathetically aware of suffering in our world, instead of feeling overwhelmed, our compassion can intensify, motivating action.

As noted in chapter 4, compassionate action can take diverse forms: providing a smile of encouragement; helping someone recognize their hidden strengths; mirroring the hidden beauty of others who don't see it in themselves; listening deeply to someone who needs an ear; being present to another's distress and suffering without immediately trying to fix it in order to make ourselves feel better; working to address systemic problems in education, health, housing, or the environment; working to meet needs of those who suffer from hunger, violence, or discrimination. As we engage in such activities, we move closer to aspects of suffering and their causes that we could not have previously noticed at a distance, and we learn from others' ways of experiencing and understanding. This fuller awareness of suffering within action can then be taken into our meditation practice, empowering stronger and more informed compassion that expresses itself in further action.

When we do daily meditation on compassion and wisdom, instead of experiencing the daily news as an enemy, it can be received as a means to inform and deepen our compassion. In a morning meditation session, we hold beings in the radiant power of compassion, wishing them free of suffering and its causes. Then throughout the day, when we see or hear of terrible difficulties others undergo, we can take that knowledge into our practice on the spot, radiating compassion that wishes them free from every outer circumstance and inner layer of the suffering, motivating various kinds of responsive action. We can do this when we encounter the tragedies reported in the media. We can do this whenever we come upon anyone in our life that is suffering or grieving. In this way, rather than hiding from the world, we can learn increasingly to open our eyes and hearts to it. Then when we sit down to meditate the next morning, the sufferings we saw or heard of the previous day further energize the meditations of compassion.

This synergy of contemplation and action is informed by getting to know people in many walks of life, by reading, and by inquiry into systemic issues, all of which empower work to address social and ecological problems.

Within this process, we can become more conscious of how our own ways of living have contributed, more than we may have noticed, to the sufferings that we are witnessing. For example, as John explains, when he and his wife first moved to the Boston area following a job offer, they looked for a neighborhood with good schools. That may sound innocuous, but since the economic support for public schools is largely based in their own towns, it ended up taking them into a community that could economically afford to support high-quality schools. At the time, they did not inquire into the social and economic arrangements through which many other neighborhoods wind up with horrible schools, to which their children are relegated. Why can't funding for all schools be equitably resourced? Like many others, they weren't asking those questions at the time.

Another example is the ecological crisis, driven by fossil fuel–based infrastructures that we virtually all participate in through our styles of living. Consequent global warming is now causing climate catastrophes that create enormous suffering for human and animal populations. As we become increasingly informed about such systemic bases of suffering and our own locations in them, we can take that awareness into our meditations for perspective, motivation, and energy for action, as noted in chapter 4 on compassion and social location.

Classical Indian and Tibetan texts instruct practitioners to elicit compassion for beings by imagining the horrors they undergo in suffering realms of rebirth as taught in Asian Buddhist cosmologies: the tortures of hell realms, the painful hunger of wandering spirits, the fearful lives of animals, as well as the manifold sufferings of human beings.[4] In a similar way, we can draw upon the visceral images of the sufferings of war, starvation, oppression, abuse, and ecological devastation that we see and hear about. Instead of turning away from the horrors of the contemporary world in helplessness, we can accept them into our meditation to inform and empower our compassion, wishing all those involved deeply free from the suffering and all of its outer and inner causes.

In this way, the suffering around us informs our meditation, and the compassion from meditation can energize our active responses to the world around us. When we learn of others' suffering or see it, we don't have to feel helpless. We can radiate the compassionate wish for their deep freedom from it and let the energy of that wish motivate us to learn and do what we can at individual and systemic levels. Suffering that cannot presently be assuaged need not become an excuse to turn our heads away. We can hold suffering beings in the energy of compassion, willing their deep freedom from it, keeping them in our minds, never forgetting them until they are freed.

FULLEST COMPASSION AS BODHICITTA: AIMING FOR UNIVERSAL FREEDOM FROM ALL LEVELS OF SUFFERING

Recall our discussion of the three levels of suffering in chapter 4: the obvious suffering of body and mind, the suffering of changeableness, and the suffering of ego-conditioning. Most of our discussion above, as with most social activism, focused on obvious sufferings, including our wish for beings to be free from that suffering and the struggle for that freedom. But there are further layers of suffering that are normally not fully conscious to people. To be freed from those layers and their causes comprises a deeper level of liberation. The *suffering of changeableness* is the futile attempt to have and hold on to changing things as if they were the very source of our well-being, when deep down we know we will lose them all. (Again, it is the power of love, compassion, and wisdom that are the actual sources of our well-being). The *suffering of ego-conditioning* refers to the subtle anxieties, fears, and reactions that are endlessly generated by the ego-centered conditioning of our minds.

While we work to address the obvious level of suffering noted in the section above, we are probably still caught in the latter two levels of suffering ourselves, driven by conditioned patterns of thought, feeling, and reaction in mind and body. The deepest inner cause of suffering, from a Buddhist perspective, is the mind's tendency to reify and grasp onto its own mental constructs of reality, mistaking everyone and everything for our own reified images and thoughts of them and endlessly reacting to them from self-grasping habits of afflictive emotion: self-clinging attachment, aversion, and so forth. Even when we think we are working to improve the world, as long as we remain caught up in those conditioned habits of mind, we contribute to the suffering around us in ways we are not conscious of. While we are identified with those conditioned habits of reaction, we cannot access a deeper source of freedom from suffering with its powers of equanimity, discernment, and unconditional compassion from which to address the suffering of ourselves and others.

But as noted in chapter 2, when we enter into deepening levels of tranquil abiding in the releasing phase of each meditation and in the Letting Be of Body, Breath, and Mind meditation, we start to settle into an unconditioned, nondual dimension of our being, the basic space and lucidity of our buddha nature, which is the ground of all our experience. That is the place of deepest freedom from all three levels of suffering and their inner causes. As noted, with the support of teachers and community who practice at that depth, we can begin to have glimpses of that nondual and unconditioned ground of experience—buddha nature—and even start to reunify with it more and more. From a Buddhist perspective, when we do so, the patterns of mind and body that condition all three levels of suffering begin to release, to "self-liberate," and we start to experience a profound relief from within.

As we reunify more and more fully with that unconditioned ground of basic space and clarity, buddha nature, we sense the same in all others, for we are undivided from them in the infinite openness of that ground. Then we can recognize more clearly how much we have all been caught up in conditioned causes of suffering for not having realized that ground of inmost freedom. From a Buddhist perspective, this recognition informs the deepest purpose of compassion—to hold all beings in the vision that knows them all in the unconditioned ground of their being, the place of their inmost freedom from suffering. The ultimate aim then is to become so unified with that enlightened ground and its qualities through practice that our presence to them can support them in their own realization of freedom from all levels of suffering, each in their own best way.

This commitment to fully realize and embody our buddha nature and its qualities in order to support all others in their process of awakening and liberation is called bodhicitta, the awakening mind of a bodhisattva. From a Buddhist point of view, it is bodhicitta that comprises the deepest form of compassion—compassion attuned to the fullest reality of beings, both in their enlightened capacity for inmost freedom and in all the layers and causes of suffering that obstruct it. It is therefore bodhicitta that is a most precious resource, perspective, and motivation for compassionate responses to the problems of the world.

Those who take up the commitment of bodhicitta to reunify with the unconditioned ground of their being—the place of deepest freedom and primal goodness—for the sake of all, have found the ultimate secure base from which to respond to the problems and needs of the world without being overwhelmed by them. That nondual ground of openness and awareness provides the discernment, awakening qualities, and energy needed to target all three levels of suffering in beings when working to meet problems and needs, not just the obvious sufferings.[5]

DRAWING ON CARING EQUANIMITY TO AVOID BURNOUT IN SERVICE AND ACTIVISM— DISTINGUISHING OUR PRIMARY CONCERN FROM OUR INSTRUMENTAL CONCERNS

The releasing phase of meditations in this book and the Letting Be meditation draw us increasingly into unity with the infinite openness, lucidity, and wisdom of our buddha nature, the unconditioned depth of our being. From that depth in us, the Inclusive-Mode Meditation and Compassion Meditations unleash powers of love and compassion that help us commune with others in their comparable depth, wishing them deeply free and well. As noted in chapter 4, several kinds of caring equanimity emerge from this synergy of wisdom and compassion, including the power to become free of expectations, from egoistic attachment to circumstances, goals, or outcomes.

We can draw on that power to avoid excessive frustration or burnout when working with and serving others. To do so, we also need to distinguish our primary concern in such work from our instrumental concerns. From the perspective of deep contemplative practice and compassion training, the primary concern is to recognize, uphold, and evoke the deep dignity and positive potential of persons when we work with them. That primary concern is never ultimately at risk as long as we stay in touch with the dignity of persons and the powers of care and compassion for them that we increasingly access in daily practice. In contrast, a second kind of concern—the expectation of accomplishing a goal, getting some particular thing done according to a certain plan within a specific time frame—is *always* at risk, *never* under our control.

As long as we know how to abide in, or come back to, the powers of wisdom, compassion, and equanimity that are supported by daily practice, the spirit of our initiative is never ultimately at risk. Only our current plan, strategy, or timeline is at risk. If one way forward doesn't work, we can try another, because the fundamental power of care that motivates our actions is not affected by any obstacles to our current plan or time frame. To know how to abide within, or reconnect with, the source of our motivation is the secret behind the perseverance of leading figures of service and action through history who have faced innumerable obstacles.

Working for Institutional and Social Change

Another kind of caring equanimity that emerges from the practice of wisdom and compassion is the power of impartial inclusiveness, which is aware of others in the depth of their being and inner sufferings, beyond superficial appearances. This kind of caring equanimity cuts through the socially conditioned tendency in all societies to care only for those in our in-groups or "on our side," not the others.

Many of us who serve others in caring roles or professions also work to change institutional or social structures that we see as harming or holding back the people we serve. To work to change such structures is often to work against the positions of other people who are committed to those structures. We are prone in such work to mistake our angry thoughts of those people for the persons. We oppose the people, not just their positions or actions, with an aversion for them that we may mistake for righteousness. This is common among social activists and can lead to growing anger and hatred toward people who oppose our positions.

Anger can get us moving for social change, but if it becomes a dominant motivation, many problems follow. Anger is typically self-protective, projecting distorted images of others that prevent us from staying in touch with their fuller human experience and potential. When we are immersed in self-righteous anger, we cannot listen deeply to others. Such anger, when cultivated as a primary motivation for social change, tends to make us increasingly defensive and abrasive, which turns people off. As a result, we can't get the help we seek, which can make us angrier in a downward spiral. Ironically, we can wind up imitating the domineering methods of our political opponents in the name of opposing them, without conscious awareness.

Many social activists take pride in their anger at injustice. "If you're not angry, you're not paying attention" is a common slogan. The understanding is that anger is not just deluded but contains important wisdom. How so? Such anger knows that something is terribly wrong; something needs to be decisively confronted in order to make things safe and well for the poor, the oppressed, and the marginalized. If the wisdom in anger could be liberated from its distorted perceptions of other persons, including one's opponents, its intense energy could clarify into a fierce form of compassion that is ferocious in upholding everyone in their essential dignity and potential by confronting the forces of narrow self-concern, greed, prejudice, hatred, and violence—forces that wield all of us more than we are conscious. For this we need to be grounded in a compassionate level of our being—the caring equanimity that is not imprisoned in the reactions of a brittle, angry sense of self that has lost touch with the unconditional worth of everyone involved, including political opponents.

As bell hooks wrote,

> We have witnessed the way in which movements for justice that denounce dominator culture, yet have an underlying commitment to corrupt uses of power, do not really create fundamental changes in our societal structure. When radical activists have not made a core break with dominator thinking. . . , there is no union of theory and practice, and real change is not sustained. That's why cultivating the mind of love is so crucial. When love is the ground of our being, a love ethic shapes our participation in politics. To work for peace and justice we begin with the individual practice of love, because it is there that we can experience firsthand love's transformative power.[6]

Inclusive-mode practices help us come from the depth of our being to sense all others in their depth as beings of great dignity and potential. The compassion meditations (including tong-len) familiarize us with our own painful feelings of fear, self-protectiveness, grief, rage, and so forth, so we can sense from inside what many of our opponents on social issues may also feel within their own perspectives. Then our vision of others can no longer be reduced to caricatures of them projected by our own self-righteous anger.

When Martin Luther King Jr. organized against social institutions of racism and economic inequality, his opponents attacked him and his people with ferocious dogs, whips, hoses, guns, and more. Yet King taught that unconditional love is the key to social change. He taught that we must confront oppressive social structures on behalf of everyone involved, including those supporting such structures. He never conceptualized his movement for positive social change as only on behalf of oppressed people. It was also on behalf of those people wielding the attack dogs and whips.

This is the essential difference between ordinary anger and fierce compassion. Ordinary anger is motivated by fear and aversion; fierce compassion is motivated by a force of love that has the courage to confront people for their own sake. Anger seeks to protect the self or one's own self-righteousness. Fierce compassion seeks to uphold all others in their deepest potential by challenging whatever in them impedes that potential.

If we learn to reconnect with the vision and energy of these meditations in daily life, repeatedly reconnecting with and gradually stabilizing our vision of everyone's deep dignity, our work for change can become more sustainable for ourselves and more effective for others. Instead of getting increasingly enraged in the work, driving away supporters and leading ourselves to burnout, we can become more caring, grounded, and energized, which can attract support from those who share our desire to work for change in a deeply grounded and sane way.

Social Action Is Not Mainly about Fighting Evil; It's about Bringing More Goodness into the World

Fighting the evil we perceive in others is never the best way to understand any work we do for social change. The evil we see in others is never just in them but also in us, and it is intensified by not recognizing that. When we act from a perception of others' evil, we evoke the evil in them. When we act from a perception of others' dignity and positive potential, we reinforce that in them.

As Thomas Merton wrote,

> The saints are what they are, not because their sanctity makes them admirable to others, but because the gift of sainthood makes it possible for them to admire everybody else. It gives them a clarity of compassion that can find good in the most terrible criminals. It delivers them from the burden of judging others, condemning other men. It teaches them to bring the good out of others by compassion, mercy and pardon. A man becomes a saint not by conviction that he is better than sinners but by the realization that he is one of them, and that all together need the mercy of God.[7]

Many are ready to fight the evil they see in others. Fewer know how to bring out the capacity for goodness in themselves and others. This is the crying need today. Our ability to do this is cultivated by all the meditations in this book. We become more present to others' humanity and potential, and the destructive tendencies that impede their potential, as we become more present to our own. As meditations reveal the underlying openness and positive power of our being, and the patterns of reaction in us that have held it back, we become more aware of the same in others—what needs to be upheld in them and what needs to be challenged for their sake as well as for the sake of others. And we listen better when others, for our sake, challenge some of the ways we think or act.

Building on the vision of Martin Luther King Jr., bell hooks wrote,

> King believed that love is "ultimately the only answer" to the problems facing this nation and the entire planet. I share that belief and the conviction that it is in choosing love, and beginning with love as the ethical foundation of politics, that we are best positioned to transform society in ways that enhance the collective good.[8]

INTRODUCING A COMPASSION MEDITATION TO
EMPOWER SOCIAL AND ECOLOGICAL ACTION

Think of some problem or injustice that you deeply care about, in empathy with those who are suffering from it—for example, protection of immigrants and refugees; protecting living beings and the natural world from environmental destruction; protecting those who suffer from racial, religious, or ethnic oppression; upholding women's rights; making health care affordable for all; helping people obtain a decent wage; protecting victims of violence or war; protecting the unborn; protecting LGBTQ+ persons; protecting communities from gun violence; assisting the incarcerated; or providing a good education for all. Think first of those who are suffering under that problem or injustice, for whom you deeply care. Then think of someone who fights for the other side of that issue, against the changes that you believe are necessary to address that suffering.

(An audio option is available at shambhala.com/howcompassionworks meditations.)

A MEDITATION FOR EXTENDING COMPASSION TO THOSE SUFFERING INJUSTICES AND TO THOSE IN OPPOSITION

STEP 1. SETTLING INTO BODY AND BREATH (2 TO 3 MINUTES) Sit in a relaxed way, with back comfortably straight, eyes gazing gently downward. Come down from the thinking mind into the body and settle into the grounded feeling of the body on your seat. (*Pause*) Let the breath flow naturally while breathing from the abdomen, so you feel the belly expand and contract with each breath. Let that feeling draw you into it more and more, breath by breath.

STEP 2. RECONNECTING WITH LOVE AND COMPASSION (3 TO 5 MINUTES) Now bring to mind your field of care as present here with you now. You are being seen and held in deep care, compassion, acceptance, and warmth beyond judgments. Relax into the felt sense of this experience, steeping in its loving energy and tender qualities and letting them infuse your whole being. Accept these loving qualities into your whole body, heart, and mind—every part of you loved in its very being.

STEP 3. EXTENDING CARE (5 TO 10 MINUTES) Let the loving energy come through you to those who are suffering under the injustice (humans or other beings). Let this caring energy help you connect with them in their dignity and potential, sensing them also in their layers of suffering, to wish them deeply well and free of the causes of the suffering. After a little while, let the loving energy come through you both to that first group who is suffering and now also to those who are fighting the changes you think are needed to address that suffering. Let this loving energy help you connect with them in their dignity and potential, sensing them also in their hidden layers of suffering, to wish them deeply well and free from the causes of their suffering.

If part of your mind is having difficulty with this practice, settle back into your field of care, reunite with its healing environment, and become compassionately aware of that part of you (that sense of self) with spacious acceptance and warmth. When that part of you settles and your mind un-blends from it, you can return to the practice of extending warmth and love.

STEP 4. RELEASING (3 TO 5 MINUTES) After some time, let this loving environment of warmth and compassion help your mind to relax, settle back a bit inwardly, release all its frameworks of worry and concern, and become naturally wide open like space. As thoughts and feelings arise, let them just metabolize themselves and release within this sky-like openness of awareness by letting everything be.

Processing the Meditation

The purpose of this meditation is to help us retain connection with the dignity, worth, and potential of all the persons involved in any issue, without erasing disagreement on the issue. The aim is to empower our ability to confront people's ways of thinking and acting, not only on behalf of those suffering from an injustice but also out of care for those who oppose the changes we see as necessary to end the injustice. From this fundamental posture of care for all involved can come a fuller capacity to hear others and the layers of pain that they may be speaking from. We need this to more fully inform any work we do for social and ecological change.

Practices like the Field of Care Meditation and the Inclusive-Mode Meditation may enhance efforts to undo structural and systemic barriers to care. In an oppressive environment, a strong sense of social support cultivated through such meditations can provide the psychological resources that help people to process painful experiences and challenge unjust conditions more effectively. This practice can help each of us learn to draw on experiences of care and connection from our life, which we can draw upon to become more compassionately present to our own feelings and reactions. Then we can learn to stay in touch with those qualities of care as we encounter situations and others in our world that need to be challenged. This enduring connection with our inner resources brings out powers of inner safeness, equanimity, wisdom, resilience, stability, courage, and responsiveness that can empower us to challenge things more effectively with care and compassion for all involved.

Several teachers and communities of practitioners point to the possibility that meditation can support efforts to challenge injustice and oppression. Through interviews with meditation practitioners who identify as people of color, the Buddhist studies scholar Ann Gleig identified several ways that contemplative practice can support engagement and response to injustice.[9] First, meditations can help us to become more aware of our own embodied conditioned defenses and heal the pain of internalized systemic conditioning. Second, for people from well-resourced social locations, meditation practices can increase tolerance for the discomfort that is generated by conversations around structural racism and privilege. Third, within meditation communities, integrating practice with discussion of social and ecological issues can help create a more inclusive communal practice setting. Finally, the presence of communal support and affinity space within meditation settings can help foster a sense of safety and relaxation, which supports the ability to relate to others beyond reductive impressions that have been conditioned by larger social structures.

THE NEED FOR SPIRITUAL COMMUNITY
AND SPIRITUAL MENTORS

Anyone can start to access capacities of love, compassion, and wisdom by regularly practicing meditations like those in this book—and by exploring ways to begin drawing on those capacities in one's relationships, work, and service. But individuals who try to practice on their own, without the support of other experienced practitioners, often have difficulty sustaining and deepening their practice over the long term. There are several reasons for this.

One reason is that meditations of unconditional love and wisdom are extremely challenging on a personal level. These meditations profoundly undercut our egos' habitual ways of labeling and reacting to everyone. Most members of society are not regularly engaged in practices to awaken all-inclusive compassion and wisdom. The social discourse around us, which is amplified by social media, routinely reduces many people to objects of contempt or apathy, which reinforces our habit of doing similarly. To integrate impartial care, compassion, and wisdom into one's life is culturally subversive. It challenges the partialities assumed in every society. Because we are learning to see the world in ways that many do *not* share, our process of awakening can feel like a lonely endeavor.

In a course in meditation theory that John taught at his university, students were required to read relevant texts, meditate daily, and explore ways that study and meditation informed their lives, for most of them as Christians and Jews. Toward the end of one semester, a student wrote that daily meditation was "blowing her mind," revealing a capacity for unconditional care that she didn't know she had. "But," she said, "this practice is *so* radical—it opens up a way of seeing and responding *so* different from what many others around me are thinking and saying. I can't imagine carrying this practice on just by myself, without the support of the others in this class." That student had begun to understand why spiritual community is considered indispensable in the world's traditions of spiritual practice, including Buddhism.

We need the support of others who practice similarly, accessing powers of compassion and wisdom in daily practice and drawing on them in their ways of being with others. When we first take up such practices, many questions typically arise that others with more experience can address. When we face inner obstacles or become discouraged, we need the input of others who have undergone similar difficulties, found their way through them, and can inform and encourage us. It also empowers our own practice for us to become such a support for others in their practice.

As noted in the introductory chapter, the contemplative path outlined in this book works with patterns of receptivity, deepening, and inclusiveness that are common to many spiritual traditions and also mirror analogous patterns in developmental psychology (as in attachment theory and social baseline theory). Support to explore those patterns of practice can be found within all such traditions, by practicing within any of their communities of deepening prayer and contemplation that you find empowering.

It is also most helpful to repeatedly receive teachings of compassion and wisdom that you find most inspiring from experienced teachers. Serious practitioners at all levels of experience regularly attend workshops or retreats in which their contemplative teachers transmit the practices that empower their process. When authentic teachers transmit a meditation in such a setting, the qualities of love, compassion, and wisdom that they embody in that moment resonate with correlative capacities in ourselves, which helps us awaken similarly as we join them in practice. When one tuning fork is struck, the energy of its vibration can cause a second tuning fork to begin to vibrate, even at a distance. Transmission of meditations and their qualities by experienced teachers to receptive students operates like that. In such settings, our teachers can also respond directly to our most pressing practice questions. There, we are also informed by the questions and insights of other experienced practitioners. Such teaching and transmission are increasingly available these days online as well as in person. Please see the Appendix on page 217 ("Resources for Ongoing Practice and Study") for suggestions for connecting with various communities, teachings, and teachers related to SCT training.

THE RELATIONAL ENDING POINT OF COMPASSION TRAINING

We began this book by introducing the concept of a *relational starting point* for meditation and compassion training. This means that we enter into the path of contemplative practice with the experience that we are seen in our deep worth and held in unwavering love, compassion, and wisdom by others, who sense us beyond any limiting judgments or stories. This outer refuge, or outer secure base, empowers our inner refuge, our inner secure base, by helping us access the same qualities of love, compassion, and wisdom from the depth of our awareness, so we can become an outer refuge for many others. The arc of contemplative practice thereby extends the scope of love, compassion, and wisdom through each of us to widening circles of other beings. In this way, the path of practice gestures toward a *relational ending point*. The very purpose of training in inclusive love and compassion is to empower our ability to respond to the fuller humanity and potential in all others and to see through the limiting impressions of ourselves and others that have been so deeply conditioned by social systems and economic structures.

This pattern of relational practice, as a means of spiritual transformation and liberation, is mirrored in many of the world's religious and spiritual traditions. In Buddhist traditions, the ultimate aim of such practice is to fully realize one's buddha nature, an unconditioned depth of inner freedom from which to realize all the qualities and activities of enlightenment. To accomplish that goal is to become an extension of Buddhist fields of refuge. Analogous ultimate goals are maintained in the contemplative practice traditions of many other religions, through which practitioners learn to become an extension of their communions of saints, fields of spiritual ancestors, assemblies of elders, and so forth for the sake of all.

Influential leaders and activists such as Martin Luther King Jr., bell hooks, Fred Rogers, Sojourner Truth, Dorothy Day, Thich Nhat Hanh, Desmond Tutu, and the Fourteenth Dalai Lama all embodied in their lives and work a sustaining and inclusive power of compassion and wisdom that was first established within the unlimited refuge (the infinitely secure base) of their own relational fields. That stable core of security supported their indomitable efforts to address some of the most difficult social problems of our time.

May this book similarly empower readers of different backgrounds, contexts, and worldviews—including those in all kinds of caring roles and professions—to access an unconditional power of love, compassion, and wisdom that can empower your lives, relationships, and work with others.

ACKNOWLEDGMENTS

We thank Chokyi Nyima Rinpoche and Tsoknyi Rinpoche for inspiring and blessing so many of us to learn how to actualize our innate capacities of love, compassion, and wisdom.

We thank all practitioners who have participated in these meditations, who have generously shared their experience and insights with us over years of engaging in these contemplative practices.

In recent years, Wendy Hasenkamp, Rob Roeser, Willa Baker, Gaëlle Desbordes, and Paula Arai have provided constructive and generous feedback on our written work concerning dialogues between science and contemplative practice.

We thank Matt Zepelin and Jenn Brown at Shambhala for shepherding this book from its inception to publication. They provided substantive support throughout the writing process.

We thank our families for their enduring support, friendship, and love.

Appendix

RESOURCES FOR ONGOING PRACTICE AND STUDY

SCT PROGRAMS AND EVENTS—AND TEACHERS THAT DRAW FROM ASPECTS OF SCT

Retreats and workshops on sustainable compassion training (SCT) led by experienced teachers are listed at the sustainablecompassion.org website. Groups that practice SCT regularly together, in person and online, can also be found at that website, as well as audio and video guided meditations and supportive reading materials. John Makransky and Paul Condon, the authors of this book, each lead SCT retreats. They can be contacted through sustainablecompassion.org. Natural Dharma Fellowship also transmits these practices in its Margha program, a core part of its contemplative training program (https://naturaldharma.org/practice/margha-program/). Courage of Care, an organization focused on social change, draws on principles of SCT in its programs (https://courageofcare.org).

The following contemplative teachers also draw from aspects of SCT in their teachings and retreats: Liz Monson (https://naturaldharma.org/practice/margha-program/), Jessica Morey (https://jessicamorey.org), Julie Forsythe (juliabforsythe@gmail.com), Rachel Cronin (AllAlong.net), Kaira Jewel Lingo (https://www.kairajewel.com), Melanie Harris (https://divinity.wfu.edu/academics/faculty/melanie-l-harris/), Lama Rod Owens (https://www.lamarod.com/), Bonnie Duran (https://washington.academia.edu/Bonnie Duran), and Donald Rothberg (https://www.donaldrothberg.com/).

TEACHINGS AND PROGRAMS WITHIN
TIBETAN BUDDHIST TRADITIONS

For those who wish to explore the Tibetan Buddhist traditions from which meditations of this book were adapted, with their full range of theory and practice, we recommend the ongoing teachings of two of our teachers, Chokyi Nyima Rinpoche and Tsoknyi Rinpoche. Points of entry to their teachings are the Tara's Triple Excellence program developed by Chokyi Nyima Rinpoche with his senior students (https://dharmasun.org/tte/), and the Fully Being program developed by Tsoknyi Rinpoche with his senior students (https://fullybeing.org/). Both teachers also continue to offer practice retreats, in person and online, in Asia and the West.

WRITINGS ON COMPASSION AND WISDOM
FROM DIVERSE SPIRITUAL TRADITIONS

Also helpful is study, not only the study of SCT materials like this book but also other materials that support your process of deepening care, compassion, and wisdom. Spiritual benefactors often come to us through their writings, which may include inspiring texts authored by teachers of your own tradition. Contemplative teachers and activists of various other traditions may also greatly inform your contemplative process through their writings, like those by Thomas Merton, Dorothy Day, Mary Oliver, Martin Luther King Jr., Desmond Tutu, Abraham Joshua Heschel, Parker J. Palmer, Martin Buber, Maya Angelou, Thich Nhat Hanh, the Dalai Lama, Pema Chödrön, Henri Nouwen, Brian Robinette, Ram Dass, Sheila Weinberg, and others.

INTERSECTION OF CONTEMPLATIVE
PRACTICE AND ANTI-OPPRESSION

A growing movement of meditation teachers and communities combine mindfulness and other contemplative practices with anti-oppression and social activism. Studying their work can also deeply inform our development with contemplative practice as a means of deconstructing social structures that reinforce internalized barriers to care and compassion. For further discussion of contemplative practice integrated with analysis of structural inequities, see Ann Gleig, *American Dharma: Buddhism Beyond Modernity*, pages

139–75; Brooke Lavelle et al., "Relationshift: The CourageRISE Model for Building Relational Cultures of Practice," in *The Arrow Journal* (2021). For recommended books, see:

- Ruth King, *Mindful of Race: Transforming Racism from the Inside Out*
- Kaira Jewel Lingo, *We Were Made for These Times: Ten Lessons on Moving through Change, Loss, and Disruption*
- Rhonda Magee, *The Inner Work of Racial Justice: Healing Ourselves and Transforming Our Communities through Mindfulness*
- Zenju Earthlyn Manuel, *The Way of Tenderness: Awakening through Race, Sexuality, and Gender*
- Resmaa Menakem, *My Grandmother's Hands: Racialized Trauma and the Pathway to Mending Our Hearts and Bodies*
- Sebene Selassie, *You Belong: A Call for Connection*
- Larry Ward, *America's Racial Karma: An Invitation to Heal*
- Angel Kyodo Williams, Rod Owens, and Jasmine Syedullah, *Radical Dharma: Talking Race, Love and Liberation*

EXPLORING THE LIVES OF PEOPLE WE CAN LEARN FROM

Supportive study can also include writings that introduce us to the lives of people beyond our own familiar worlds; that communicate their struggles, difficulties, and courageous ways of responding to them, such as the writings of W. E. B. Du Bois, James Baldwin, and Etty Hillesum, *Nickled and Dimed* by Barbara Ehrenreich, *The Working Poor* by David Shipler, *Evicted* by Matthew Desmond, *Savage Inequalities* by Jonathan Kozol, *The New Jim Crow* by Michelle Alexander, or *Stories from the Shadows: Reflections of a Street Doctor* by James O'Connell.

SCIENTIFIC CONTEXT OF CONTEMPLATIVE PRACTICE

Our understanding of the scientific context of contemplative practice can also be informed by readings that summarize relevant findings in contemplative science, psychology, neuroscience, and attachment theory. For recommended books, see:

- Tania Singer and Matthias Bolz, eds., *Compassion: Bridging Practice and Science*
- Matthieu Ricard, *Altruism: The Power of Compassion to Change Yourself and the World*
- Thupten Jinpa, *A Fearless Heart: How the Courage to Be Compassionate Can Transform Our Lives*
- Paul Gilbert, ed., *Compassion: Concepts, Research, and Application*
- Daniel Goleman and Richard J. Davidson, *Altered Traits: Science Reveals How Meditation Changes Your Mind, Brain, and Body*
- Francisco Varela, *Ethical Know-How: Action, Wisdom, and Cognition*
- Lisa Feldman Barrett, *How Emotions Are Made: The Secret Life of the Brain*
- Jamil Zaki, *The War for Kindness: Building Empathy in a Fractured World*
- James Kirby, *Choose Compassion: Why It Matters and How It Works*
- Robert Karen, *Becoming Attached: First Relationships and How They Shape Our Capacity to Love*
- Bethany Saltman, *Strange Situation: A Mother's Journey into the Science of Attachment*
- Kent Hoffman, Glen Cooper, and Bert Powell, *Raising a Secure Child: How Circle of Security Parenting Can Help You Nurture Your Child's Attachment, Emotional Resilience, and Freedom to Explore*

READINGS THAT INFORM MEDITATIONS OF SUSTAINABLE COMPASSION TRAINING

John Makransky, *Awakening through Love: Unveiling Your Deepest Goodness* (Boston: Wisdom Publications, 2007).

John Makransky, "Compassion in Buddhist Psychology," in *Wisdom and Compassion in Psychotherapy*, ed. Christopher Germer and Ronald Siegel, 61–74 (New York. Guilford Press, 2012).

Paul Condon and John Makransky, "Sustainable Compassion Training: Integrating Meditation Theory with Psychological Science," *Frontiers in Psychology* 11 (2020): 2249.

Paul Condon and John Makransky, "Recovering the Relational Starting Point of Compassion Training," *Perspectives on Psychological Science* 15 (2020): 1346–62.

Paul Condon and John Makransky, "Compassion and Skillful Means: Cultural Adaptation, Psychological Science, and Creative Responsiveness," *Mindfulness* 14 (2023): 2331–41.

Paul Condon, "You Can Take Refuge Right Here," *Lion's Roar*, 2021, https://www.lionsroar.com/you-can-take-refuge-right-here/.

Paul Condon, "Venturing beyond Our Fear of Emptiness," *Lion's Roar*, 2023, https://www.lionsroar.com/venturing-beyond-our-fear-of-emptiness/.

Tsoknyi Rinpoche, *Open Heart, Open Mind: Awakening the Power of Essence Love* (New York: Harmony Books, 2012).

Dzigar Kongtrul Rinpoche, *Training in Tenderness: Buddhist Teachings on Tsewa, the Radical Openness of Heart That Can Change the World* (Boulder, CO: Shambhala, 2018).

Chokyi Nyima Rinpoche and David Shlim, *Medicine and Compassion: A Tibetan Lama's Guidance for Caregivers* (Boston: Wisdom Publications, 2006).

Tulku Thondup, *The Healing Power of Mind: Simple Meditation Exercises for Health, Well-Being, and Enlightenment* (Boston: Shambhala, 1996),

Tulku Thondup, *The Heart of Unconditional Love: A Powerful New Approach to Loving-Kindness Meditation* (Boston: Shambhala, 2015).

Phakchok Rinpoche and Sophie Wu, *Awakening Dignity: A Guide to Living a Life of Deep Fulfillment* (Boulder, CO: Shambhala, 2022).

Nyoshul Khenpo and Surya Das, *Natural Great Perfection: Dzogchen Teachings* (Ithaca, NY: Snow Lion Publications, 1995).

Khenchen Thrangu Rinpoche, *Crystal Clear: Practical Advice for Mahāmudrā Meditators* (Hong Kong: Rangjung Yeshe Publications, 2003).

Pema Chödrön, *Start Where You Are: A Guide to Compassionate Living* (Boston: Shambhala, 1994).

Martin Luther King Jr., *A Gift of Love: Sermons from "Strength to Love" and Other Preachings* (Boston: Beacon Press, 2018).

Cheryl Giles and Pamela Ayo Yetunde, *Black and Buddhist: What Buddhism Can Teach Us about Race, Resilience, and Freedom* (Boulder, CO: Shambhala, 2020).

Lama Rod Owens, *Love & Rage: The Path of Liberation through Anger* (Berkeley, CA: North Atlantic Books, 2020).

Willa Blythe Baker, *The Wakeful Body: Somatic Mindfulness as a Path to Freedom* (Boulder, CO: Shambhala, 2021).

NOTES

INTRODUCTION

1. For fuller discussion of these points, see John Makransky, *Awakening through Love: Unveiling Your Deepest Goodness* (Boston: Wisdom Publications, 2007), 1–10; Thupten Jinpa, *A Fearless Heart: How the Courage to Be Compassionate Can Transform Our Lives* (New York: Hudson Street Press, 2015), 12–21, 182–92.

2. Sarah Blaffer Hrdy, *Mothers and Others: The Evolutionary Origins of Mutual Understanding* (Cambridge, MA: Harvard University Press, 2009), 18–20; Abigail A. Marsh, "The Caring Continuum: Evolved Hormonal and Proximal Mechanisms Explain Prosocial and Antisocial Extremes," *Annual Review of Psychology* 70, no. 1 (2019): 347–71, https://doi.org/10.1146/annurev-psych-010418-103010.

3. Phillip R. Shaver et al., "A Lifespan Perspective on Attachment and Care for Others: Empathy, Altruism, and Prosocial Behavior," in *Handbook of Attachment: Theory, Research, and Clinical Applications*, ed. Jude Cassidy and Phillip R. Shaver, 3rd ed. (New York: Guilford Press, 2016), 878–916; Mario Mikulincer and Phillip R. Shaver, "Boosting Attachment Security in Adulthood: The 'Broaden-and-Build' Effects of Security-Enhancing Mental Representations and Interpersonal Contexts," in *Attachment Theory and Research: New Directions and Emerging Themes*, ed. Jeffry A. Simpson and W. Steven Rholes (New York: Guilford Press, 2015), 124–44; Glenn I. Roisman et al., "Earned–Secure Attachment Status in Retrospect and Prospect," *Child Development* 73, no. 4 (2002): 1204–19, https://doi.org/10.1111/1467-8624.00467; Rachel Saunders et al., "Pathways to Earned-Security: The Role of Alternative Support Figures," *Attachment and Human Development* 13, no. 4 (July 1, 2011): 403–20, https://doi.org/10.1080/14616734.2011.584405.

4. Frank Rogers, *Practicing Compassion* (Nashville, TN: Fresh Air Books, 2015), 11–15, 18–20, 38; Jamil Zaki, *The War for Kindness: Building Empathy in a Fractured World* (New York: Crown, 2019), 94–118.

5. David McMahan and Erik Braun, "Introduction—From Colonialism to Brainscans: Modern Transformations of Buddhist Meditation," in *Meditation, Buddhism,*

and Science, ed. David McMahan and Erik Braun (New York: Oxford University Press, 2017), 1–20.

6. Funie Hsu, "American Cultural Baggage: The Racialized Secularization of Mindfulness in Schools," in *Secularizing Buddhism: New Perspectives on a Dynamic Tradition*, ed. Richard K. Payne (Boulder, CO: Shambhala Publications, 2021), 79–93.

7. Daniel Goleman, *Social Intelligence: The New Science of Social Relationships* (New York: Bantam Books, 2006), 55–56, 60–61; Hrdy, *Mothers and Others*, 5–7, 28–29, 39.

8. Paul Condon and John Makransky, "Recovering the Relational Starting Point of Compassion Training: A Foundation for Sustainable and Inclusive Care," *Perspectives on Psychological Science* 15 (2020): 1346–62, https://doi.org/10.1177/1745691620922200; Jinpa, *Fearless Heart*; Jude Cassidy, "The Nature of the Child's Ties," in *Handbook of Attachment: Theory, Research, and Clinical Applications*, ed. Jude Cassidy and Phillip R. Shaver, 3rd ed. (New York: Guilford Press, 2016), 3–24; Paul Gilbert, "Explorations into the Nature and Function of Compassion," in "Mindfulness," special issue, *Current Opinion in Psychology* 28 (August 1, 2019): 108–14, https://doi.org/10.1016/j.copsyc.2018.12.002; Jennifer L. Goetz, Dacher Keltner, and Emiliana Simon-Thomas, "Compassion: An Evolutionary Analysis and Empirical Review," *Psychological Bulletin* 136, no. 3 (2010): 351–74, https://doi.org/10.1037/a0018807; Hrdy, *Mothers and Others*; James N. Kirby, Jamin Day, and Vinita Sagar, "The 'Flow' of Compassion: A Meta-Analysis of the Fears of Compassion Scales and Psychological Functioning," *Clinical Psychology Review* 70 (June 1, 2019): 26–39, https://doi.org/10.1016/j.cpr.2019.03.001.

9. Hrdy, *Mothers and Others*; Matthieu Ricard, *Altruism: The Power of Compassion to Change Yourself and the World* (New York: Little, Brown, 2015), 173; Michael Tomasello et al., "Understanding and Sharing Intentions: The Origins of Cultural Cognition," *Behavioral and Brain Sciences* 28, no. 5 (2005): 675–91, https://doi.org/10.1017/S0140525X05000129.

10. Penny Spikins, "Prehistoric Origins: The Compassion of Far Distant Strangers," in *Compassion: Concepts, Research and Applications*, ed. Paul Gilbert (London: Routledge, 2017), 16–30.

11. Hrdy, *Mothers and Others*, 10, 25, 28–29.

12. Felix Warneken and Michael Tomasello, "The Roots of Human Altruism," *British Journal of Psychology* 100, no. 3 (2009): 455–71, https://doi.org/10.1348/000712608X379061; Michael Tomasello, *Why We Cooperate* (Cambridge, MA: MIT Press, 2009).

13. Felix Warneken and Michael Tomasello, "Altruistic Helping in Human Infants and Young Chimpanzees," *Science* 311, no. 5765 (March 3, 2006): 1301–3, https://doi.org/10.1126/science.1121448.

14. Tomasello, *Why We Cooperate*; Tomasello et al., "Understanding and Sharing Intentions."

15. David G. Rand, Joshua D. Greene, and Martin A. Nowak, "Spontaneous Giving and Calculated Greed," *Nature* 489, no. 7416 (September 2012): 427–30, https://

doi.org/10.1038/nature11467; David G. Rand, "Cooperation, Fast and Slow: Meta-Analytic Evidence for a Theory of Social Heuristics and Self-Interested Deliberation," *Psychological Science* 27, no. 9 (September 1, 2016): 1192–1206, https://doi.org/10.1177/0956797616654455.

16. David G. Rand and Ziv G. Epstein, "Risking Your Life without a Second Thought: Intuitive Decision-Making and Extreme Altruism," *PLOS ONE* 9, no. 10 (October 15, 2014): e109687, https://doi.org/10.1371/journal.pone.0109687.

17. Alain Cohn et al., "Civic Honesty around the Globe," *Science* 365, no. 6448 (July 5, 2019): 70–73, https://doi.org/10.1126/science.aau8712.

18. Hrdy, *Mothers and Others*, 28.

19. Cassidy, "Nature of the Child's Ties"; Mario Mikulincer and Phillip R. Shaver, *Attachment in Adulthood: Structure, Dynamics, and Change*, 2nd ed. (New York: Guilford Press, 2016), 3–74; Robert W. Roeser, Blake A. Colaianne, and Mark A. Greenberg, "Compassion and Human Development: Current Approaches and Future Directions," *Research in Human Development* 15, no. 3–4 (October 2, 2018): 238–51, https://doi.org/10.1080/15427609.2018.1495002.

20. Mario Mikulincer and Phillip R. Shaver, "Adult Attachment and Compassion: Normative and Individual Difference Components," in *The Oxford Handbook of Compassion Science*, ed. Emma M. Seppälä et al. (New York: Oxford University Press, 2017), 79–89, https://doi.org/10.1093/oxfordhb/9780190464684.013.7; Mario Mikulincer and Philip R. Shaver, "An Attachment Perspective on Compassion and Altruism," in *Compassion: Concepts, Research and Applications*, ed. Paul Gilbert (London: Routledge, 2017), 187–208, https://doi.org/10.4324/9781315564296-11; Jinpa, *Fearless Heart*, 54–55, 60–61; Shaver et al., "Lifespan Perspective on Attachment and Care for Others."

21. Jeremy Holmes and Arietta Slade, *Attachment in Therapeutic Practice* (Thousand Oaks, CA: Sage Publications, 2018); Mikulincer and Shaver, "Boosting Attachment Security in Adulthood."

22. Mikulincer and Shaver, "Attachment Perspective on Compassion and Altruism," 195.

23. Condon and Makransky, "Recovering the Relational Starting Point of Compassion Training"; Sharon Begley, *Train Your Mind, Change Your Brain: How a New Science Reveals Our Extraordinary Potential to Transform Ourselves* (New York: Ballantine Books, 2007), 194–97.

24. Paul Bloom, *Against Empathy: The Case for Rational Compassion* (New York: Ecco, 2016); Jamil Zaki and Mina Cikara, "Addressing Empathic Failures," *Current Directions in Psychological Science*, December 10, 2015, https://doi.org/10.1177/0963721415599978.

25. Paul Condon and John Makransky, "Recovering the Relational Starting Point of Compassion Training"; Kristin Neff and Christopher Germer, "Self-Compassion and Psychological Well-Being," in *The Oxford Handbook of Compassion Science*, ed. Emma Seppälä et al. (New York: Oxford University Press, 2017), 375, https://doi.org/10.1093/oxfordhb/9780190464684.001.0001.

26. Mikulincer and Shaver, "Adult Attachment and Compassion"; Ricard, *Altruism*, 63–64; C. Daryl Cameron and B. Keith Payne, "The Cost of Callousness: Regulating Compassion Influences the Moral Self-Concept," *Psychological Science* 23, no. 3 (March 1, 2012): 225–29, https://doi.org/10.1177/0956797611430334.

27. Paul Gilbert and Jennifer Mascaro, "Compassion Fears, Blocks, and Resistances: An Evolutionary Investigation," in *The Oxford Handbook of Compassion Science*, ed. Emma Seppälä et al. (New York: Oxford University Press, 2017), 399–418; Christina Maslach, Wilmar B. Schaufeli, and Michael P. Leiter, "Job Burnout," *Annual Review of Psychology* 52, no. 1 (2001): 397–422, https://doi.org/10.1146/annurev.psych.52.1.397.

28. Richard J. Davidson and Bruce S. McEwen, "Social Influences on Neuroplasticity: Stress and Interventions to Promote Well-Being," *Nature Neuroscience* 15, no. 5 (May 2012): 689–95, https://doi.org/10.1038/nn.3093; Cortland J. Dahl, Christine D. Wilson-Mendenhall, and Richard J. Davidson, "The Plasticity of Well-Being: A Training-Based Framework for the Cultivation of Human Flourishing," *Proceedings of the National Academy of Sciences* 117, no. 51 (December 22, 2020): 32197–206, https://doi.org/10.1073/pnas.2014859117.

29. Eleanor A. Maguire, Katherine Woollett, and Hugo J. Spiers, "London Taxi Drivers and Bus Drivers: A Structural MRI and Neuropsychological Analysis," *Hippocampus* 16, no. 12 (2006): 1091–1101, https://doi.org/10.1002/hipo.20233.

30. Recent research findings have demonstrated that meditation does not necessarily change brain structure, which has been a common assumption in the popular portrayal of scientific research. In that study, eight weeks of mindfulness-based training did not yield structural changes in the brain. See Tammi R. A. Kral et al., "Absence of Structural Brain Changes from Mindfulness-Based Stress Reduction: Two Combined Randomized Controlled Trials," *Science Advances* 8, no. 20 (May 20, 2022): eabk3316, https://doi.org/10.1126/sciadv.abk3316. Nevertheless, habits of mind that are repeated in any activity have the potential to shape physiological patterns of the brain and body (Dahl, Wilson-Mendenhall, and Davidson, "Plasticity of Well-Being"), including those relevant to compassion. Christine D. Wilson-Mendenhall, John D. Dunne, and Richard J. Davidson, "Visualizing Compassion: Episodic Simulation as Contemplative Practice," *Mindfulness* 14, no. 10 (October 1, 2023): 2532–48, https://doi.org/10.1007/s12671-022-01842-6. Further research is needed to uncover the contextual variables that impact the effects of meditation.

31. Mario Mikulincer and Phillip R. Shaver, "Attachment Theory and Intergroup Bias: Evidence That Priming the Secure Base Schema Attenuates Negative Reactions to out-Groups," *Journal of Personality and Social Psychology* 81, no. 1 (2001): 97–115, https://doi.org/10.1037/0022-3514.81.1.97; Begley, *Train Your Mind, Change Your Brain*, 198–211; Elle M. Boag and Katherine B. Carnelley, "Attachment and Prejudice: The Mediating Role of Empathy," *British Journal of Social Psychology* 55, no. 2 (2016): 337–56, https://doi.org/10.1111/bjso.12132.

32. Paul Condon, "Meditation in Context: Factors That Facilitate Prosocial Behavior," *Current Opinion in Psychology* 28 (2019): 15–19, https://doi.org/10.1016/j.copsyc.2018.09.011.

33. Olga M. Klimecki et al., "Differential Pattern of Functional Brain Plasticity after Compassion and Empathy Training," *Social Cognitive and Affective Neuroscience* 9, no. 6 (June 1, 2014): 873–79, https://doi.org/10.1093/scan/nst060; Jennifer S. Mascaro et al., "Compassion Meditation Enhances Empathic Accuracy and Related Neural Activity," *Social Cognitive and Affective Neuroscience* 8, no. 1 (January 1, 2013): 48–55, https://doi.org/10.1093/scan/nss095.

34. Helen Y. Weng et al., "Compassion Training Alters Altruism and Neural Responses to Suffering," *Psychological Science* 24 (2013): 1171–80, https://doi.org/10.1177/0956797612469537; Helen Y. Weng et al., "The Role of Compassion in Altruistic Helping and Punishment Behavior," *PLOS ONE* 10, no. 12 (December 10, 2015), https://doi.org/10.1371/journal.pone.0143794; Yoni K. Ashar et al., "Effects of Compassion Meditation on a Psychological Model of Charitable Donation," *Emotion* 16, no. 5 (August 2016): 691–705, http://dx.doi.org/10.1037/emo0000119.

35. Paul Condon et al., "Meditation Increases Compassionate Responses to Suffering," *Psychological Science* 24 (2013): 2125–27, https://doi.org/10.1177/0956797613485603.

36. Yoona Kang, Jeremy R. Gray, and John F. Dovidio, "The Nondiscriminating Heart: Lovingkindness Meditation Training Decreases Implicit Intergroup Bias," *Journal of Experimental Psychology: General* 143, no. 3 (2014): 1306–13, https://doi.org/10.1037/a0034150.

37. Daniel R. Berry et al., "Short-Term Training in Mindfulness Predicts Helping Behavior Toward Racial Ingroup and Outgroup Members," *Social Psychological and Personality Science* 14, no. 1 (January 1, 2023): 60–71, https://doi.org/10.1177/19485506211053095; Denise Zheng, Daniel R. Berry, and Kirk Warren Brown, "Effects of Brief Mindfulness Meditation and Compassion Meditation on Parochial Empathy and Prosocial Behavior Toward Ethnic Out-Group Members," *Mindfulness* 14, no. 10 (October 1, 2023): 2454–70, https://doi.org/10.1007/s12671-023-02100-z.

38. Condon and Makransky, "Recovering the Relational Starting Point of Compassion Training."

39. This pattern of ritual, prayer, and/or contemplation can be found in parts of each of the religious traditions surveyed in Huston Smith, *The World's Religions* (San Francisco: HarperSanFrancisco, 1991). For further examples of this pattern in diverse faiths, see, e.g., Peter Harvey, *An Introduction to Buddhism: Teachings, History and Practices* (New York: Cambridge University Press, 2013), 103–8, 151–93, 237–63; David Kinsley, *Hinduism: A Cultural Perspective* (Englewood Cliffs, NJ: Prentice Hall, 1982), 105–21; Laurence Thompson, *Chinese Religion: An Introduction* (Belmont, CA: Wadsworth, 1989), 36–74; H. Byron Earhart, *Religion in the Japanese Experience: Sources and Interpretations* (Belmont, CA: Wadsworth, 1974);

Karen Armstrong, *A History of God: The 4,000 Year Quest of Judaism, Christianity and Islam* (New York: Ballantine Books, 1993); from Christianity, Andrew Dreitcer, *Living Compassion, Loving Like Jesus* (Nashville, TN: Upper Room Books, 2017); from Judaism, Sheila Weinberg, *God Loves the Stranger: Stories, Poems and Prayers* (Amherst, MA: White River Books, 2017); from Sufism in Islam, Natana DeLong-Bas, *Islam: A Living Faith* (Winona, MN: Anselm Academic, 2018), 162–84.

40. Condon and Makransky, "Recovering the Relational Starting Point of Compassion Training."

41. See, e.g., Bhikku Ñāṇamoli and Bhikku Bodhi, *The Middle Length Discourses of the Buddha: A Translation of the Majjhima Nikāya* (Somerville, MA: Wisdom Publications, 1995), 120, 221–23, 374–75, 419–20, 434, 456–57, 474–75.

42. Buddhaghosa, *The Path of Purification: Visuddhimagga*, trans. Bhikku Ñāṇamoli (Colombo, Sri Lanka: A. Semage, 1964), 206–30.

43. David McMahan, *Empty Vision: Metaphor and Visionary Imagery in Mahāyāna Buddhism* (New York: Routledge Curzon, 2002), 149–58; see also Śāntideva, *Śikṣā Samuccaya*, trans. Cecil Bendall and W. H. D. Rouse (Delhi: Motilal Banaarsidass, 1981), 284–88.

44. McMahan, *Empty Vision*, 168–72; Bokar Rinpoche, *Chenrezig: Lord of Love* (San Francisco: ClearPoint Press, 1991), 11–17, 43–51; Tulku Urgyen Rinpoche, *As It Is*, vol. 1 (Hong Kong: Rangjung Yeshe, 1999), 31–38 (this section points directly to the enlightened nature of the reader); Tulku Thondup, *The Heart of Unconditional Love: A Powerful New Approach to Loving-Kindness Meditation* (Boston: Shambhala, 2015), 209–13.

45. Condon and Makransky, "Recovering the Relational Starting Point of Compassion Training."

46. Condon and Makransky, "Recovering the Relational Starting Point of Compassion Training"; David L. McMahan, *The Making of Buddhist Modernism* (New York: Oxford University Press, 2008), 183–214; Ronald E. Purser, *McMindfulness: How Mindfulness Became the New Capitalist Spirituality* (London: Repeater Books, 2019).

47. Purser, *McMindfulness.*

48. Francisco J. Varela, *Ethical Know-How: Action, Wisdom, and Cognition* (Stanford, CA: Stanford University Press, 1999), 74.

49. Simone Schnall et al., "Social Support and the Perception of Geographical Slant," *Journal of Experimental Social Psychology* 44, no. 5 (September 1, 2008): 1246–55, https://doi.org/10.1016/j.jesp.2008.04.011.

50. James A. Coan, Hillary S. Schaefer, and Richard J. Davidson, "Lending a Hand: Social Regulation of the Neural Response to Threat," *Psychological Science* 17, no. 12 (December 1, 2006): 1032–39, https://doi.org/10.1111/j.1467-9280.2006.01832.x.

51. James A. Coan and Erin L. Maresh, "Social Baseline Theory and the Social Regulation of Emotion," in *Handbook of Emotion Regulation*, ed. James J. Gross, 2nd ed. (New York: Guilford Press, 2014), 221–36; James A Coan and David A Sbarra, "Social Baseline Theory: The Social Regulation of Risk and Effort," in "Relationship Science," special issue, *Current Opinion in Psychology* 1 (February 1, 2015): 87–91, https://doi.org/10.1016/j.copsyc.2014.12.021.

52. SCT has also been referred to as innate compassion training (ICT) in prior publications, e.g., John Makransky, "Compassion beyond Fatigue: Contemplative Training for People Who Serve Others," in *Meditation and the Classroom: Contemplative Pedagogy for Religious Studies*, ed. Judith Simmer-Brown and Fran Grace (Albany: State University of New York Press, 2011), 85–94.

53. Condon and Makransky, "Recovering the Relational Starting Point of Compassion Training"; Roeser, Colaianne, and Greenberg, "Compassion and Human Development."

54. Figure adapted from Paul Condon and John Makransky, "Sustainable Compassion Training: Integrating Meditation Theory with Psychological Science," *Frontiers in Psychology* 11 (2020), https://www.frontiersin.org/articles/10.3389/fpsyg.2020.02249.

55. Lawrence W. Barsalou, "Perceptual Symbol Systems," *Behavioral and Brain Sciences* 22, no. 4 (August 1999): 577–660, https://doi.org/10.1017/S0140525X99002149; Lawrence W. Barsalou, "Simulation, Situated Conceptualization, and Prediction," *Philosophical Transactions of the Royal Society B: Biological Sciences* 364, no. 1521 (May 12, 2009): 1281–89, https://doi.org/10.1098/rstb.2008.0319; Lawrence W. Barsalou, "Grounded Cognition," *Annual Review of Psychology* 59 (2008): 617–45, https://doi.org/10.1146/annurev.psych.59.103006.093639.

56. For parallel descriptions of deepening modes of contemplative practice toward buddha nature, see Makransky, *Awakening through Love*, 33–68; Tulku Thondup, *The Healing Power of Mind: Simple Meditation Exercises for Health, Well-Being, and Enlightenment* (Boston: Shambhala Publications, 1996), 93–97; Tsoknyi Rinpoche, *Open Heart, Open Mind: Awakening the Power of Essence Love* (New York: Harmony Books, 2012), 41–80.

57. SCT constructs an "open" secular space in which a specific worldview is not prescribed but rather diverse religious and scientific perspectives are welcome within dialogue and practice. This contrasts with a "closed" secular space where discussions of religion or spirituality are avoided. When we teach aspects of SCT in medical centers to doctors, nurses, social workers, chaplains, and researchers, everyone in the room is invited to engage the practice at hand from within their own worldview, whether spiritual, scientific, or both. For more on open versus close secular space, see Brooke D. Lavelle, "Against One Method: Contemplation in Context," in *Handbook of Mindfulness: Culture, Context, and Social Engagement*, ed. Ronald E. Purser, David Forbes, and Adam Burke, Mindfulness in Behavioral Health (Cham: Springer, 2016), 233–42, https://doi.org/10.1007/978-3-319-44019-4_16; Condon and Makransky, "Sustainable Compassion Training."

58. Jared R. Lindahl et al., "The Varieties of Contemplative Experience: A Mixed-Methods Study of Meditation-Related Challenges in Western Buddhists," *PLOS ONE* 12, no. 5 (May 24, 2017): e0176239, https://doi.org/10.1371/journal .pone.0176239; David A. Treleaven, *Trauma-Sensitive Mindfulness: Practices for Safe and Transformative Healing* (New York: W. W. Norton, 2018).

59. We are grateful to Ana Hristić for conversations about trauma-informed approaches to meditation.

60. Treleaven, *Trauma-Sensitive Mindfulness*.

61. For further discussion, see Harvey Aronson, *Buddhist Practice on Western Ground: Reconciling Eastern Ideals and Western Psychology* (Boston: Shambhala, 2004).

1. RECEPTIVE MODE

1. Marsh, "The Caring Continuum"; Stephanie D. Preston, "The Origins of Altruism in Offspring Care," *Psychological Bulletin* 139, no. 6 (2013): 1305–41, https://doi .org/10.1037/a0031755.

2. It is important to note that meditation is not an activity that only happens inside the brain or head of an individual. According to theories of enactive cognition, activities such as meditation occur within a social and cultural context that includes others, just as an activity such as a bird flying through the sky doesn't only happen in the bird's brain. See Evan Thompson, "What Is Mind?" Insights: Journey into the Heart of Contemplative Science, August 29, 2022, https://www.mindandlife.org/insight /what-is-mind/. Enactive cognition further underscores the importance of a relational approach to meditation—that is, the relational environment is part of the supportive context that helps enact capacities of our underlying awareness.

3. Research confirms that we can access our capacities for care by observing others engage in prosocial acts. Scientists refer to this as moral elevation. See Simone Schnall and Jean Roper, "Elevation Puts Moral Values into Action," *Social Psychological and Personality Science* 3, no. 3 (May 1, 2012): 373–78, https://doi .org/10.1177/1948550611423595; Simone Schnall, Jean Roper, and Daniel M. T. Fessler, "Elevation Leads to Altruistic Behavior," *Psychological Science* 21, no. 3 (March 1, 2010): 315–20, https://doi.org/10.1177/0956797609359882.

4. Jacqueline Brenner et al., "Mindfulness with Paced Breathing Reduces Blood Pressure," *Medical Hypotheses* 142 (September 1, 2020): 109780, https://doi.org/10.1016/j .mehy.2020.109780.

5. Katie Hoemann et al., "Expertise in Emotion: A Scoping Review and Unifying Framework for Individual Differences in the Mental Representation of Emotional Experience," *Psychological Bulletin* 147 (2021): 1159–83, https://doi.org/10.1037 /bul0000327.

6. See, for example, Todd B. Kashdan, Lisa Feldman Barrett, and Patrick E. Mc-Knight, "Unpacking Emotion Differentiation: Transforming Unpleasant Experi-

ence by Perceiving Distinctions in Negativity," *Current Directions in Psychological Science* 24, no. 1 (February 1, 2015): 10–16, https://doi.org/10.1177/0963721414550708; Jacob Israelashvili et al., "Knowing Me, Knowing You: Emotion Differentiation in Oneself Is Associated with Recognition of Others' Emotions," *Cognition and Emotion* 33, no. 7 (February 8, 2019): 1–11, https://doi.org/10.1080/02699931.2019.157 7221; Marc A. Brackett et al., "Enhancing Academic Performance and Social and Emotional Competence with the RULER Feeling Words Curriculum," in "Noncognitive Skills in Education: Emerging Research and Applications in a Variety of International Contexts," special issue, *Learning and Individual Differences* 22, no. 2 (April 1, 2012): 218–24, https://doi.org/10.1016/j.lindif.2010.10.002.

7. Hoemann et al., "Expertise in Emotion"; Tse Yen Tan, Louise Wachsmuth, and Michele M. Tugade, "Emotional Nuance: Examining Positive Emotional Granularity and Well-Being," *Frontiers in Psychology* 13 (2022), https://www.frontiersin.org/articles/10.3389/fpsyg.2022.715966.

8. Theodore E. A. Waters and Glenn I. Roisman, "The Secure Base Script Concept: An Overview," in "Attachment in Adulthood," special issue, *Current Opinion in Psychology* 25 (February 1, 2019): 162–66, https://doi.org/10.1016/j.copsyc.2018.08.002; Harriet S. Waters and Everett Waters, "The Attachment Working Models Concept: Among Other Things, We Build Script-like Representations of Secure Base Experiences," *Attachment & Human Development* 8, no. 3 (September 1, 2006): 185–97, https://doi.org/10.1080/14616730600856016.

9. Daniel J. Simons and Christopher F. Chabris, "Gorillas in Our Midst: Sustained Inattentional Blindness for Dynamic Events," *Perception* 28, no. 9 (1999): 1059–74, https://doi.org/10.1068/p281059; for a replication of this basic concept with expert radiologists, see Trafton Drew, Melissa L.-H. Võ, and Jeremy M. Wolfe, "The Invisible Gorilla Strikes Again: Sustained Inattentional Blindness in Expert Observers," *Psychological Science* 24, no. 9 (September 1, 2013): 1848–53, https://doi.org/10.1177/0956797613479386.

10. N. L. Collins and B. C. Feeney, "Working Models of Attachment Shape Perceptions of Social Support: Evidence from Experimental and Observational Studies," *Journal of Personality and Social Psychology* 87, no. 3 (2004): 363–83, https://doi.org/10.1037/0022-3514.87.3.363; Matthew J. Dykas and Jude Cassidy, "Attachment and the Processing of Social Information across the Life Span: Theory and Evidence," *Psychological Bulletin* 137, no. 1 (2011): 19–46, https://doi.org/10.1037/a0021367.

11. Wilson-Mendenhall, Dunne, and Davidson, "Visualizing Compassion."

12. We are grateful to John Dunne for this example.

13. This approach was developed by our colleagues Paul Gilbert and Thupten Jinpa, inspired, in part, by practices of Indigenous traditions; Jinpa, *Fearless Heart*, 143–44; Paul Gilbert and Choden, *Mindful Compassion: How the Science of Compassion Can Help You Understand Your Emotions, Live in the Present, and Connect Deeply with Others*

(Oakland, CA: New Harbinger Publications, 2014), 243; see also Thondup, *Healing Power of Mind*, 93ff., on establishing a "source of power" that evokes the energies and wisdom for deep healing and awakening.

14. This practice draws from a meditation form developed by Paul Gilbert and Brooke Lavelle.

15. A note on terminology: Our use of the term *parts* is inspired by the internal family systems (IFS) model in psychotherapy. See Richard C. Schwartz and Martha Sweezy, *Internal Family Systems Therapy,* 2nd ed. (New York Guilford Press, 2019). Analogous terms are found in social psychology and developmental psychology, such as *self-concepts, self-representations,* and *internalized working models.* These terms each refer to a constructed sense of self with corresponding mental patterns and expectations about the self, others, and the world. We use the terms *part of us* and *sense of self* interchangeably to capture the possibility of different self-concepts or internalized working models that may be active in various moments, consciously or subconsciously. In contrast with IFS, we do not adopt the perspective that these "parts" refer to various subpersonalities or different autonomous beings within us. In our view, a "part of us" is a habit of mind that has been inhabited frequently enough such that it becomes concretized as a self-concept that a person identifies with. From a grounded cognition perspective, a "part of us" refers to a fully embodied simulation of an experience that we become identified with, as in the constructed experience of an emotion, such as anger, jealousy, pride, or enthusiasm.

16. Attachment theory explains why we tend to think that loving qualities come only from external sources. Attachment scripts are imprinted in the course of our development as a strategy to predict and control access to external sources of protection and love. Some of us have learned to be avoidant, for example, because we may have experienced others as unreliable sources of protection in our childhood. Scripts that tell us to dismiss others' signals of care, then, have served us since childhood to avoid being let down. In turn, we may adapt strategies of exaggerated self-reliance and may even become attracted to meditation as a self-help technique for an isolated sense of self. Phillip R. Shaver et al., "Social Foundations of the Capacity for Mindfulness: An Attachment Perspective," *Psychological Inquiry* 18, no. 4 (October 19, 2007): 264–71, https://doi.org/10.1080/10478400701598389; Varela, *Ethical Know-How*. But as we stated in the introductory chapter, that narrow kind of starting point for meditation can limit its larger ethical and social purposes.

17. The integration of attachment strategies and parts of us within meditation raises another point. First, people do not have only one attachment style or strategy—such as an "avoidant" strategy that dismisses external sources of support from fear that they are not reliable or an "anxious" strategy that nervously clings to external sources of support from fear of being abandoned. While people tend to have

one primary attachment strategy, we all have many attachment strategies with a diversity of attachment scripts and senses of self. These stem from our various experiences with different caregivers, mentors, friends, romantic partners, and so forth. These different scripts can alternate with each other so that we might feel anxious within one relationship and avoidant within another. N. L. Collins and Stephen J. Read, "Cognitive Representations of Attachment: The Structure and Function of Working Models," in *Attachment Processes in Adulthood*, Advances in Personal Relationships, vol. 5. (London: Jessica Kingsley, 1994), 53–90; Phillip R. Shaver, Mario Mikulincer, and Jude Cassidy, "Attachment, Caregiving in Couple Relationships, and Prosocial Behavior in the Wider World," in "Attachment in Adulthood," special issue, *Current Opinion in Psychology* 25 (February 1, 2019): 16–20, https://doi.org/10.1016/j.copsyc.2018.02.009.

18. Our use of the term *metabolize* was inspired by Resmaa Menakem, *My Grand-mother's Hands: Racialized Trauma and the Pathway to Mending Our Hearts and Bodies* (Las Vegas, NV: Central Recovery Press, 2017).

19. Lawrence W. Barsalou, "Grounded Cognition"; Wilson-Mendenhall, Dunne, and Davidson, "Visualizing Compassion"; for further discussion of caring moments in connection with grounded cognition, see Condon and Makransky, "Recovering the Relational Starting Point of Compassion Training."

20. We borrow the term *unblending* from internal family systems. See Schwartz and Sweezy, *Internal Family Systems Therapy*. In our view, the term *unblending* encompasses two key psychological processes: (1) Stepping back from any given sense of self or identity so as to observe it, i.e., "disidentification." Shauna L. Shapiro et al., "Mechanisms of Mindfulness," *Journal of Clinical Psychology* 62, no. 3 (2006): 373–86, https://doi.org/10.1002/jclp.20237; and (2) Experiencing our own thoughts as contingent mental events rather than true representations of the world, a process called "dereification" that is inspired by Tibetan Buddhist traditions. See Paul Condon, John Dunne, and Christine Wilson-Mendenhall, "Wisdom and Compassion: A New Perspective on the Science of Relationships," *Journal of Moral Education* 48, no. 1 (January 2, 2019): 98–108, https://doi.org/10.1080/03057240.2018.1439828. In Tibetan Buddhist terms, then, to unblend from a part enables the mind to release its identification with that particular sense of self and its goals so the mind can access more capacities of its buddha nature: spaciousness, fuller awareness, clarity, compassion, discernment, etc.

21. This process of unblending from senses of self is similar to increasing granularity for emotion. Research has shown that granularity also supports discernment of emotions that are unrelated to our current situation and the corresponding ability to unblend from such emotions, lessening their distorting influence on judgment and behavior. For example, after a difficult day at work, people commonly experience projecting their stress onto family members. However, training in emotion granularity can support unblending such that judgments of

others are immune to this carry-over effect. See C. Daryl Cameron, B. Keith Payne, and John M. Doris, "Morality in High Definition: Emotion Differentiation Calibrates the Influence of Incidental Disgust on Moral Judgments," *Journal of Experimental Social Psychology* 49, no. 4 (July 1, 2013): 719–25, https://doi .org/10.1016/j.jesp.2013.02.014.

22. Difficulties can also arise in the Field of Care Meditation when the mind prefers to continue to identify with a familiar part or sense of self, even if it is negative, rather than to have it challenged. Social psychologists refer to this tendency as "self-verification," and have discovered that people often prefer to spend time with others that verify our familiar sense of self, even if that sense of self is negative. See William B. Swann Jr. and Jennifer K. Bosson, "Self and Identity," in *Handbook of Social Psychology*, vol. 1, 5th ed. (Hoboken, NJ: John Wiley & Sons, 2010), 589–628, https://doi.org/10.1002/9780470561119.socpsy001016. Since various protective parts of us are very ingrained in the mind, the mind is often hesitant at first to learn how to unblend from them in the receptive mode. But with patience and repeated practice, these parts of the mind can catch on to the process in time, with repetition and patience and care for them.

23. While increasing granularity for senses of self will help deepen practice, it is also important to keep in mind that constant analysis of mental content can itself become an impediment to practice. We are drawing on psychological theories to help inform and support meditation practice. But during the meditations themselves, the practitioner should just follow the meditation instruction; not ruminate about psychological theories, since psychological analysis during meditation can become an impediment to the practice. See Aronson, *Buddhist Practice on Western Ground*. Constant analysis of experience is a barrier to deeper levels of meditative relaxation and settling into the source of loving qualities from our fundamental awareness, i.e., the deepening mode of SCT practice.

24. This image has been published in various forms throughout psychological science dating back to as early as 1899. For more on the history of this image in psychological research, see John F. Kihlstrom, "Joseph Jastrow and His Duck—Or Is It a Rabbit?" https://www.ocf.berkeley.edu/~jfkihlstrom/JastrowDuck.htm.

25. Katie Hoemann, Maria Gendron, and Lisa Feldman Barrett, "Mixed Emotions in the Predictive Brain," in "Mixed Emotions," special issue, *Current Opinion in Behavioral Sciences* 15 (June 1, 2017): 51–57, https://doi.org/10.1016/j.co beha.2017.05.013.

26. See, for example, Zhechen Gyaltsab Padma Gyurmed Namgyal, *Path of Heroes: Birth of Enlightenment*, vol. 2 (Oakland, CA: Dharma Publishing, 1995), 355–418.

27. Paul Gilbert, "Compassion as a Social Mentality: An Evolutionary Approach," in *Compassion: Concepts, Research and Applications* (London: Routledge, 2017), 31–68.

28. For further reading on trauma-sensitive mindfulness, see Treleaven, *Trauma-Sensitive Mindfulness*, 2018.

2. DEEPENING MODE

1. On these three aspects of fundamental awareness, see Longchen Rabjam, *The Precious Treasury of the Way of Abiding*, trans. Richard Barron (Junction City, CA: Padma Publishing, 2001), 36–41; Longchen Rabjam, *The Precious Treasury of the Basic Space of Phenomena*, trans. Richard Barron (Junction City, CA: Padma Publishing, 2001), 52–55; Tulku Urgyen Rinpoche, *Rainbow Painting* (Hong Kong: Rangjung Yeshe, 1995), 52–57; Chokyi Nyima Rinpoche, *Present Fresh Wakefulness: A Meditation Manual on Nonconceptual Wisdom* (Hong Kong: Rangjung Yeshe, 2002), 46–47; John Reynolds, *The Golden Letters: The Three Statements of Garab Dorje with Commentary by Dza Patrul Rinpoche* (Ithaca, NY: Snow Lion Publications, 1996), 84–89.

2. When first learning the meditations in chapter 2, it is helpful to notice these "parts of the mind" as various senses of self. With increasing practice, we can begin to experience these senses of self as mere patterns of mind rather than concretized entities or substantial identities. Experiencing parts of mind as mere patterns of thought is part of the process of the deepening-mode practices in this chapter, which cultivate the wisdom that recognizes the constructed nature, and therefore the emptiness, of all those senses of self. We will explore this further in this chapter.

3. Longchen Rabjam, *Precious Treasury of the Way of Abiding*, 34–37; Reginald Ray, *Indestructible Truth: The Living Spirituality of Tibetan Buddhism* (Boston: Shambhala, 2000), 421–22, 434–37; Makransky, *Awakening through Love*, 34–35; Reginald Ray, *Secret of the Vajra World: The Tantric Buddhism of Tibet* (Boston: Shambhala, 2001), 265–69; John Welwood, *Toward a Psychology of Awakening* (Boston: Shambhala, 2002), 157, 165.

4. Karl Rahner, "The Experience of God Today," in *Theological Investigations*, vol. 11, trans. David Bourke (London: Darton, Longman and Todd, 1974), 154–56; Anne Carr, "Starting with the Human," in *A World of Grace: An Introduction to the Themes and Foundations of Karl Rahner's Theology*, ed. Leo O'Donovan (Washington DC: Georgetown University Press, 1995), 21–22; Elizabeth Johnson, *Quest for the Living God: Mapping Frontiers in the Theology of God* (London: Bloomsbury, 2007), 33–37, 41–42.

5. Varela, *Ethical Know-How*, 43–75; E. Fucci et al., "Differential Effects of Non-Dual and Focused Attention Meditations on the Formation of Automatic Perceptual Habits in Expert Practitioners," *Neuropsychologia* 119 (October 1, 2018): 92–100, https://doi.org/10.1016/j.neuropsychologia.2018.07.025; Ruben E. Laukkonen and Heleen A. Slagter, "From Many to (n)One: Meditation and the Plasticity of the Predictive Mind," *Neuroscience & Biobehavioral Reviews* 128 (September 1, 2021): 199–217, https://doi.org/10.1016/j.neubiorev.2021.06.021.

6. Jinpa, *Fearless Heart*, 131.

7. When people seek to avoid or suppress feelings, over time those feelings ironically increase. See Daniel M. Wegner, "When the Antidote Is the Poison: Ironic Mental Control Processes," *Psychological Science* 8, no. 3 (May 1, 1997): 148–50, https://doi .org/10.1111/j.1467-9280.1997.tb00399.x; Daniel M. Wegner, Ralph Erber, and Sophia Zanakos, "Ironic Processes in the Mental Control of Mood and Mood-Related Thought," *Journal of Personality and Social Psychology* 65, no. 6 (1993): 1093–1104, https://doi.org/10.1037/0022-3514.65.6.1093.

8. Emotional suppression can yield greater sympathetic nervous system reactivity which manifests as physical and emotional tightness, including heightened blood pressure, vasoconstriction, and avoidance motivation. See James J. Gross and Robert W. Levenson, "Emotional Suppression: Physiology, Self-Report, and Expressive Behavior," *Journal of Personality and Social Psychology* 64, no. 6 (1993): 970–86, https://doi.org/10.1037/0022-3514.64.6.970; Iris B. Mauss and James J. Gross, "Emotion Suppression and Cardiovascular Disease: Is Hiding Feelings Bad for Your Heart?," in *Emotional Expression and Health: Advances in Theory, Assessment and Clinical Applications*, ed. Ivan Nyklicek, Lydia Temoshok, and A. J. J. M. Vingerhoets (New York: Brunner-Routledge, 2004), 61–81; Wendy Berry Mendes et al., "Cardiovascular Correlates of Emotional Expression and Suppression: Do Content and Gender Context Matter?" *Journal of Personality and Social Psychology* 84, no. 4 (2003): 771–92, https://doi.org/10.1037/0022-3514.84.4.771.

9. Emotional suppression can also disrupt interpersonal communication and relationship quality. See Emily A. Butler et al., "The Social Consequences of Expressive Suppression," *Emotion* 3, no. 1 (2003): 48–67, https://doi.org/10.1037/1528-3542.3.1.48; Jane M. Richards, Emily A. Butler, and James J. Gross, "Emotion Regulation in Romantic Relationships: The Cognitive Consequences of Concealing Feelings," *Journal of Social and Personal Relationships* 20, no. 5 (October 1, 2003): 599–620, https://doi.org/10.1177/02654075030205002.

10. For a summary of this dilemma in relation to health-care settings, see Paul Condon and John Makransky, "Compassion Practices," in *Integrative Medicine*, ed. David Rakel and Vincent J. Minichiello, 5th ed. (New York: Elsevier, 2023), 831–35.

11. Lisa Feldman Barrett, *How Emotions Are Made: The Secret Life of the Brain* (New York: Houghton Mifflin, 2017), 112–27.

12. Lisa Feldman Barrett, "Emotions Are Real," *Emotion* 12, no. 3 (2012): 413–29, https://doi.org/10.1037/a0027555.

13. Lisa Feldman Barrett, "Your Brain Predicts (Almost) Everything You Do," *Mindful*, April 29, 2021, https://www.mindful.org/your-brain-predicts-almost -everything-you-do/.

14. This analysis of emotions in light of the theory of constructed emotion and the Compassionate Presence to Feelings Meditation also applies to other psychological categories in this book: "parts of the mind" "senses of self" "attachment scripts" "internalized working models," and so forth. According to constructiv-

ist views in psychological science and in Buddhist theories of the mind, every experience is utterly unique. Yet most of the time, we do not notice that, because the words that we use to describe our experiences suppress the uniqueness of each moment. Each time we experience a "part of me" or a particular "attachment script," the mind is constructing that experience anew by drawing on past experiences to make meaning of the current unique moment. This means that "parts of the mind," "self-identities," "attachment scripts," or "internalized working models" are not static entities that occur in the exact same way, each time, like a computer algorithm repeating itself, but are constantly being reconstructed based on the accrued experience of our lives. Because of this, with increasing meditation practice, the experienced qualities of the practices (like warmth, acceptance, spaciousness, and discernment) can become associated with the various parts, scripts, or models of ourselves, which transforms our experience of them. For more on the Buddhist theories of mind that emphasize the utter uniqueness of each moment, see John Dunne, "Key Features of Dharmakīrti's Apoha Theory," in *Apoha: Buddhist Nominalism and Human Cognition*, ed. Mark Siderits, Tom Tillemans, and Arindam Chakrabarti (New York: Columbia University Press, 2011), 84–108; Georges B. J. Dreyfus, *Recognizing Reality: Dharmakīrti's Philosophy and Its Tibetan Interpretations* (Albany: State University of New York Press, 1997), 56. For analogous perspectives in psychology, see Hoemann, Gendron, and Barrett, "Mixed Emotions in the Predictive Brain"; Barsalou, "Perceptual Symbol Systems."

15. On the "holding environment," see D. W. Winnicott, "The Theory of the Parent-Infant Relationship," *International Journal of Psycho-Analysis* 41 (December 1960): 585–95; Kent Hoffman, "Taking Refuge in the Family of Things," *The Arrow* 2 (2015): 1–30.

16. This nondual view from Dzogchen, Mahāmudrā, and Zen Buddhist traditions aligns with research on mindfulness and emotional reactivity, which shows that acceptance is a key ingredient of mindfulness meditation. See Emily K. Lindsay and J. David Creswell, "Mechanisms of Mindfulness Training: Monitor and Acceptance Theory (MAT)," *Clinical Psychology Review* 51 (February 1, 2017): 48–59, https://doi.org/10.1016/j.cpr.2016.10.011. Acceptance is also a central process in allied therapies that relieve stress. See Steven C. Hayes, "Buddhism and Acceptance and Commitment Therapy," *Cognitive and Behavioral Practice* 9, no. 1 (December 1, 2002): 58–66, https://doi.org/10.1016/S1077-7229(02)80041-4; Clive J. Robins, Henry Schmidt III, and Marsha M. Linehan, "Dialectical Behavior Therapy: Synthesizing Radical Acceptance with Skillful Means," in *Mindfulness and Acceptance: Expanding the Cognitive-Behavioral Tradition* (New York: Guilford Press, 2004), 30–44.

17. Welwood, *Toward a Psychology of Awakening*, 116–20, 137–47.

18. Welwood, 143.

19. Welwood, 145.

20. Jodi Halpern, "What Is Clinical Empathy?" *Journal of General Internal Medicine* 18, no. 8 (August 1, 2003): 670–74, https://doi.org/10.1046/j.1525-1497.2003.21017.x.

21. Zaki, *War for Kindness*, 94–118; Jamil Zaki, "The Caregiver's Dilemma: In Search of Sustainable Medical Empathy," *Lancet* 396, no. 10249 (August 15, 2020): 458–59, https://doi.org/10.1016/S0140-6736(20)31685-8.

22. Shane Sinclair et al., "Healthcare Providers Perspectives on Compassion Training: A Grounded Theory Study," *BMC Medical Education*. 20, no. 249 (2020), doi:10.1186 /s12909-020-02164-8; Antonio T. Fernando and Nathan S. Consedine, "Beyond Compassion Fatigue: The Transactional Model of Physician Compassion," *Journal of Pain and Symptom Management* 42, no. 2 (2014): 289–298, 2014; 48(2): 289–98. doi:10.1016/j.jpainsymman.2013.09.014.

23. Jeremy P. Jamieson, Matthew K. Nock, and Wendy Berry Mendes, "Mind over Matter: Reappraising Arousal Improves Cardiovascular and Cognitive Responses to Stress," *Journal of Experimental Psychology: General* 141, no. 3 (2012): 417–22, https:// doi.org/10.1037/a0025719; Jeremy P. Jamieson et al., "Reappraising Stress Arousal Improves Performance and Reduces Evaluation Anxiety in Classroom Exam Situations," *Social Psychological and Personality Science* 7, no. 6 (August 1, 2016): 579–87, https://doi.org/10.1177/1948550616644656.

24. See, e.g., Pema Chödrön, *Start Where You Are: A Guide to Compassionate Living* (Boston: Shambhala, 2001); Dilgo Khyentse Rinpoche, *Enlightened Courage: An Explanation of the Seven Point Mind Training* (Ithaca, NY: Snow Lion Publications, 1993); Ryōkan, *Dewdrops on a Lotus Leaf: Zen Poems of Ryōkan*, trans. John Stevens (Boston: Shambhala, 1996).

25. Tsoknyi Rinpoche, *Open Heart, Open Mind*, 41–81.

26. Cher Weixia Chen and Paul C. Gorski, "Burnout in Social Justice and Human Rights Activists: Symptoms, Causes and Implications," *Journal of Human Rights Practice* 7, no. 3 (November 1, 2015): 366–90, https://doi.org/10.1093/jhuman/huv011.

27. Welwood, *Toward a Psychology of Awakening*, 134, 144–47.

28. Rod Owens, *Love and Rage: The Path of Liberation through Anger* (Berkeley, CA: North Atlantic Books, 2020), 27.

29. John Makransky, "Confronting the 'Sin' Out of Love for the 'Sinner': Fierce Compassion as a Force for Social Change," *Buddhist-Christian Studies* 36, no. 1 (October 10, 2016): 87–96, https://doi.org/10.1353/bcs.2016.0009.

30. Wangchuk Dorje, *Mahāmudrā: The Ocean of Definitive Meaning*, trans. Elizabeth Callahan (Seattle: Nitartha International, 2001), 110–12; Dakpo Tashi Namgyal, *Clarifying the Natural State*, trans. Erik Kunzang (Hong Kong: Rangjung Yeshe, 2001), 55; Chokyi Nyima Rinpoche, *Sadness, Love, Openness* (Boulder, CO: Shambhala, 2018), 101; Reynolds, *Golden Letters*, 101; Willa Blythe Baker, *The Wakeful Body: Somatic Mindfulness as a Path to Freedom* (Boulder, CO: Shambhala, 2021), 141–43.

31. The "zoom lens" metaphor has been used by Tsoknyi Rinpoche when teaching śamatha without support.

32. Tsoknyi Rinpoche, *Fearless Simplicity: The Dzogchen Way of Living Freely in a Complex World* (Hong Kong: Rangjung Yeshe, 2003), 78.

33. Tsoknyi Rinpoche, *Fearless Simplicity*, 66, 73; Orgyen Chowang, *Our Pristine Mind* (Boulder, CO: Shambhala, 2016), 44–52.

34. Traleg Kyabgon, *Mind at Ease: Self-Liberation through Mahāmudrā Meditation* (Boston: Shambhala, 2004), 156–58; Dakpo Tashi Namgyal, *Moonbeams of Mahamudra* (Ithaca, NY: Snow Lion, 2019), 193–94, 197, 199; Dorje, *Mahāmudrā*, 116; Chowang, *Our Pristine Mind*, 46–48; Tsoknyi Rinpoche, *Fearless Simplicity*, 50–80; Tsoknyi Rinpoche, *Open Heart, Open Mind*, 223–24.

35. Lawrence W. Barsalou, "Deriving Categories to Achieve Goals," in *Psychology of Learning and Motivation*, ed. Gordon H. Bower, vol. 27 (San Diego: Academic Press, 1991), 1–64, https://doi.org/10.1016/S0079-7421(08)60120-6; Lisa Feldman Barrett and Barbara L Finlay, "Concepts, Goals and the Control of Survival-Related Behaviors," in "Survival Circuits," special issue, *Current Opinion in Behavioral Sciences* 24 (December 1, 2018): 172–79, https://doi.org/10.1016/j.cobeha.2018.10.001.

36. Tsoknyi Rinpoche, *Fearless Simplicity*, 67.

37. Tsoknyi Rinpoche, 55–59; Chowang, *Our Pristine Mind*, 46–52

38. Tsoknyi Rinpoche, *Fearless Simplicity*, 77.

39. John D. Dunne, "Toward an Understanding of Non-Dual Mindfulness," *Contemporary Buddhism* 12, no. 1 (May 1, 2011): 71–88, https://doi.org/10.1080/14639947.2011.564820; Evan Thompson, "What's in a Concept? Conceptualizing the Nonconceptual in Buddhist Philosophy and Cognitive Science," MindRxiv, August 14, 2020, https://doi.org/10.31231/osf.io/2m84e; Paul Condon and John Makransky, "Compassion and Skillful Means: Cultural Adaptation, Psychological Science, and Creative Responsiveness," *Mindfulness* 14 (2023): 2231–41, https://link.springer.com/article/10.1007/s12671-022-01866-y.

40. Sogyal Rinpoche, "Dharma Talk: A Mind Like a Clear Pool," *Tricycle: The Buddhist Review* (Fall 2002): 45–46, on shamatha without support settling naturally toward the view of Dzogchen; Reynolds, *Golden Letters*, 78; Chokyi Nyima Rinpoche, *Sadness, Love, Openness*, 98–103; Chowang, *Our Pristine Mind*, 48–49, 94.

41. Chokyi Nyima Rinpoche, *Sadness, Love, Openness*, 102.

42. Tsoknyi Rinpoche, *Fearless Simplicity*, 148–53; Reynolds, *Golden Letters*, 114–15.

43. Eleanor J. Gibson and Richard D. Walk, "The 'Visual Cliff,'" *Scientific American* 202, no. 4 (1960): 64–71; James F. Sorce et al., "Maternal Emotional Signaling: Its Effect on the Visual Cliff Behavior of 1-Year-Olds," *Developmental Psychology* 21, no. 1 (1985): 195–200, https://doi.org/10.1037/0012-1649.21.1.195.

44. Paul Condon, "Venturing Beyond Our Fear of Emptiness," *Lion's Roar*, November 16, 2023, https://www.lionsroar.com/venturing-beyond-our-fear-of-emptiness/.

45. Namgyal, *Clarifying the Natural State*, 27–39; Thrangu Rinpoche, *Crystal Clear: Practical Advice for Mahamudra Meditators* (Hong Kong: Rangjung Yeshe, 2003), 56–76; Tsoknyi Rinpoche, *Open Heart, Open Mind*, 2012, 180–98; Tsoknyi Rinpoche, *Fearless Simplicity*, 118–26; Makransky, *Awakening through Love*, 55–62.

46. Paul Condon, "Buddhanature beyond Mere Concept," *Buddhadharma: The Practitioner's Guide* 21, no. 4 (2023): 77–76.

3. INCLUSIVE MODE

1. Analogously, the eighth-century Indian Buddhist teacher Śāntideva declared that we should learn to protect all beings like we protect all parts of our bodies. Śāntideva, *A Guide to the Bodhisattva Way of Life*, trans. B. Alan Wallace and Vesna Wallace (Ithaca, NY: Snow Lion Publications, 1997), 100–101 (Bodhicaryāvatāra, ch. 8, vv. 91, 99).

2. On "communing," see the section on "inclusive mode" in Condon and Makransky, "Sustainable Compassion Training"; on the related concept of "resonance" as a key element of love and compassion, see Barbara Fredrickson and Daniel Siegel, "Broaden and Build Theory Meets Interpersonal Neurobiology as a Lens on Compassion and Positivity Resonance," in *Compassion: Concepts, Research and Applications*, ed. Paul Gilbert (London: Routledge, 2017), 203–18.

3. On taking ancestors and intergenerational trauma into the field of care practice as a basis of deep healing and awakening, see Cheryl Giles, "They Say the People Could Fly: Disrupting the Legacy of Sexual Violence through Myth, Memory, and Connection," in *Black and Buddhist: What Buddhism Can Teach Us about Race, Resilience, Transformation, and Freedom*, ed. Cheryl Giles and Pamela Ayo Yetunde (Boulder, CO: Shambhala, 2020), 25–43; Owens, *Love and Rage*, 67–91, 177–87.

4. Within attachment theory, psychologists understand this preverbal level of connection as moments of emotional attunement that are experienced between a parent and infant before language is learned, which then establishes patterns of relationality for the future, called implicit relational knowing. See Karlen Lyons-Ruth et al., "Implicit Relational Knowing: Its Role in Development and Psychoanalytic Treatment," *Infant Mental Health Journal* 19, no. 3 (1998): 282–89, https://doi.org/10.1002/(SICI)1097-0355(199823)19:3<282::AID-IMHJ3>3.0.CO;2-O. Moments of emotional attunement between people are also the basis for an expansion of one's consciousness to greater levels of emotional awareness, complexity, and meaning. See Ed Tronick and Marjorie Beeghly, "Infants' Meaning-Making and the Development of Mental Health Problems," *American Psychologist* 66, no. 2 (2011): 107–19, https://doi.org/10.1037/a0021631; Fabia Eleonora Banella and Ed Tronick, "Mutual Regulation and Unique Forms of Implicit Relational Knowing," in *Early Interaction and Developmental Psychopathology: Volume I: Infancy*, ed. Gisèle Apter, Emmanuel Devouche, and Maya Gratier (Cham: Springer, 2019), 35–53, https://doi.org/10.1007/978-3-030-04769-6_3.

5. Erica J. Boothby, Margaret S. Clark, and John A. Bargh, "Shared Experiences Are Amplified," *Psychological Science* 25, no. 12 (December 1, 2014): 2209–16, https://doi.org/10.1177/0956797614551162.

6. According to Buddhist perspectives of concept formation, there are two errors that occur when we form concepts of self and others: First, the mind attributes a false sameness to utterly unique instances that suppresses their differences. We might notice this when meeting someone new, when we have an immediate dislike for them because they look like or remind us of someone we had difficulty with in the past. Second, the mind engages in a process of fusion in which it mistakes the conceptual representation of self or other for the actual being. We relate to our thought of another person as if it were that person, without noticing their fuller humanity and subjectivity. This perspective is drawn from the seventh-century Buddhist philosopher Dharmakirti as explained by Dunne, "Key Features of Dharmakīrti's Apoha Theory"; for integration with psychological research on reification and cognitive fusion, see Condon and Makransky, "Recovering the Relational Starting Point of Compassion Training," 1350–51.

7. On holding our identities lightly from a place of depth, see Tsoknyi Rinpoche, *Open Heart, Open Mind*, 108–10.

8. Thanks to Paul Knitter for sharing this story.

9. Martin Buber, *I and Thou*, trans. Walter Kaufman (New York: Charles Scribner's Sons, 1970), 67–68.

10. Martin Luther King Jr., *A Gift of Love: Sermons from "Strength to Love" and Other Preachings* (Boston: Beacon Press, 2012), 45–48.

11. See Dzigar Kongtrul, *Training in Tenderness* (Boulder, CO: Shambhala, 2018), 43–61, for an impressively thorough deconstructive analysis of all tendencies to hold grudges. Dilgo Khyentse Rinpoche taught, "If you subdue the hatred within, you will discover that there is not a single enemy left outside." Dilgo Khyentse Rinpoche and Matthieu Ricard, *The Spirit of Tibet* (New York: Aperture, 2001), 61.

12. This is another example of enactive cognition: the processes of the mind are not occurring only in one's head but are enacted and embedded in a wider social web. See Thompson, "What Is Mind?"

4. GENERATING ALL-INCLUSIVE COMPASSION AND WISDOM

1. E. A. Burtt, ed., *Teachings of the Compassionate Buddha* (New York: Mentor, 1955), 45–46; Eugene Watson Burlingame, *Buddhist Legends in the Pali Text of the Dhammapada Commentary*, vol. 30, Harvard Oriental Series (Cambridge MA: Harvard University Press, 1921), 165–66.

2. Ricard, *Altruism*, 58.

3. For aspects of compassion in Buddhist psychology and contemplative training, see Dalai Lama, *Dalai Lama, an Open Heart: Practicing Compassion in Everyday Life* (New York: Little, Brown, 2001), 91–106; Ricard, *Altruism*, 25–29, 57–64; John Makransky, "Compassion in Buddhist Psychology," in *Wisdom and Compassion in Psychotherapy*, ed. Christopher Germer and Ronald Siegel (New York: Guilford

Press, 2012); Harvey, *Introduction to Buddhism*, 151–53, 278–82; Yangsi Rinpoche, *Practicing the Path: A Commentary on the Lamrim Chenmo* (Boston: Wisdom Publications, 2003), 300–342; Anālayo, *Compassion and Emptiness in Early Buddhist Meditation* (Cambridge, UK: Windhorse, 2015); Harvey Aronson, *Love and Sympathy in Theravāda Buddhism* (Delhi: Motilal Banarsidass, 1980).

4. This definition of empathy includes the three dimensions of empathy that have been identified by neuroscientists and psychologists: (1) perspective-taking, which involves imaging what others are feeling; (2) experience sharing, which involves mirroring or feeling the emotions that others experience; and (3) empathic concern, which involves a motivation to extend care to others. See Jamil Zaki and Kevin N. Ochsner, "The Neuroscience of Empathy: Progress, Pitfalls and Promise," *Nature Neuroscience* 15, no. 5 (May 2012): 675–80, https://doi.org/10.1038/nn.3085. The last dimension is sometimes equated with compassion in psychological research.

5. This definition of compassion is similar to psychological definitions of compassion as (1) a state of concern in response to another's needs or suffering, and (2) a desire to alleviate their suffering. See Goetz, Keltner, and Simon-Thomas, "Compassion"; yet our definition also includes more features because it draws heavily on Tibetan Buddhism, known for its sophistication in the theory and practice of compassion. Those features are the focus of this chapter. For similar approaches to defining compassion and its qualities, see Gilbert and Choden, *Mindful Compassion*, 95–120; Ricard, *Altruism*. Both of these sources, like us, draw both from Buddhism and psychology.

6. Zaki and Cikara, "Addressing Empathic Failures."

7. C. Daryl Cameron and B. Keith Payne, "Escaping Affect: How Motivated Emotion Regulation Creates Insensitivity to Mass Suffering," *Journal of Personality and Social Psychology* 100, no. 1 (2011): 1–15, https://doi.org/10.1037/a0021643.

8. On kinds of wisdom that inform compassion, also see Dalai Lama, *Dalai Lama, an Open Heart*, 91–106; Ricard, *Altruism*, 26–38.

9. A frequent quote in Buddhist traditions. See, e.g., Zhechen Gyaltsab Padma Gyurmed Namgyal, *Path of Heroes: Birth of Enlightenment*, vol. 1 (Oakland, CA: Dharma Publishing, 1995), 81; Kelsang Gyatso, *Joyful Path of Good Fortune* (New York: Tharpa, 2016), 285.

10. On the three levels of suffering as basis of compassion in Buddhist understanding, see also Dalai Lama, *Dalai Lama, an Open Heart*, 93–96; Yangsi Rinpoche, *Practicing the Path*, 317.

11. Dalai Lama, *Dalai Lama, an Open Heart*, 93, 95.

12. Dzogchen Ponlop Rinpoche, *Trainings in Compassion* (Ithaca, NY: Snow Lion Publications, 2004), 18; Namgyal, *Path of Heroes*, vol. 2, 345, 585–86.

13. For evidence that granularity supports recognition of others' emotions, see Israelashvili et al., "Knowing Me, Knowing You"; Yasemin Erbas et al., "Feeling

Me, Feeling You: The Relation Between Emotion Differentiation and Empathic Accuracy," *Social Psychological and Personality Science* 7, no. 3 (April 1, 2016): 240–47, https://doi.org/10.1177/1948550616633504.

14. See also Owens, *Love and Rage*, 239–52; Rod Owens, "The Dharma of Trauma," in *Black and Buddhist: What Buddhism Can Teach Us about Race, Resilience, Transformation and Freedom*, ed. Cheryl Giles and Pamela Ayo Yetunde (Boulder, CO: Shambhala, 2020), 44–64; Giles, "They Say the People Could Fly," 39–43.

15. Research has shown that the mere physical presence of a supportive person, especially someone with whom we have a close relationship, can help attenuate emotional reactivity to threat. See Coan, Schaefer, and Davidson, "Lending a Hand"; Coan and Maresh, "Social Baseline Theory and the Social Regulation of Emotion"; see also our discussion of social baseline theory in the introduction to this book.

16. Research on experiences of security evoked through attachment priming (first introduced in chapters 1 and 2) has shown that a feeling of security can help us to experience these outcomes—including greater emotional resource and patience to listen to others in their difficulties. See Mario Mikulincer et al., "Security Enhancement, Self-Esteem Threat, and Mental Depletion Affect Provision of a Safe Haven and Secure Base to a Romantic Partner," *Journal of Social and Personal Relationships* 31, no. 5 (2014): 630–50, https://doi.org/10.1177/0265407514525887. For reduced in-group/out-group biases, see Boag and Carnelley, "Attachment and Prejudice"; Mikulincer and Shaver, "Attachment Theory and Intergroup Bias." The field of care and compassionate presence to feelings components of the meditations introduced above help establish that kind of secure base.

17. Annie Murphy Paul, "Your Brain on Fiction," Opinion, *New York Times*, March 17, 2012, https://www.nytimes.com/2012/03/18/opinion/sunday/the-neuroscience -of-your-brain-on-fiction.html; Raymond A. Mar, "Stories and the Promotion of Social Cognition," *Current Directions in Psychological Science* 27, no. 4 (August 1, 2018): 257–62, https://doi.org/10.1177/0963721417749654; John F. Dovidio et al., "Reducing Intergroup Bias through Intergroup Contact: Twenty Years of Progress and Future Directions," *Group Processes & Intergroup Relations* 20, no. 5 (September 1, 2017): 606–20, https://doi.org/10.1177/1368430217712052; Tal Eyal, Mary Steffel, and Nicholas Epley, "Perspective Mistaking: Accurately Understanding the Mind of Another Requires Getting Perspective, Not Taking Perspective," *Journal of Personality and Social Psychology* 114, no. 4 (April 2018): 547–71, https://doi.org/10.1037 /pspa0000115.

18. Personal communication, 2014, originally quoted in John Makransky, "A Buddhist Critique of, and Learning from, Christian Liberation Theology," *Theological Studies* 75, no. 3 (September 1, 2014): 635–57, https://doi.org/10.1177/0040563914541028.

19. The instructions in this meditation cultivate our capacity to choose empathy as a path to compassion instead of empathic distress. The ability to convert feelings of empathy into compassion aligns with psychological perspectives

that suggest empathy is a motivated choice—we can become more skillful at empathy by making a choice to empathize with others, which overcomes the tendency to shut down our emotional responsiveness. See C. Daryl Cameron, "Compassion Collapse: Why We Are Numb to Numbers," in *The Oxford Handbook of Compassion Science*, ed. Emma M. Seppälä et al., Oxford Library of Psychology (New York: Oxford University Press, 2017), 261–71, https://doi.org/10.1093 /oxfordhb/9780190464684.001.0001; Jamil Zaki, "Empathy: A Motivated Account," *Psychological Bulletin* 140, no. 6 (2014): 1608–47, https://doi.org/10.1037 /a0037679; James Kirby, *Choose Compassion: Why It Matters and How It Works* (St. Lucia, Queensland: University of Queensland Press, 2022), 155–70.

20. Henri Nouwen, *Reaching Out: The Three Movements of the Spiritual Life* (New York: Doubleday, 1975), 50.

21. C. D. Batson et al., "Influence of Self-Reported Distress and Empathy on Egoistic versus Altruistic Motivation to Help," *Journal of Personality and Social Psychology* 45, no. 3 (1983): 706–18, https://doi.org/10.1037/0022-3514.45.3.706; C. Daryl Cameron, Lasana T. Harris, and B. Keith Payne, "The Emotional Cost of Humanity: Anticipated Exhaustion Motivates Dehumanization of Stigmatized Targets," *Social Psychological and Personality Science* 7, no. 2 (March 1, 2016): 105–12, https:// doi.org/10.1177/1948550615604453; Cameron and Payne, "Escaping Affect." See also recent research that shows that the mere thought of compassion as taxing can result in empathic distress and reduced compassion. Izzy Gainsburg and Julia Lee Cunningham, "Compassion Fatigue as a Self-Fulfilling Prophecy: Believing Compassion Is Limited Increases Fatigue and Decreases Compassion," *Psychological Science* 34 (2023): 1206–19, https://doi.org/10.1177/09567976231194537.

22. Matthieu Ricard provides a vivid description of his own contemplative experience of the difference between empathy becoming empathic distress and empathy becoming compassion. See Ricard, *Altruism*, 57–64. His contemplative self-report contributed to neuroscience research directed by Tania Singer that tracked different neural networks for those two different kinds of empathic experience. Some neuroscience research has supported the idea that meditation training in compassion can channel empathic awareness of another's suffering into compassion instead of empathic distress. Pascal Vrtička, Pauline Favre, and Tania Singer, "Compassion and the Brain," in *Compassion: Concepts, Research, and Applications*, ed. Paul Gilbert (London: Routledge, 2017), 135–45.

23. Research in health-care settings has shown that the caring, empathic presence of a provider can have many tangible benefits, e.g., by informing the provider's discernment of a patient's condition, building trust, improving diagnoses, and promoting physical and emotional benefits for patients. Such benefits include reduced pain, better medical adherence, faster physical recovery, and better mental health. See Sundip Patel et al., "Curricula for Empathy and Compassion Training in Medical Education: A Systematic Review," *PLOS ONE* 14, no. 8 (August 22, 2019):

e0221412, https://doi.org/10.1371/journal.pone.0221412; David Rakel, *The Compassionate Connection: The Healing Power of Empathy and Mindful Listening* (New York: W. W. Norton, 2018).

24. "Whatever virtues I may have . . ., may I dispense them equally to the beings of the six realms. By means of the suffering I undergo as the result of various ills, may I draw forth all the suffering of those realms. . . . From now until I obtain enlightenment, may whatever emotions I experience, whether as cause or effect, become the means for bringing all beings to perfection. May I devote myself to this end right now, on this very day." Maitriyogin, quoted in Namgyal, *Path of Heroes*, vol. 2, 332.

25. John first learned tong-len from Lama Zopa Rinpoche in 1978, then from many other lamas in Tibetan Gelug, Kagyu, and Nyingma traditions. He has also benefited from Pema Chödrön's adaptive approaches to tong-len.

26. On this first type of equanimity, the all-inclusiveness of compassion and wisdom, see e.g., Maitreya, Khenpo Shenga, and Ju Mipham, *Ornament of the Great Vehicle Sutras: Maitreya's Mahāyānasūtrālaṃkāra with Commentaries by Khenpo Shenga and Ju Mipham* (Ithaca, NY: Snow Lion Publications, 2014), 634; Khyentse Rinpoche and Ricard, *Spirit of Tibet*, 72, 82, 86, 124; Kunzang Pelden, *The Nectar of Manjushri's Speech: A Detailed Commentary on Shantideva's Way of the Bodhisattva*, trans. Padmakara Translation Group (New Delhi: Shechen Publications, 2008), 228–29, 354–55; Nyoshul Khenpo, *Natural Great Perfection*, trans. Surya Das (Ithaca, NY: Snow Lion Publications, 1995), 43–44, 50, 120; Longchen Rabjam, *Precious Treasury of the Way of Abiding*, 20–21; Namgyal, *Path of Heroes*, vol. 2, 307, 362–64, 586.

27. On this second type of equanimity, freedom from attachment to personal expectations and goals: See Maitreya, Shenga, and Mipham, *Ornament of the Great Vehicle Sutras*, 655, on wisdom-compassion as unaffected by changing conditions. See Pelden, *Nectar of Manjushri's Speech*, 382–83, on "the signless, the empty, and the goalless" as beyond frameworks of ego-clinging. See Edward Conze, *The Perfection of Wisdom in Eight Thousand Lines* (Bolinas, CA: Four Seasons Foundation, 1975), 225–26, 235, on the perfection of wisdom operative in love and compassion as beyond discouragement. See Namgyal, *Path of Heroes*, vol. 2, 489, 518, on relinquishing ego-centered goals and not depending on external conditions.

28. On this third type of equanimity, experiencing suffering as encompassed in unconditional openness and compassion, see Maitreya, Shenga, and Mipham, *Ornament of the Great Vehicle Sutras*, 604–5, 615, 620–23; Khyentse Rinpoche and Ricard, *Spirit of Tibet*, 86; Khenpo, *Natural Great Perfection*, 120; Pelden, *Nectar of Manjushri's Speech*, 388–89; Namgyal, *Path of Heroes*, vol. 2, 413–14; Welwood, *Toward a Psychology of Awakening*, 137–47; Makransky, "Compassion in Buddhist Psychology," 68–71.

5. INTEGRATING PRACTICES OF LOVE, COMPASSION AND WISDOM WITH OUR LIVES

1. Mikulincer and Shaver, "Boosting Attachment Security in Adulthood"; Omri Gillath, Emre Selcuk, and Phillip R. Shaver, "Moving Toward a Secure Attachment Style: Can Repeated Security Priming Help?" *Social and Personality Psychology Compass* 2, no. 4 (2008): 1651–66, https://doi.org/10.1111/j.1751-9004.2008.00120.x; Dahl, Wilson-Mendenhall, and Davidson, "Plasticity of Well-Being"; Wilson-Mendenhall, Dunne, and Davidson, "Visualizing Compassion"; Goleman, *Social Intelligence*; Begley, *Train Your Mind, Change Your Brain*.

2. Jeanette Skowronek, Andreas Seifert, and Sven Lindberg, "The Mere Presence of a Smartphone Reduces Basal Attentional Performance," *Scientific Reports* 13, no. 1 (June 8, 2023): 9363, https://doi.org/10.1038/s41598-023-36256-4.

3. Treleaven, *Trauma-Sensitive Mindfulness*, 150–76.

4. See, for example, Tsong-kha-pa, *The Great Treatise on the Stages of the Path to Enlightenment: Lam Rim Chen Mo*, vol. 1, ed. Joshua Cutler and Guy Newland, trans. Lamrim Chenmo Translation Committee (Ithaca, NY: Snow Lion Publications, 2000), 161–75, 271–95.

5. See, e.g., Maitreya, Shenga, and Mipham, *Ornament of the Great Vehicle Sutras*, 607, 633, which notes that the great compassion of bodhisattvas includes beings that are undergoing all three levels of suffering, not just obvious suffering.

6. bell hooks, "Toward a Revolution of Love," *Lion's Roar*, February 13, 2024, https://www.lionsroar.com/toward-a-revolution-of-love/.

7. Thomas Merton, *New Seeds of Contemplation* (New York: New Directions, 1972), 57.

8. bell hooks, *Outlaw Culture: Resisting Representations* (New York: Routledge, 2006), 247.

9. Ann Gleig, *American Dharma: Buddhism beyond Modernity* (New Haven, CT: Yale University Press, 2019), 139–75.

REFERENCES

Anālayo. *Compassion and Emptiness in Early Buddhist Meditation*. Cambridge, UK: Windhorse, 2015.

Armstrong, Karen. *A History of God: The 4,000 Year Quest of Judaism, Christianity and Islam*. New York: Ballantine Books, 1993.

Aronson, Harvey. *Buddhist Practice on Western Ground: Reconciling Eastern Ideals and Western Psychology*. Boston: Shambhala Publications, 2004.

————. *Love and Sympathy in Theravāda Buddhism*. Delhi: Motilal Banarsidass, 1980.

Ashar, Yoni K., Jessica R. Andrews-Hanna, Tal Yarkoni, Jenifer Sills, Joan Halifax, Sona Dimidjian, and Tor D. Wager. "Effects of Compassion Meditation on a Psychological Model of Charitable Donation." *Emotion* 16, no. 5 (August 2016): 691–705. http://dx.doi.org/10.1037/emo0000119.

Baker, Willa Blythe. *The Wakeful Body*. Boulder, CO: Shambhala, 2021.

Banella, Fabia Eleonora, and Ed Tronick. "Mutual Regulation and Unique Forms of Implicit Relational Knowing." In *Early Interaction and Developmental Psychopathology: Volume I: Infancy*, edited by Gisèle Apter, Emmanuel Devouche, and Maya Gratier, 35–53. Cham: Springer International Publishing, 2019. https://doi.org/10.1007/978-3-030-04769-6_3.

Barrett, Lisa Feldman. "Emotions Are Real." *Emotion* 12, no. 3 (2012): 413–29. https://doi.org/10.1037/a0027555.

————. *How Emotions Are Made: The Secret Life of the Brain*. New York: Houghton Mifflin, 2017.

————. "Your Brain Predicts (Almost) Everything You Do." Mindful, April 29, 2021. https://www.mindful.org/your-brain-predicts-almost-everything-you-do/.

Barrett, Lisa Feldman, and Barbara L Finlay. "Concepts, Goals and the Control of Survival-Related Behaviors." Current Opinion in Behavioral Sciences 24 (December 1, 2018): 172–79. https://doi.org/10.1016/j.cobeha.2018.10.001.

Barsalou, Lawrence W. "Deriving Categories to Achieve Goals." In *Psychology of Learning and Motivation*, edited by Gordon H. Bower, 27:1–64. San Diego: Academic Press, 1991. https://doi.org/10.1016/S0079-7421(08)60120-6.

———. "Grounded Cognition." *Annual Review of Psychology* 59 (2008): 617–45. https://doi.org/10.1146/annurev.psych.59.103006.093639.

———. "Perceptual Symbol Systems." *Behavioral and Brain Sciences* 22, no. 4 (August 1999): 577–660. https://doi.org/10.1017/S0140525X99002149.

———. "Simulation, Situated Conceptualization, and Prediction." *Philosophical Transactions of the Royal Society B: Biological Sciences* 364, no. 1521 (May 12, 2009): 1281–89. https://doi.org/10.1098/rstb.2008.0319.

Batson, C. D., Karen O'Quin, Jim Fultz, Mary Vanderplas, and Alice M. Isen. "Influence of Self-Reported Distress and Empathy on Egoistic versus Altruistic Motivation to Help." *Journal of Personality and Social Psychology* 45, no. 3 (1983): 706–18. https://doi.org/10.1037/0022-3514.45.3.706.

Begley, Sharon. *Train Your Mind, Change Your Brain: How a New Science Reveals Our Extraordinary Potential to Transform Ourselves.* New York: Ballantine Books, 2007.

Berry, Daniel R., Catherine S. J. Wall, Justin D. Tubbs, Fadel Zeidan, and Kirk Warren Brown. "Short-Term Training in Mindfulness Predicts Helping Behavior Toward Racial Ingroup and Outgroup Members." *Social Psychological and Personality Science* 14, no. 1 (January 1, 2023): 60–71. https://doi.org/10.1177/19485506211053095.

Bloom, Paul. *Against Empathy: The Case for Rational Compassion.* New York: Ecco, 2016.

Boag, Elle M., and Katherine B. Carnelley. "Attachment and Prejudice: The Mediating Role of Empathy." *British Journal of Social Psychology* 55, no. 2 (2016): 337–56. https://doi.org/10.1111/bjso.12132.

Bokar Rinpoche. *Chenrezig: Lord of Love.* San Francisco: ClearPoint Press, 1991.

Boothby, Erica J., Margaret S. Clark, and John A. Bargh. "Shared Experiences Are Amplified." *Psychological Science* 25, no. 12 (December 1, 2014): 2209–16. https://doi.org/10.1177/0956797614551162.

Brackett, Marc A., Susan E. Rivers, Maria R. Reyes, and Peter Salovey. "Enhancing Academic Performance and Social and Emotional Competence with the RULER Feeling Words Curriculum." *Learning and Individual Differences* 22, no. 2 (April 1, 2012): 218–24. https://doi.org/10.1016/j.lindif.2010.10.002.

Brenner, Jacqueline, Suzanne LeBlang, Michelle Lizotte-Waniewski, Barbara Schmidt, Patricio S. Espinosa, David L. DeMets, Andrew Newberg, and Charles H. Hennekens. "Mindfulness with Paced Breathing Reduces Blood Pressure." *Medical Hypotheses* 142 (September 1, 2020): 109780. https://doi.org/10.1016/j.mehy.2020.109780.

Buber, Martin. *I and Thou.* Translated by Walter Kaufman. New York: Charles Scribner's Sons, 1970.

Buddhaghosa. *The Path of Purification: Visuddhimagga.* Translated by Bhikku Ñāṇamoli. Colombo: A. Semage, 1964.

Burlingame, Eugene Watson. *Buddhist Legends in the Pali Text of the Dhammapada Commentary.* Vol. 30. Harvard Oriental Series. Cambridge, MA: Harvard University Press, 1921.

Burtt, E. A., ed. *Teachings of the Compassionate Buddha.* New York: Mentor, 1955.

Butler, Emily A., Boris Egloff, Frank H. Wlhelm, Nancy C. Smith, Elizabeth A. Erickson, and James J. Gross. "The Social Consequences of Expressive Suppression." *Emotion* 3, no. 1 (2003): 48–67. https://doi.org/10.1037/1528-3542.3.1.48.

Cameron, C. Daryl. "Compassion Collapse: Why We Are Numb to Numbers." In *The Oxford Handbook of Compassion Science,* 261–71. Oxford Library of Psychology. New York: Oxford University Press, 2017. https://doi.org/10.1093/ox fordhb/9780190464684.001.0001.

Cameron, C. Daryl, Lasana T. Harris, and B. Keith Payne. "The Emotional Cost of Humanity: Anticipated Exhaustion Motivates Dehumanization of Stigmatized Targets." *Social Psychological and Personality Science* 7, no. 2 (March 1, 2016): 105–12. https://doi.org/10.1177/1948550615604453.

Cameron, C. Daryl, and B. Keith Payne. "The Cost of Callousness: Regulating Compassion Influences the Moral Self-Concept." *Psychological Science* 23, no. 3 (March 1, 2012): 225–29. https://doi.org/10.1177/0956797611430334.

———. "Escaping Affect: How Motivated Emotion Regulation Creates Insensitivity to Mass Suffering." *Journal of Personality and Social Psychology* 100, no. 1 (2011): 1–15. https://doi.org/10.1037/a0021643.

Cameron, C. Daryl, B. Keith Payne, and John M. Doris. "Morality in High Definition: Emotion Differentiation Calibrates the Influence of Incidental Disgust on Moral Judgments." *Journal of Experimental Social Psychology* 49, no. 4 (July 1, 2013): 719–25. https://doi.org/10.1016/j.jesp.2013.02.014.

Carr, Anne. "Starting with the Human." In *A World of Grace: An Introduction to the Themes and Foundations of Karl Rahner's Theology,* edited by Leo O'Donovan. Washington DC: Georgetown University Press, 1995.

Cassidy, Jude. "The Nature of the Child's Ties." In *Handbook of Attachment: Theory, Research, and Clinical Applications,* edited by Jude Cassidy and Phillip R. Shaver, 3rd ed., 3–24. New York: Guilford Press, 2016.

Chen, Cher Weixia, and Paul C. Gorski. "Burnout in Social Justice and Human Rights Activists: Symptoms, Causes and Implications." *Journal of Human Rights Practice* 7, no. 3 (November 1, 2015): 366–90. https://doi.org/10.1093/jhuman/huv011.

Chödrön, Pema. *Start Where You Are: A Guide to Compassionate Living.* Boston: Shambhala, 2001.

Chokyi Nyima Rinpoche. *Present Fresh Wakefulness: A Meditation Manual on Nonconceptual Wisdom.* Hong Kong: Rangjung Yeshe, 2002.

———. *Sadness, Love, Openness.* Boulder, CO: Shambhala, 2018.

Chowang, Orgyen. *Our Pristine Mind.* Boulder, CO: Shambhala, 2016.

Coan, James A., and Erin L. Maresh. "Social Baseline Theory and the Social Regulation of Emotion." In *Handbook of Emotion Regulation,* 2nd ed., 221–36. New York: Guilford Press, 2014.

Coan, James A., and David A. Sbarra. "Social Baseline Theory: The Social Regulation of Risk and Effort." *Current Opinion in Psychology* 1 (February 1, 2015): 87–91. https://doi.org/10.1016/j.copsyc.2014.12.021.

Coan, James A., Hillary S. Schaefer, and Richard J. Davidson. "Lending a Hand: Social Regulation of the Neural Response to Threat." *Psychological Science* 17, no. 12 (December 1, 2006): 1032–39. https://doi.org/10.1111/j.1467-9280.2006.01832.x.

Cohn, Alain, Michel André Maréchal, David Tannenbaum, and Christian Lukas Zünd. "Civic Honesty around the Globe." *Science* 365, no. 6448 (July 5, 2019): 70–73. https://doi.org/10.1126/science.aau8712.

Collins, N. L., and B. C. Feeney. "Working Models of Attachment Shape Perceptions of Social Support: Evidence from Experimental and Observational Studies." *Journal of Personality and Social Psychology* 87, no. 3 (2004): 363–83. https://doi.org/10.1037/0022-3514.87.3.363.

Collins, N. L., and Stephen J. Read. "Cognitive Representations of Attachment: The Structure and Function of Working Models." In *Attachment Processes in Adulthood*, Advances in Personal Relationships, vol. 5, edited by Kim Bartholomew and Daniel Perlman, 53–90. London, England: Jessica Kingsley Publishers, 1994.

Condon, Paul. "Buddhanature beyond Mere Concept." *Buddhadharma: The Practitioner's Guide* 21, no. 4 (2023): 77–76.

———. "Meditation in Context: Factors That Facilitate Prosocial Behavior." *Current Opinion in Psychology* 28 (2019): 15–19. https://doi.org/10.1016/j.copsyc.2018.09.011.

———. "Venturing Beyond Our Fear of Emptiness." *Lion's Roar*, November 16, 2023. https://www.lionsroar.com/venturing-beyond-our-fear-of-emptiness/.

Condon, Paul, Gaëlle Desbordes, Willa B. Miller, and David DeSteno. "Meditation Increases Compassionate Responses to Suffering." *Psychological Science* 24 (2013): 2125–27. https://doi.org/10.1177/0956797613485603.

Condon, Paul, John Dunne, and Christine Wilson-Mendenhall. "Wisdom and Compassion: A New Perspective on the Science of Relationships." *Journal of Moral Education* 48, no. 1 (January 2, 2019): 98–108. https://doi.org/10.1080/03057240.2018.1439828.

Condon, Paul, and John Makransky. "Compassion and Skillful Means: Cultural Adaptation, Psychological Science, and Creative Responsiveness." *Mindfulness* 14 (2023): 2331–41. https://link.springer.com/article/10.1007/s12671-022-01866-y.

———. "Compassion Practices." In *Integrative Medicine*, edited by David Rakel and Vincent J. Minichiello, 5th ed., 831–35. New York: Elsevier, 2023.

———. "Recovering the Relational Starting Point of Compassion Training: A Foundation for Sustainable and Inclusive Care." *Perspectives on Psychological Science* 15 (2020): 1346–62. https://doi.org/doi.org/10.1177/1745691620922200.

———. "Sustainable Compassion Training: Integrating Meditation Theory with Psychological Science." *Frontiers in Psychology* 11 (2020). https://www.frontiersin.org/articles/10.3389/fpsyg.2020.02249.

Conze, Edward. *The Perfection of Wisdom in Eight Thousand Lines.* Bolinas, CA: Four Seasons Foundation, 1975.

Dahl, Cortland J., Christine D. Wilson-Mendenhall, and Richard J. Davidson. "The Plasticity of Well-Being: A Training-Based Framework for the Cultivation of Human Flourishing." *Proceedings of the National Academy of Sciences* 117, no. 51 (December 22, 2020): 32197–206. https://doi.org/10.1073/pnas.2014859117.

Dalai Lama. *Dalai Lama, an Open Heart: Practicing Compassion in Everyday Life.* New York: Little, Brown, 2001.

Davidson, Richard J., and Bruce S. McEwen. "Social Influences on Neuroplasticity: Stress and Interventions to Promote Well-Being." *Nature Neuroscience* 15, no. 5 (May 2012): 689–95. https://doi.org/10.1038/nn.3093.

DeLong-Bas, Natana. *Islam: A Living Faith.* Winona, MN: Anselm Academic, 2018.

Dorje, Wangchuk. *Mahāmudrā: The Ocean of Definitive Meaning.* Translated by Elizabeth Callahan. Seattle: Nitartha International, 2001.

Dovidio, John F., Angelika Love, Fabian M. H. Schellhaas, and Miles Hewstone. "Reducing Intergroup Bias through Intergroup Contact: Twenty Years of Progress and Future Directions." *Group Processes and Intergroup Relations* 20, no. 5 (September 1, 2017): 606–20. https://doi.org/10.1177/1368430217712052.

Dreitcer, Andrew. *Living Compassion, Loving Like Jesus.* Nashville, TN: Upper Room Books, 2017.

Drew, Trafton, Melissa L.-H. Võ, and Jeremy M. Wolfe. "The Invisible Gorilla Strikes Again: Sustained Inattentional Blindness in Expert Observers." *Psychological Science* 24, no. 9 (September 1, 2013): 1848–53. https://doi.org/10.1177/0956797613479386.

Dreyfus, Georges, B. J. *Recognizing Reality: Dharmakīrti's Philosophy and Its Tibetan Interpretations.* Albany: State University of New York Press, 1997.

Dunne, John. "Key Features of Dharmakīrti's Apoha Theory." In *Apoha: Buddhist Nominalism and Human Cognition*, edited by Mark Siderits, Tom Tillemans, and Arindam Chakrabarti, 84–108. New York: Columbia University Press, 2011.

Dunne, John D. "Toward an Understanding of Non-Dual Mindfulness." *Contemporary Buddhism* 12, no. 1 (May 1, 2011): 71–88. https://doi.org/10.1080/14639947.2011.564820.

Dykas, Matthew J., and Jude Cassidy. "Attachment and the Processing of Social Information across the Life Span: Theory and Evidence." *Psychological Bulletin* 137, no. 1 (2011): 19–46. https://doi.org/10.1037/a0021367.

Dzogchen Ponlop Rinpoche. *Trainings in Compassion.* Ithaca, NY: Snow Lion Publications, 2004.

Earhart, H. Byron. *Religion in the Japanese Experience: Sources and Interpretations.* Belmont, CA: Wadsworth, 1974.

Erbas, Yasemin, Laura Sels, Eva Ceulemans, and Peter Kuppens. "Feeling Me, Feeling You: The Relation Between Emotion Differentiation and Empathic Accuracy." *Social Psychological and Personality Science* 7, no. 3 (April 1, 2016): 240–47. https://doi.org/10.1177/1948550616633504.

Eyal, Tal, Mary Steffel, and Nicholas Epley. "Perspective Mistaking: Accurately Understanding the Mind of Another Requires Getting Perspective, Not Taking Perspective." *Journal of Personality and Social Psychology* 114, no. 4 (April 2018): 547–71. https://doi.org/10.1037/pspa0000115.

Fernando, Antonio T., and Nathan S. Consedine. "Beyond Compassion Fatigue: The Transactional Model of Physician Compassion," *Journal of Pain and Symptom Management* 48, no. 2 (2014):289–298, https://doi.org/10.1016/j.jpainsym man.2013.09.014.

Fredrickson, Barbara, and Daniel Siegel. "Broaden and Build Theory Meets Interpersonal Neurobiology as a Lens on Compassion and Positivity Resonance." In *Compassion: Concepts, Research and Applications*, edited by Paul Gilbert, 203–18. London: Routledge, 2017.

Fucci, E., O. Abdoun, A. Caclin, A. Francis, J. D. Dunne, M. Ricard, R. J. Davidson, and A. Lutz. "Differential Effects of Non-Dual and Focused Attention Meditations on the Formation of Automatic Perceptual Habits in Expert Practitioners." *Neuropsychologia* 119 (October 1, 2018): 92–100. https://doi.org/10.1016/j.neuropsychologia.2018.07.025.

Gainsburg, Izzy, and Julia Lee Cunningham. "Compassion Fatigue as a Self-Fulfilling Prophecy: Believing Compassion Is Limited Increases Fatigue and Decreases Compassion." *Psychological Science* 34 (2023): 1206-1219. https://doi.org/10.1177/09567976231194537.

Gibson, Eleanor J., and Richard D. Walk. "The 'Visual Cliff.'" *Scientific American* 202, no. 4 (1960): 64–71.

Gilbert, Paul. "Compassion as a Social Mentality: An Evolutionary Approach." In *Compassion: Concepts, Research and Applications*, 31–68. London: Routledge, 2017.

———. "Explorations into the Nature and Function of Compassion." *Current Opinion in Psychology*, Mindfulness 28 (August 1, 2019): 108–14. https://doi.org/10.1016/j.copsyc.2018.12.002.

Gilbert, Paul, and Choden. *Mindful Compassion: How the Science of Compassion Can Help You Understand Your Emotions, Live in the Present, and Connect Deeply with Others.* Oakland, CA: New Harbinger Publications, 2014.

Gilbert, Paul, and Jennifer Mascaro. "Compassion Fears, Blocks, and Resistances: An Evolutionary Investigation." In *The Oxford Handbook of Compassion Science*, edited by Emma Seppälä, Emiliana Simon-Thomas, Stephanie L. Brown, Monica C. Worline, C. Daryl Cameron, and James R. Doty, 399–418. New York: Oxford University Press, 2017.

Giles, Cheryl. "They Say the People Could Fly: Disrupting the Legacy of Sexual Violence through Myth, Memory, and Connection." In *Black and Buddhist: What Buddhism Can Teach Us about Race, Resilience, Transformation, and Freedom*, edited by Cheryl Giles and Pamela Ayo Yetunde, 25–43. Boulder, CO: Shambhala, 2020.

Gillath, Omri, Emre Selcuk, and Phillip R. Shaver. "Moving Toward a Secure Attachment Style: Can Repeated Security Priming Help?" *Social and Personality Psychology Compass* 2, no. 4 (2008): 1651–66. https://doi.org/10.1111/j.1751-9004.2008.00120.x.

Gleig, Ann. *American Dharma: Buddhism Beyond Modernity*. New Haven, CT: Yale University Press, 2019.

Goetz, Jennifer L., Dacher Keltner, and Emiliana Simon-Thomas. "Compassion: An Evolutionary Analysis and Empirical Review." *Psychological Bulletin* 136, no. 3 (2010): 351–74. https://doi.org/10.1037/a0018807.

Goleman, Daniel. *Social Intelligence: The New Science of Social Relationships*. New York: Bantam Books, 2006.

Gross, James J., and Robert W. Levenson. "Emotional Suppression: Physiology, Self-Report, and Expressive Behavior." *Journal of Personality and Social Psychology* 64, no. 6 (1993): 970–86. https://doi.org/10.1037/0022-3514.64.6.970.

Gyatso, Kelsang. *Joyful Path of Good Fortune*. New York: Tharpa, 2016.

Halpern, Jodi. "What Is Clinical Empathy?" *Journal of General Internal Medicine* 18, no. 8 (August 1, 2003): 670–74. https://doi.org/10.1046/j.1525-1497.2003.21017.x.

Harvey, Peter. *An Introduction to Buddhism: Teachings, History and Practices*. New York: Cambridge University Press, 2013.

Hayes, Steven C. "Buddhism and Acceptance and Commitment Therapy." *Cognitive and Behavioral Practice* 9, no. 1 (December 1, 2002): 58–66. https://doi.org/10.1016/S1077-7229(02)80041-4.

Hoemann, Katie, Maria Gendron, and Lisa Feldman Barrett. "Mixed Emotions in the Predictive Brain." *Current Opinion in Behavioral Sciences* 15 (June 1, 2017): 51–57. https://doi.org/10.1016/j.cobeha.2017.05.013.

Hoemann, Katie, Catie Nielson, Ashley Yuen, J. W. Gurera, Karen S. Quigley, and Lisa F. Barrett. "Expertise in Emotion: A Scoping Review and Unifying Framework for Individual Differences in the Mental Representation of Emotional Experience." *Psychological Bulletin* 147 (2021): 1159–83. https://doi.org/10.1037/bul0000327.

Hoffman, Kent. "Taking Refuge in the Family of Things." *The Arrow* 2 (2015): 1–30.

Holmes, Jeremy, and Arietta Slade. *Attachment in Therapeutic Practice*. Thousand Oaks, CA: Sage Publications, 2018.

hooks, bell. *Outlaw Culture: Resisting Representations*. New York: Routledge, 2006.

———. "Toward a Revolution of Love." *Lion's Roar*, February 13, 2024. https://www.lionsroar.com/toward-a-revolution-of-love/.

Hrdy, Sarah Blaffer. *Mothers and Others: The Evolutionary Origins of Mutual Understanding*. Cambridge MA: Belknap Press, 2009.

Hsu, Funie. "American Cultural Baggage: The Racialized Secularization of Mindfulness in Schools." In *Secularizing Buddhism: New Perspectives on a Dynamic Tradition*, edited by Richard K. Payne, 79–93. Boulder, CO: Shambhala Publications, 2021.

Israelashvili, Jacob, Suzanne Oosterwijk, Disa Sauter, and Agneta Fischer. "Knowing Me, Knowing You: Emotion Differentiation in Oneself Is Associated with Recognition of Others' Emotions." *Cognition and Emotion* 33, no. 7 (February 8, 2019): 1–11. https://doi.org/10.1080/02699931.2019.1577221.

Jamieson, Jeremy P., Matthew K. Nock, and Wendy Berry Mendes. "Mind over

Matter: Reappraising Arousal Improves Cardiovascular and Cognitive Responses to Stress." *Journal of Experimental Psychology: General* 141, no. 3 (2012): 417–22. https://doi.org/10.1037/a0025719.

Jamieson, Jeremy P., Brett J. Peters, Emily J. Greenwood, and Aaron J. Altose. "Reappraising Stress Arousal Improves Performance and Reduces Evaluation Anxiety in Classroom Exam Situations." *Social Psychological and Personality Science* 7, no. 6 (August 1, 2016): 579–87. https://doi.org/10.1177/1948550616644656.

Jinpa, Thupten. *A Fearless Heart: How the Courage to Be Compassionate Can Transform Our Lives.* New York: Hudson Street Press, 2015.

Johnson, Elizabeth. *Quest for the Living God: Mapping Frontiers in the Theology of God.* London: Bloomsbury, 2007.

Kang, Yoona, Jeremy R. Gray, and John F. Dovidio. "The Nondiscriminating Heart: Lovingkindness Meditation Training Decreases Implicit Intergroup Bias." *Journal of Experimental Psychology: General* 143, no. 3 (2014): 1306–13. https://doi.org/10.1037/a0034150.

Kashdan, Todd B., Lisa Feldman Barrett, and Patrick E. McKnight. "Unpacking Emotion Differentiation: Transforming Unpleasant Experience by Perceiving Distinctions in Negativity." *Current Directions in Psychological Science* 24, no. 1 (February 1, 2015): 10–16. https://doi.org/10.1177/0963721414550708.

Khenpo, Nyoshul. *Natural Great Perfection.* Translated by Surya Das. Ithaca, NY: Snow Lion Publications, 1995.

Khyentse Rinpoche, Dilgo. *Enlightened Courage: An Explanation of the Seven Point Mind Training.* Ithaca, NY: Snow Lion Publications, 1993.

Khyentse Rinpoche, Dilgo, and Matthieu Ricard. *The Spirit of Tibet.* New York: Aperture, 2001.

King, Martin Luther, Jr. *A Gift of Love: Sermons from "Strength to Love" and Other Preachings.* Boston: Beacon Press, 2012.

Kinsley, David. *Hinduism; A Cultural Perspective.* Englewood Cliffs, NJ: Prentice Hall, 1982.

Kirby, James. *Choose Compassion: Why It Matters and How It Works.* St. Lucia, Queensland: University of Queensland Press, 2022.

Kirby, James N., Jamin Day, and Vinita Sagar. "The 'Flow' of Compassion: A Meta-Analysis of the Fears of Compassion Scales and Psychological Functioning." *Clinical Psychology Review* 70 (June 1, 2019): 26–39. https://doi.org/10.1016/j.cpr.2019.03.001.

Klimecki, Olga M., Susanne Leiberg, Matthieu Ricard, and Tania Singer. "Differential Pattern of Functional Brain Plasticity after Compassion and Empathy Training." *Social Cognitive and Affective Neuroscience* 9, no. 6 (June 1, 2014): 873–79. https://doi.org/10.1093/scan/nst060.

Kongtrul, Dzigar. *Training in Tenderness: Buddhist Teachings on Tsewa, the Radical Openness of Heart That Can Change the World.* Boulder, CO: Shambhala, 2018.

Kral, Tammi R. A., Kaley Davis, Cole Korponay, Matthew J. Hirshberg, Rachel Hoel,

Lawrence Y. Tello, Robin I. Goldman, Melissa A. Rosenkranz, Antoine Lutz, and Richard J. Davidson. "Absence of Structural Brain Changes from Mindfulness-Based Stress Reduction: Two Combined Randomized Controlled Trials." *Science Advances* 8, no. 20 (May 20, 2022): eabk3316. https://doi.org/10.1126/sciadv.abk3316.

Kyabgon, Traleg. *Mind at Ease: Self-Liberation through Mahāmudrā Meditation*. Boston: Shambhala, 2004.

Laukkonen, Ruben E., and Heleen A. Slagter. "From Many to (n)One: Meditation and the Plasticity of the Predictive Mind." *Neuroscience & Biobehavioral Reviews* 128 (September 1, 2021): 199–217. https://doi.org/10.1016/j.neubiorev.2021.06.021.

Lavelle, Brooke D. "Against One Method: Contemplation in Context." In *Handbook of Mindfulness: Culture, Context, and Social Engagement*, edited by Ronald E. Purser, David Forbes, and Adam Burke, 233–42. Mindfulness in Behavioral Health. Cham: Springer International Publishing, 2016. https://doi.org/10.1007/978-3-319-44019-4_16.

Lavelle, Brooke, Abra Vigna, Zack Walsh, and Ed Porter. "Relationshift: The Courage-RISE Model for Building Relational Cultures of Practice," The Arrow Journal 8, no. 2 (2021): 130–152.

Lindahl, Jared R., Nathan E. Fisher, David J. Cooper, Rochelle K. Rosen, and Willoughby B. Britton. "The Varieties of Contemplative Experience: A Mixed-Methods Study of Meditation-Related Challenges in Western Buddhists." *PLOS ONE* 12, no. 5 (May 24, 2017): e0176239. https://doi.org/10.1371/journal.pone.0176239.

Lindsay, Emily K., and J. David Creswell. "Mechanisms of Mindfulness Training: Monitor and Acceptance Theory (MAT)." *Clinical Psychology Review* 51 (February 1, 2017): 48–59. https://doi.org/10.1016/j.cpr.2016.10.011.

Longchen Rabjam. *The Precious Treasury of the Basic Space of Phenomena*. Translated by Richard Barron. Junction City, CA: Padma Publishing, 2001.

———. *The Precious Treasury of the Way of Abiding*. Translated by Richard Barron. Junction City, CA: Padma Publishing, 2001.

Lyons-Ruth, Karlen, Nadia Bruschweiler-Stern, Alexandra M. Harrison, Alexander C. Morgan, Jeremy P. Nahum, Louis Sander, Daniel N. Stern, and Edward Z. Tronick. "Implicit Relational Knowing: Its Role in Development and Psychoanalytic Treatment." *Infant Mental Health Journal* 19, no. 3 (1998): 282–89. https://doi.org/10.1002/(SICI)1097-0355(199823)19:3<282::AID-IMHJ3>3.0.CO;2-O.

Maguire, Eleanor A., Katherine Woollett, and Hugo J. Spiers. "London Taxi Drivers and Bus Drivers: A Structural MRI and Neuropsychological Analysis." *Hippocampus* 16, no. 12 (2006): 1091–1101. https://doi.org/10.1002/hipo.20233.

Maitreya, Khenpo Shenga, and Ju Mipham. *Ornament of the Great Vehicle Sutras: Maitreya's Mahāyānasūtrālaṃkāra with Commentaries by Khenpo Shenga and Ju Mipham*. Ithaca, NY: Snow Lion Publications, 2014.

Makransky, John. *Awakening through Love: Unveiling Your Deepest Goodness*. Boston: Wisdom Publications, 2007.

―――. "A Buddhist Critique of, and Learning from, Christian Liberation Theology." *Theological Studies* 75, no. 3 (September 1, 2014): 635–57. https://doi .org/10.1177/0040563914541028.

―――. "Compassion beyond Fatigue: Contemplative Training for People Who Serve Others." In *Meditation and the Classroom: Contemplative Pedagogy for Religious Studies*, edited by Judith Simmer-Brown and Fran Grace, 85–94. Albany: State University of New York Press, 2011.

―――. "Compassion in Buddhist Psychology." In *Wisdom and Compassion in Psychotherapy*, edited by Christopher Germer and Ronald Siegel, 61–74. New York: Guilford Press, 2012.

―――. "Confronting the 'Sin' out of Love for the 'Sinner': Fierce Compassion as a Force for Social Change." *Buddhist-Christian Studies* 36, no. 1 (October 10, 2016): 87–96. https://doi.org/10.1353/bcs.2016.0009.

Mar, Raymond A. "Stories and the Promotion of Social Cognition." *Current Directions in Psychological Science* 27, no. 4 (August 1, 2018): 257–62. https://doi .org/10.1177/0963721417749654.

Marsh, Abigail A. "The Caring Continuum: Evolved Hormonal and Proximal Mechanisms Explain Prosocial and Antisocial Extremes." *Annual Review of Psychology* 70, no. 1 (2019): 347–71. https://doi.org/10.1146/annurev-psych-010418-103010.

Mascaro, Jennifer S., James K. Rilling, Lobsang Tenzin Negi, and Charles L. Raison. "Compassion Meditation Enhances Empathic Accuracy and Related Neural Activity." *Social Cognitive and Affective Neuroscience* 8, no. 1 (January 1, 2013): 48–55. https:// doi.org/10.1093/scan/nss095.

Maslach, Christina, Wilmar B. Schaufeli, and Michael P. Leiter. "Job Burnout." *Annual Review of Psychology* 52, no. 1 (2001): 397–422. https://doi.org/10.1146/annurev .psych.52.1.397.

Mauss, Iris B., and James J. Gross. "Emotion Suppression and Cardiovascular Disease: Is Hiding Feelings Bad for Your Heart?" In *Emotional Expression and Health: Advances in Theory, Assessment and Clinical Applications*, edited by Ivan Nyklicek, Lydia Temoshok, and A. J. J. M. Vingerhoets, 61–81. New York: Brunner-Routledge, 2004.

McMahan, David. *Empty Vision: Metaphor and Visionary Imagery in Mahāyāna Buddhism.* New York: RoutledgeCurzon, 2002.

―――. *The Making of Buddhist Modernism.* New York: Oxford University Press, 2008.

McMahan, David, and Erik Braun. "Introduction-From Colonialism to Brainscans: Modern Transformations of Buddhist Meditation." In *Meditation, Buddhism, and Science*, edited by David McMahan and Erik Braun, 1–20. New York: Oxford University Press, 2017.

Menakem, Resmaa. *My Grandmother's Hands: Racialized Trauma and the Pathway to Mending Our Hearts and Bodies.* Las Vegas, NV: Central Recovery Press, 2017.

Mendes, Wendy Berry, Harry T. Reis, Mark D. Seery, and Jim Blascovich. "Cardiovascular Correlates of Emotional Expression and Suppression: Do Content and

Gender Context Matter?" *Journal of Personality and Social Psychology* 84, no. 4 (2003): 771–92. https://doi.org/10.1037/0022-3514.84.4.771.

Merton, Thomas. *New Seeds of Contemplation.* New York: New Directions, 1972.

Mikulincer, Mario, and Philip R. Shaver. "An Attachment Perspective on Compassion and Altruism." In *Compassion: Concepts, Research and Applications,* edited by Paul Gilbert, 187–202. London: Routledge, 2017. https://doi.org/10.4324/9781315564296-11.

Mikulincer, Mario, and Phillip R. Shaver. "Adult Attachment and Compassion: Normative and Individual Difference Components." In *The Oxford Handbook of Compassion Science,* edited by Emma M. Seppälä, Emiliana Simon-Thomas, Stephanie L. Brown, Monica C. Worline, C. Daryl Cameron, and James R. Doty, 79–90. New York: Oxford University Press, 2017. https://doi.org/10.1093/oxfordhb/9780190464684.013.7.

———. *Attachment in Adulthood: Structure, Dynamics, and Change.* 2nd ed. New York: Guilford Publications, 2016.

———. "Attachment Theory and Intergroup Bias: Evidence That Priming the Secure Base Schema Attenuates Negative Reactions to Out-Groups." *Journal of Personality and Social Psychology* 81, no. 1 (2001): 97–115. https://doi.org/10.1037/0022-3514.81.1.97.

———. "Boosting Attachment Security in Adulthood: The 'Broaden-and-Build' Effects of Security-Enhancing Mental Representations and Interpersonal Contexts." In *Attachment Theory and Research: New Directions and Emerging Themes,* edited by Jeffry A. Simpson and W. Steven Rholes, 124–44. New York: Guilford Press, 2015.

Mikulincer, Mario, Phillip R. Shaver, Naama Bar-On, and Baljinder K. Sahdra. "Security Enhancement, Self-Esteem Threat, and Mental Depletion Affect Provision of a Safe Haven and Secure Base to a Romantic Partner." *Journal of Social and Personal Relationships* 31, no. 5 (2014): 630–50. https://doi.org/10.1177/0265407514525887.

Namgyal, Dakpo Tashi. *Clarifying the Natural State.* Translated by Erik Kunzang. Hong Kong: Rangjung Yeshe, 2001.

———. *Moonbeams of Mahamudra.* Ithaca, NY: Snow Lion Publications, 2019.

Ñāṇamoli, Bhikku, and Bhikku Bodhi. *The Middle Length Discourses of the Buddha: A Translation of the Majjhima Nikāya.* Somerville, MA: Wisdom Publications, 1995.

Neff, Kristin, and Christopher Germer. "Self-Compassion and Psychological Well-Being." In *The Oxford Handbook of Compassion Science,* edited by Emma M. Seppälä, Emiliana Simon-Thomas, Stephanie L. Brown, Monica C. Worline, C. Daryl Cameron, and James R. Doty, 371–85. Oxford Library of Psychology. New York: Oxford University Press, 2017. https://doi.org/10.1093/oxfordhb/9780190464684.001.0001.

Nouwen, Henri. *Reaching Out: The Three Movements of the Spiritual Life.* New York: Doubleday, 1975.

Owens, Rod. *Love and Rage: The Path of Liberation through Anger.* Berkeley, CA: North Atlantic Books, 2020.

———. "The Dharma of Trauma." In *Black and Buddhist; What Buddhism Can Teach Us about Race, Resilience, Transformation, and Freedom,* edited by Cheryl Giles and Pamela Ayo Yetunde. Boulder, CO: Shambhala, 2020.

Patel, Sundip, Alexis Pelletier-Bui, Stephanie Smith, Michael B. Roberts, Hope Kilgannon, Stephen Trzeciak, and Brian W. Roberts. "Curricula for Empathy and Compassion Training in Medical Education: A Systematic Review." *PLOS ONE* 14, no. 8 (August 22, 2019): e0221412. https://doi.org/10.1371/journal.pone.0221412.

Paul, Annie Murphy. "Your Brain on Fiction." Opinion. *New York Times*, March 17, 2012. https://www.nytimes.com/2012/03/18/opinion/sunday/the-neuroscience-of-your-brain-on-fiction.html.

Pelden, Kunzang. *The Nectar of Manjushri's Speech: A Detailed Commentary on Shantideva's Way of the Bodhisattva*. Translated by Padmakara Translation Group. New Delhi: Shechen Publications, 2008.

Preston, Stephanie D. "The Origins of Altruism in Offspring Care." *Psychological Bulletin* 139, no. 6 (2013): 1305–41. https://doi.org/10.1037/a0031755.

Purser, Ronald E. *McMindfulness: How Mindfulness Became the New Capitalist Spirituality*. London: Repeater Books, 2019.

Rahner, Karl. "The Experience of God Today." In *Theological Investigations*, vol. 11, translated by David Bourke. London: Darton, Longman and Todd, 1974.

Rakel, David. *The Compassionate Connection: The Healing Power of Empathy and Mindful Listening*. New York: W. W. Norton, 2018.

Rand, David G. "Cooperation, Fast and Slow: Meta-Analytic Evidence for a Theory of Social Heuristics and Self-Interested Deliberation." *Psychological Science* 27, no. 9 (September 1, 2016): 1192–1206. https://doi.org/10.1177/0956797616654455.

Rand, David G., and Ziv G. Epstein. "Risking Your Life without a Second Thought: Intuitive Decision-Making and Extreme Altruism." *PLOS ONE* 9, no. 10 (October 15, 2014): e109687. https://doi.org/10.1371/journal.pone.0109687.

Rand, David G., Joshua D. Greene, and Martin A. Nowak. "Spontaneous Giving and Calculated Greed." *Nature* 489, no. 7416 (September 2012): 427–30. https://doi.org/10.1038/nature11467.

Ray, Reginald. *Indestructible Truth: The Living Spirituality of Tibetan Buddhism*. Boston: Shambhala, 2000.

———. *Secret of the Vajra World: The Tantric Buddhism of Tibet*. Boston: Shambhala, 2001.

Reynolds, John. *The Golden Letters: The Three Statements of Garab Dorje with Commentary by Dza Patrul Rinpoche*. Ithaca, NY: Snow Lion Publications, 1996.

Ricard, Matthieu. *Altruism: The Power of Compassion to Change Yourself and the World*. New York: Little, Brown, 2015.

Richards, Jane M., Emily A. Butler, and James J. Gross. "Emotion Regulation in Romantic Relationships: The Cognitive Consequences of Concealing Feelings." *Journal of Social and Personal Relationships* 20, no. 5 (October 1, 2003): 599–620. https://doi.org/10.1177/0265407503020205002.

Robins, Clive J., Henry Schmidt III, and Marsha M. Linehan. "Dialectical Behavior Therapy: Synthesizing Radical Acceptance with Skillful Means." In *Mindfulness and Acceptance: Expanding the Cognitive-Behavioral Tradition*, edited by Steven C.

Hayes, Victoria Follette, and Marsha Linehan, 30–44. New York: Guilford Press, 2004.

Roeser, Robert W., Blake A. Colaianne, and Mark A. Greenberg. "Compassion and Human Development: Current Approaches and Future Directions." *Research in Human Development* 15, no. 3–4 (October 2, 2018): 238–51. https://doi.org/10.1080/154 27609.2018.1495002.

Rogers, Frank. *Practicing Compassion*. Nashville, TN: Fresh Air Books, 2015.

Roisman, Glenn I., Elena Padrón, L. Alan Sroufe, and Byron Egeland. "Earned–Secure Attachment Status in Retrospect and Prospect." *Child Development* 73, no. 4 (2002): 1204–19. https://doi.org/10.1111/1467-8624.00467.

Ryōkan. *Dewdrops on a Lotus Leaf: Zen Poems of Ryōkan*. Translated by John Stevens. Boston: Shambhala, 1996.

Śāntideva. *A Guide to the Bodhisattva Way of Life*. Translated by B. Alan Wallace and Vesna Wallace. Ithaca, NY: Snow Lion Publications, 1997.

———. *Śikṣā Samuccaya*. Translated by Cecil Bendall and W. H. D. Rouse. Delhi: Motilal Banaarsidass, 1981.

Saunders, Rachel, Deborah Jacobvitz, Maria Zaccagnino, Lauren M. Beverung, and Nancy Hazen. "Pathways to Earned-Security: The Role of Alternative Support Figures." *Attachment and Human Development* 13, no. 4 (July 1, 2011): 403–20. https://doi.org/10.1080/14616734.2011.584405.

Schnall, Simone, Kent D. Harber, Jeanine K. Stefanucci, and Dennis R. Proffitt. "Social Support and the Perception of Geographical Slant." *Journal of Experimental Social Psychology* 44, no. 5 (September 1, 2008): 1246–55. https://doi.org/10.1016/j .jesp.2008.04.011.

Schnall, Simone, and Jean Roper. "Elevation Puts Moral Values into Action." *Social Psychological and Personality Science* 3, no. 3 (May 1, 2012): 373–78. https://doi .org/10.1177/1948550611423595.

Schnall, Simone, Jean Roper, and Daniel M. T. Fessler. "Elevation Leads to Altruistic Behavior." *Psychological Science* 21, no. 3 (March 1, 2010): 315–20. https://doi .org/10.1177/0956797609359882.

Schwartz, Richard C., and Martha Sweezy. *Internal Family Systems Therapy*. 2nd ed. New York: Guilford Press, 2019.

Shapiro, Shauna L., Linda E. Carlson, John A. Astin, and Benedict Freedman. "Mechanisms of Mindfulness." *Journal of Clinical Psychology* 62, no. 3 (2006): 373–86. https:// doi.org/10.1002/jclp.20237.

Shaver, Phillip R., Shiri Lavy, Clifford D. Saron, and Mario Mikulincer. "Social Foundations of the Capacity for Mindfulness: An Attachment Perspective." *Psychological Inquiry* 18, no. 4 (October 19, 2007): 264–71. https://doi.org/10.1080/10478400701598389.

Shaver, Phillip R., Mario Mikulincer, and Jude Cassidy. "Attachment, Caregiving in Couple Relationships, and Prosocial Behavior in the Wider World." *Current Opinion in Psychology* 25 (February 1, 2019): 16–20. https://doi.org/10.1016/j.copsyc.2018.02.009.

Shaver, Phillip R., Mario Mikulincer, Jacquelyn T. Gross, Jessica A. Stern, and Jude Cassidy. "A Lifespan Perspective on Attachment and Care for Others: Empathy, Altruism, and Prosocial Behavior." In *Handbook of Attachment: Theory, Research, and Clinical Applications*, 3rd ed., edited by Jude Cassidy and Phillip R. Shaver, 878–916. New York: Guilford Press, 2016.

Simons, Daniel J., and Christopher F. Chabris. "Gorillas in Our Midst: Sustained Inattentional Blindness for Dynamic Events." *Perception* 28, no. 9 (1999): 1059–74. https://doi.org/10.1068/p281059.

Sinclair, Shane, Thomas F. Hack, Susan McClement, Selley Raffin-Bouchal, Harvey Max Chochinov, and Neil A. Hagen. "Healthcare Providers Perspectives on Compassion Training: A Grounded Theory Study." *BMC Medical Education* 20, no. 249 (2020), https://doi.org/10.1186/s12909-020-02164-8.

Skowronek, Jeanette, Andreas Seifert, and Sven Lindberg. "The Mere Presence of a Smartphone Reduces Basal Attentional Performance." *Scientific Reports* 13, no. 1 (June 8, 2023): 9363. https://doi.org/10.1038/s41598-023-36256-4.

Smith, Huston. *The World's Religions*. San Francisco: HarperSanFrancisco, 1991.

Sogyal Rinpoche. "Dharma Talk: A Mind Like a Clear Pool." *Tricycle: The Buddhist Review*, no. Fall (2002): 43–61.

Sorce, James F., Robert N. Emde, Joseph J. Campos, and Mary D. Klinnert. "Maternal Emotional Signaling: Its Effect on the Visual Cliff Behavior of 1-Year-Olds." *Developmental Psychology* 21, no. 1 (1985): 195–200. https://doi.org/10.1037/0012-1649.21.1.195.

Spikins, Penny. "Prehistoric Origins: The Compassion of Far Distant Strangers." In *Compassion: Concepts, Research and Applications*, edited by Paul Gilbert, 16–30. London: Routledge, 2017.

Swann, William B., Jr., and Jennifer K. Bosson. "Self and Identity." In *Handbook of Social Psychology*, vol. 1, 5th ed., Susan T. Fiske, Daniel T. Gilbert, and Gardner Lindzey, 589–628. Hoboken, NJ: John Wiley & Sons, 2010. https://doi.org/10.1002/9780470561119.socpsy001016.

Tan, Tse Yen, Louise Wachsmuth, and Michele M. Tugade. "Emotional Nuance: Examining Positive Emotional Granularity and Well-Being." *Frontiers in Psychology* 13 (2022). https://www.frontiersin.org/articles/10.3389/fpsyg.2022.715966.

Thompson, Evan. "What Is Mind?" Insights: Journey into the Heart of Contemplative Science, August 29, 2022. https://www.mindandlife.org/insight/what-is-mind/.

———. "What's in a Concept? Conceptualizing the Nonconceptual in Buddhist Philosophy and Cognitive Science." MindRxiv, August 14, 2020. https://doi.org/10.31231/osf.io/2m84e.

Thompson, Laurence. *Chinese Religion: An Introduction*. Belmont, CA: Wadsworth, 1989.

Thondup, Tulku. *The Healing Power of Mind: Simple Meditation Exercises for Health, Well-Being, and Enlightenment*. Boston: Shambhala Publications, 1996.

———. *The Heart of Unconditional Love: A Powerful New Approach to Loving-Kindness Meditation*. Boston: Shambhala, 2015.

Thrangu Rinpoche. *Crystal Clear: Practical Advice for Mahamudra Meditators*. Hong Kong: Rangjung Yeshe, 2003.

Tomasello, Michael. *Why We Cooperate*. Cambridge, MA: MIT Press, 2009.

Tomasello, Michael, Malinda Carpenter, Josep Call, Tanya Behne, and Henrike Moll. "Understanding and Sharing Intentions: The Origins of Cultural Cognition." *Behavioral and Brain Sciences* 28, no. 5 (2005): 675–91. https://doi.org/10.1017/S0140525X05000129.

Treleaven, David A. *Trauma-Sensitive Mindfulness: Practices for Safe and Transformative Healing*. New York: W. W. Norton, 2018.

Tronick, Ed, and Marjorie Beeghly. "Infants' Meaning-Making and the Development of Mental Health Problems." *American Psychologist* 66, no. 2 (2011): 107–19. https://doi.org/10.1037/a0021631.

Tsoknyi Rinpoche. *Fearless Simplicity: The Dzogchen Way of Living Freely in a Complex World*. Hong Kong: Rangjung Yeshe, 2003.

———. *Open Heart, Open Mind: Awakening the Power of Essence Love*. New York: Harmony Books, 2012.

Tsong-kha-pa. *The Great Treatise on the Stages of the Path to Enlightenment: Lam Rim Chen Mo*. Vol. 1. Edited by Joshua Cutler and Guy Newland. Translated by Lamrim Chenmo Translation Committee. Ithaca, NY: Snow Lion Publications, 2000.

Tulku Urgyen Rinpoche. *As It Is*. Vol. I. Hong Kong: Rangjung Yeshe, 1999.

———. *Rainbow Painting*. Hong Kong: Rangjung Yeshe, 1995.

Varela, Francisco J. *Ethical Know-How: Action, Wisdom, and Cognition*. Stanford, CA: Stanford University Press, 1999.

Vrtička, Pascal, Pauline Favre, and Tania Singer. "Compassion and the Brain." In *Compassion: Concepts, Research, and Applications*, edited by Paul Gilbert, 135–45. London: Routledge, 2017.

Warneken, Felix, and Michael Tomasello. "Altruistic Helping in Human Infants and Young Chimpanzees." *Science* 311, no. 5765 (March 3, 2006): 1301–3. https://doi.org/10.1126/science.1121448.

———. "The Roots of Human Altruism." *British Journal of Psychology* 100, no. 3 (2009): 455–71. https://doi.org/10.1348/000712608X379061.

Waters, Harriet S., and Everett Waters. "The Attachment Working Models Concept: Among Other Things, We Build Script-like Representations of Secure Base Experiences." *Attachment & Human Development* 8, no. 3 (September 1, 2006): 185–97. https://doi.org/10.1080/14616730600856016.

Waters, Theodore E. A., and Glenn I. Roisman. "The Secure Base Script Concept: An Overview." *Current Opinion in Psychology* 25 (February 1, 2019): 162–66. https://doi.org/10.1016/j.copsyc.2018.08.002.

Wegner, Daniel M. "When the Antidote Is the Poison: Ironic Mental Control Processes." *Psychological Science* 8, no. 3 (May 1, 1997): 148–50. https://doi.org/10.1111/j.1467-9280.1997.tb00399.x.

Wegner, Daniel M., Ralph Erber, and Sophia Zanakos. "Ironic Processes in the Mental Control of Mood and Mood-Related Thought." *Journal of Personality and Social Psychology* 65, no. 6 (1993): 1093–1104. https://doi.org/10.1037/0022-3514.65.6.1093.

Weinberg, Sheila. *God Loves the Stranger: Stories, Poems and Prayers.* Amherst, MA: White River Books, 2017.

Welwood, John. *Toward a Psychology of Awakening.* Boston: Shambhala, 2002.

Weng, Helen Y., Andrew S. Fox, Heather C. Hessenthaler, Diane E. Stodola, and Richard J. Davidson. "The Role of Compassion in Altruistic Helping and Punishment Behavior." *PLOS ONE* 10, no. 12 (December 10, 2015). https://doi.org/10.1371/journal.pone.0143794.

Weng, Helen Y., Andrew S. Fox, Alexander J. Shackman, Diane E. Stodola, Jessica Z. K. Caldwell, Matthew C. Olson, Gregory M. Rogers, and Richard J. Davidson. "Compassion Training Alters Altruism and Neural Responses to Suffering." *Psychological Science* 24 (2013): 1171–80. https://doi.org/10.1177/0956797612469537.

Wilson-Mendenhall, Christine D., John D. Dunne, and Richard J. Davidson. "Visualizing Compassion: Episodic Simulation as Contemplative Practice." *Mindfulness* 14, no. 10 (October 1, 2023): 2532–48. https://doi.org/10.1007/s12671-022-01842-6.

Winnicott, D. W. "The Theory of the Parent-Infant Relationship." *International Journal of Psycho-Analysis* 41 (December 1960): 585–95.

Yangsi Rinpoche. *Practicing the Path: A Commentary on the Lamrim Chenmo.* Boston: Wisdom Publications, 2003.

Zaki, Jamil. "The Caregiver's Dilemma: In Search of Sustainable Medical Empathy." *The Lancet* 396, no. 10249 (August 15, 2020): 458–59. https://doi.org/10.1016/S0140-6736(20)31685-8.

———. "Empathy: A Motivated Account." *Psychological Bulletin* 140, no. 6 (2014): 1608–47. https://doi.org/10.1037/a0037679.

———. *The War for Kindness: Building Empathy in a Fractured World.* New York: Crown, 2019.

Zaki, Jamil, and Mina Cikara. "Addressing Empathic Failures:" *Current Directions in Psychological Science,* December 10, 2015. https://doi.org/10.1177/0963721415599978.

Zaki, Jamil, and Kevin N. Ochsner. "The Neuroscience of Empathy: Progress, Pitfalls and Promise." *Nature Neuroscience* 15, no. 5 (May 2012): 675–80. https://doi.org/10.1038/nn.3085.

Zhechen Gyaltsab Padma Gyurmed Namgyal. *Path of Heroes: Birth of Enlightenment.* Vol. 1. Oakland, CA: Dharma Publishing, 1995.

———. *Path of Heroes: Birth of Enlightenment.* Vol. 2. Oakland, CA: Dharma Publishing, 1995.

Zheng, Denise, Daniel R. Berry, and Kirk Warren Brown. "Effects of Brief Mindfulness Meditation and Compassion Meditation on Parochial Empathy and Prosocial Behavior Toward Ethnic Out-Group Members." *Mindfulness* 14, no. 10 (October 1, 2023): 2454–70. https://doi.org/10.1007/s12671-023-02100-z.

INDEX

inclusive mode (*continued*)
  Field of Care Meditation and, 110–13
  overview, 113–14
  reductive images in, 129–31
Inclusive-Mode Meditation
  benefits, 117
  blessing circles of beings in, 142–43
  compassion-focused, instructions on, 163–65
  and daily life, integrating, 133–34, 137, 195
  difficulties in, 116, 125, 126
  effects of, 131, 143
  empowering, 123
  instructions, 114–16, 126–28
  preparing for, 191–92
  progressive stages of, 132–33
  purposes, 128, 162
  and receptive mode, relationship of, 118–19
  resistance in, 129
  in service and activism, 204
  on the spot practice, 198
  systemic barriers and, 211
  when to practice, 194
Indian Mahayana tradition, 12
Indigenous religions, 10, 15, 30–31, 45–46
infants' visual systems study, 104
in-groups, 8, 73, 129, 141, 148, 149, 158, 181, 185, 205
insight (Tib. *lhag mthong*; Skt. *vipaśyanā*), 102–3
interdependence, recalling, 140–41
intuition, 116–17
Islam, 10, 15, 30–31. *See also* Sufism

Jinpa, Thupten, 75
joy
  from compassion practices, 176, 186
  empathetic/sympathetic, 11, 173, 179, 180
  in others' happiness, 33
  sharing, mentally, 181, 184
Judaism, contemplative, 30–31, 72

Kagyu tradition, 22. *See also* Mahāmudrā tradition
King, Martin Luther, Jr., 11, 136, 137, 188, 207, 208, 214
Kisā Gotamī, 145–47, 150, 152, 153
Knitter, Paul, 167

labels, 122, 125
  awareness of, 128, 129
  goals and, 96
  habitual, 213
  limiting, 149, 198
  reductive, 11, 129, 142
  See also reductive images
Letting Be of Body, Breath, and Mind, 184, 191
  difficulties in, 99
  distractions in, 96–97
  effects of, 92
  as entry point, 190
  gaze in, 90, 93
  goals in, relaxing, 96
  in inclusive mode, 119
  instructions, 91–92
  purposes, 73–74, 89, 90, 95, 107
  settling into openness in, 196, 198, 204
  when to practice, 194
love
  accessing, 1–2, 131
  activism and, 206, 208
  altruistic, 147
  capacity for, 30, 55, 124–25, 138–39
  as confirming and confronting, 137–38
  for enemies, 136
  "essence," 86
  manifesting, 119–20
  in nondual experiences, 102
  for others, extending, 61, 130, 135
  purpose of training in, 214
  source, 68, 107
  thoroughness of, 117–18
  unconditional, 11, 12, 38–39
  vastness of, 118–19
  and wisdom, synergy of, 108
  from within, 106
loving environments, 110, 113, 117, 125, 133, 150
loving qualities, 59
  accessing, 38, 44, 50, 51
  in daily life, connecting with, 67–68
  extending to others, 117–18
  as external, 53, 54, 59, 71
  impediments to, 51–53
  noticing and naming, 36–37
  source, 55
  unconditional experience of, 38–39

nature of mind, 69
    as compassion's ground, 173–74
    dawning, 103, 105
    fear and, 104
    as natural state, 70
    reunifying with, 101, 107
    as secure base, ultimate, 74
    settling into, 177, 181, 196
Nechung Rinpoche, 29–30, 45, 174
nervous system, parasympathetic, 36
neural systems, 60
neuroplasticity, 8–9
neuroscience, 14–15, 81
Nouwen, Henri, 168–69
Nyingma tradition, 22. *See also* Dzogchen
    tradition

out-groups, 8, 9, 129, 147, 181
Owens, Rod, 88

peer support, 27
perceptions
    arising of, 103
    emotions and, 81
    of others, narrow, 123, 134
    of others, opening, 124, 130, 185, 197, 198
    of others as evil, 208
    as primordial awareness, 105
    reductive, 135
    of world conditions, 199
person and person's behaviors,
    distinguishing, 188
post-meditation, 186
presence, 25, 74, 82–83, 197. *See also*
    compassionate presence
psychological science, 4, 16, 21, 22
psychology
    Buddhist, 100, 121–22, 123, 175
    constructed emotion in, 81
    relational training and, 14–15
psychotherapy, 27
pure cognizance, 93–94, 102, 103
pure perception, 12

Rahner, Karl, 72
reappraisal, 86, 131, 154, 157, 170, 176–77
receptive mode, 16, 18–19, 30, 213
    access points in, 51

awareness and, 61, 70
caring moments in, 33–35
and daily life, integrating, 67–68
and deepening mode, alternating, 73
difficulties in, 53, 83
field of care in, 30, 31, 70, 106
nondual awareness and, 103
principles of, 58–60, 63, 110–11
purposes, 36, 37, 64, 107
suffering, awareness of in, 152, 153
reductive images, 6–8, 13, 129–31, 134, 135, 138,
    141, 147, 153
refuge, 12, 18, 103–4, 106–7, 214
relational ending point, 214
relational starting point, 10–12, 213–14
relaxation response, 36
resilience, 1, 37, 61, 87, 134, 211
resting in nowness, 94
Ricard, Matthieu, 147
Rogers, Fred, 11, 214

sameness, threefold, 122–23, 125, 133, 135,
    136–37
samsara, 181
sangha, recollecting, 12
science
    and Buddhism, relationship of, 3–4
    cognitive, 96
    contemplative, 192–93
    of emotion, 37
    on nondual awareness, 72
    worldview of, 22
secure base
    buddha nature as, 20
    cultivating, 154
    establishing, 34, 54
    infinitely, 11, 13, 21, 214
    lacking, 6–8, 10
    of loving qualities, 192
    outer and inner, support of, 64–65
    strengthening, 18, 67, 90
    of teachers and practitioners, 104
    three levels, 106–7
    ultimate, 61, 74, 107, 204
security, inner, 7, 8, 11, 19, 39, 68, 87
selective attention, 40
self-awareness, 37, 152
self-clinging, 73, 103–4, 181, 196, 203

ABOUT THE AUTHORS

JOHN MAKRANSKY, PHD, has been a professor of Buddhism and Comparative Theology at Boston College, senior academic advisor at Rangjung Yeshe Institute in Nepal, president of the Society of Buddhist-Christian studies, fellow of the Mind & Life Institute, and senior editor for the Buddhism section of the St. Andrews Encyclopedia of Theology. John's scholarly writings focus on connections between devotion, compassion, and wisdom in Buddhism, adapting Buddhist practices to meet contemporary minds, and theoretical issues in interfaith learning. In 2000, John was ordained as a lama in the Nyingma tradition of Tibetan Buddhism—a teacher of innate love and wisdom practices. For the past twenty-five years, John has taught meditations of innate compassion and wisdom adapted from Tibetan Buddhism for modern Buddhists, those in other spiritual traditions, and for people in caring roles and professions. In consultation with participants from those settings, John developed the Sustainable Compassion Training model of contemplative practice (SCT) to help Western Buddhists, people of diverse faiths, and those in caring roles and professions generate a more sustaining and unconditional power of compassion and awareness to support their lives and work.

PAUL CONDON is an associate professor of psychology at Southern Oregon University and a research fellow at the Mind & Life Institute. He has also served as a visiting lecturer for the Centre for Buddhist Studies at Rangjung Yeshe Institute. His research examines the relational basis for empathy, compassion, wellbeing, and prosocial action and the influence of compassion and mindfulness training on those capacities. His writings and teachings also explore the use of scientific theories in dialogue with contemplative traditions to inform meditation practices of compassion, mindfulness, and wisdom. His research and writings have appeared in leading psychology journals and Buddhist magazines, and his work on meditation has been cited in media outlets such as *New York Times*, *Wall Street Journal*, and *Smithsonian Magazine*. Paul is codeveloper of the Sustainable Compassion Training model, and he teaches meditation practices adapted from the Tibetan Nyingma and Kagyu traditions for multi-faith and secular application.